HEINRICH HEINE

Heinrich Heine

Writing the Revolution

◆·◆·◆

GEORGE PROCHNIK

Yale

UNIVERSITY

PRESS

New Haven and London

Yale University Press books may be purchased in quantity for educational, business, or promotional use. For information, please e-mail sales.press@yale.edu (U.S. office) or sales@yaleup.co.uk (U.K. office).

Frontispiece: Ludwig Emil Grimm, *Portrait of Heinrich Heine*, 1827. Etching (228 × 191 mm). Rijksmuseum, Amsterdam (Wikimedia Commons/Public Domain).

Set in Janson Oldstyle type by Integrated Publishing Solutions.
Printed in the United States of America.

Library of Congress Control Number: 2020936895
ISBN 978-0-300-23654-5 (hardcover : alk. paper)

A catalogue record for this book is available from the British Library.

This paper meets the requirements of ANSI/NISO Z39.48-1992
(Permanence of Paper).

10 9 8 7 6 5 4 3 2 1

For Rebecca

CONTENTS

HEINRICH HEINE

Chapter One

WHAT'S LIFE without glory, blazing love affairs, and apple tarts?

That's to say, what is life without song and true liberation for all?

Heinrich Heine at thirteen, diminutive and dashing with wavy chestnut hair and a passion for play, charged into the crowd beneath the linden trees of Düsseldorf's palace garden. Napoleon and his cortege were riding down the avenue. The emperor's triumphs drummed through his imagination as he struggled for a view: fiery battles in which the general raised aloft the flag adorned with Jupiter's eagles; proclamations bestowing equality on all the world's peoples. Now Napoleon's revolutionary vision would ignite Düsseldorf. The torpid, pretty riverside hamlet of sixteen thousand souls, where Heine and his sister once hid under hay in a chicken coop, clucking and crowing to confuse the passersby, was receiving the greatest man in the world. On a contemporary map, the town is just a fortified blister attached to the lumpy blue hose of the Rhine, surrounded by fields and loose woody patches. Wreathed in pipe and chimney smoke, with irregular streets, brick houses, errant dogs, a picture gallery, and a handful of silk, glass, vinegar, and sugar manufactories, it was a pleasant place from which to dream of waking.

When Heine wrote about that day in November 1811, he switched the scene to spring and made it a tragicomic stage show of Christ's entry to Jerusalem. "Hosannah! The Emperor!" Trees bowed as the general rode by. Light rays trembled with nervous curiosity. Napoleon's "hand of sunny marble" held the reins, Heine noted, while his countenance resembled an antique bust. "I have loved only the dead and statues," he remarked elsewhere.

Heine never lost his allegiance to Napoleon, that ghost colossus, even when he saw through his pretenses and took the measure of his ego. He would not relinquish the idea that without our heroes and our gods we wither. Or we deify money. Or we crown the mob. Even after we've seen through the dazzle to the little man in dress-up clothes, we can't afford to shed all our starry-eyed enthusiasms. They're too tangled with the sheer love of being alive. "Red life is boiling in my veins, the earth is quivering under my feet, I clasp trees and marble statues with ardent love, and they come to life in my embrace," Heine vowed. He disdained the priest's promise of a second life. There was plenty to experience here—including the eternity of the past, which he could conquer by living backward through his predecessors.

In Napoleon, Heine found the personification of the French Revolution, which was itself the overture to "world revolution," a term Heine coined to represent "the gigantic battle of the disinherited and the inheritors of fortune." In that struggle there would be "no question of nationality or religion, for there will be . . . but one religion, that of happiness in *this life.*" Such was Heine's contention, from youth on through his final, devastating illness: there is no real justice or freedom without joy. And what did joy consist in? Erotic delight. Plenty of money. Beauty. Coruscating wit. Artistic jags. Fair laws. No idiotic censorship. High-spirited fun and shameless comedy. It wasn't all that complicated.

Heine wasn't greedy. He lived most of his adult life in cramped, drab flats with few belongings, complaining only when things got too noisy. But his prose and poetry glow with the desire to revolutionize society in a manner that will give more or less everything to everyone. The Great Man gave palpable form to that ideal potential of the community at large—some sublime order just the other side of this jangly animal carnival in which we dance and wrestle now.

"I have gone through every phase of modern thought and feeling," he told a visitor in 1852, four years before his death. "I have been Werther, René, Lara, Faust, Mephistopheles. . . . But I have never wavered in my faith in the Emperor." Heine was always changing into others, or channeling their voices. The day Napoleon came to Düsseldorf, he envied the white pony the emperor straddled with such ease—patted by the hand that tamed the many-headed monster of anarchy and brought order to the dueling nations. Extraordinary characters trigger a moral thunderstorm in the uncallused minds of young people akin to the effect that meteorological ones have on cats, Heine wrote. Napoleon smiled benevolently at the crowd; but all he had to do was whistle and the clergy fell dumb, or Prussia ceased to exist. Everyone knew it was against the law to ride down the central avenue of the Hofgarten—doing so would incur a sharp fine. But Napoleon advanced straight down the path and no one budged to stop him. His eyes were clear as heaven, absorbing everything on earth simultaneously.

Not that absolute power meant bliss. The future wars Napoleon would have to fight were carved across his brow like hieroglyphics, and every so often his forehead twitched. Each time that happened, tremendous, creative thoughts were taking place behind the emperor's furrows. Any one of which could supply a German writer with enough material to occupy him for the remainder of his life, Heine argued.

That's another reason he could never surrender faith in Napoleon. The artist and the emperor were locked in an uncanny symbiosis. Napoleon was "the man of the idea, the idea become man," as Heine stated in a letter. And he himself was the idea become lyric, the kind of musical picture-writing he attributed to Paganini in a sequence from his novella *Florentine Nights* that depicts the violinist as sorcerer: spinning myriad, disarming stories around his audience as he runs his bow across the strings; producing tones that kiss, then swirl away again before melting together and becoming lost inside the listener. Tones filled with "melodious torments, into which the *obbligato*-goat-laughter comes bleating in," heralding kaleidoscopic flashes of the apocalypse that dissolve into a sweeping chorus where all Creation performs the artist's bidding; prefiguring the advent of a song which no ear has heard.

Yet it's just possible, the narrator interjects, that the heart *can* grasp this music when lost in contemplation of classical art.

Or when a man has had a bottle too much of champagne, blurts a voice from nowhere that jerks the speaker from his reverie.

Such glissandos are everywhere in Heine. At one point he alludes to "the chimney of my head, in which imagination climbs up and down as a chimney sweep." Elsewhere he describes a torrent of visions unspooling from the conked-out deity who created us—"the Iliad, Plato, the Battle of Marathon, Moses, the Medici Venus, Strasbourg Cathedral, the French Revolution, Hegel, steamships"—each bright idea becoming reality at the instant of conception, although the sleeper doesn't know this. "The world is so delightfully confused; it is the dream of an intoxicated god," Heine wrote.

So God is another great individual Heine pairs the poet with. Or rather, God's far livelier unconscious—the fertile source of gorgeous mutiny, and a much less woeful, peevish character than the sober, woken deity.

Chapter Two

Heinrich Heine's mother, Betty, deplored the drowsy provincial sensibility that hung like haze from grilling sausages over most of eighteenth-century Germany. The daughter of a reasonably well-to-do physician, from a Jewish family with intellectual routines and fortune-chasing ancestors, Betty learned some Latin, French, and English. Also Rousseau, Goethe, and the flute. At the age of twenty-four she told a friend that only the weak depended on the crutch of social custom. "Although I combine an ordinary face and figure with an equally ordinary mind, yet I feel that I have the power to rise above the chimeras of prejudice, convention and etiquette," Betty insisted. She made her children promise never to create their homes in some piddling German principality. "Choose large towns in big states," she commanded. In a sentimental yet barbed sonnet to his mother, the young Heine acknowledged his own arrogance and rough temper. "But much as my haughty pride may swell and puff / I feel submissive and subdued enough / when thy much cherished, darling form is nigh," he wrote, adding that her spirit ruled with "hidden might." Hidden in what way, he didn't say.

How Betty came to fixate on the winsome but feckless Samson for a husband—a man who had turned up in Düsseldorf from Hanover in his early thirties, with neither employment nor prospects—is uncertain. Yet she successfully fought the rabbinic authorities who sought to banish him for his insolvency. And she did her best to clean up Samson's act once they settled in together, forcing him, in Heine's telling, to relinquish his playing cards and high-stakes actresses. Even his pack of hounds got sold off, except for Joly, an astoundingly ugly dog that couldn't hunt and reminded Heine of a walking barracks full of fleas.

These renunciations were the prerequisite for Betty's larger program of turning her man into a successful draper. It never worked. But he kept his dreamy smile and decent heart. When Heine found him of a morning at his desk, his father would extend a pale, delicately blue-veined hand up behind him to be kissed, often without even bothering to turn his head. But one day, he embraced his son with great tenderness. "Last night I had a lovely dream about you, and I am very pleased with you, my dear," he said.

The dream had generated real esteem—Heine absorbed this lesson.

It was fitting that his father's portrait had been sketched in pastels since this medium conveyed the indistinctness of his features, along with the film of pollenlike dust that coated his skin: a residue of the high-grade starch shaken daily through his coiffure. That sweet, rococo likeness of his father "bore all the character of an age that had no character," Heine observed. An age that loved the pretty and the dainty rather than the beautiful. An era that elevated insipidity to poetry. "In his heart, there was always a party going on," Heine wrote. Even when his father looked most solemn, the sight evoked those antique bas-reliefs in which a merry child holds a giant tragic mask before his face. Heine loved him with an unconditional amusement.

Things were always more complex with his mother. Betty chastised the maids if they told him ghost stories. She expressed a "dread" of poetry. She plucked novels from his hands and barred him from attending the theater. Artistic fantasy and superstition were allied in her mind, and she did everything she could to minimize Heine's exposure to both. When he pronounced his mother sanity personified, it wasn't entirely complimentary. But neither was the allusion to her dogmatic rationalism scornful. Heine's character was torn unevenly along the seam between the twin countenances of a Janus deity, one side looking toward the Age of Reason and the other at Romanticism, with ageless irony laughing from the darkness in between.

In later years, Betty peers out from her portrait with a tight black gaze that misses nothing, excuses little, and warns idle onlookers what it means to take life's business with due seriousness. But her thin-lipped countenance is framed by a fancy, ruffled bonnet fastened with a giant satin bow. Heine loved to buy them for her when he had the cash; he loved to play her chevalier. The copious correspondence between mother and son is rife with tender regrets from Heine about their separation, and pledges of his perfect faith. "You have no idea how often I think of you," he repeatedly reminds her. "Write me frequently and at great length, how you are and how all goes." He did his best to project a dauntless spirit of high cheer throughout the grisly stations of his physical deterioration. "I am as lucky as a man can be, since nothing in this world is perfect," he assured her after one visit home in 1844, four years before he collapsed for keeps into what he would dub his "mattress grave." He felt so well now, he added, that it was clear all he needed to recuperate was her company.

Chapter Three

WHEN NAPOLEON'S ARMIES first appeared in Düsseldorf, in 1795, Betty's equanimity gave way to lamentation. French artillery shelled the town, turning its famous castle into rubble and felling all the trees at her favorite spot at the Hofgarten, where she loved to stroll in the midday heat. Soon there would be no cool place left except the grave, she told a friend.

The initial occupation didn't signal Düsseldorf's legal incorporation into the French Empire, however. Arrangements for the city's governance shifted back and forth for years in tandem with the intricate negotiations that accompanied Napoleon's military adventures. The aftermath of the French Revolution demonstrated that shock waves produced by huge events don't mimic the steadily outward-spreading rings triggered by explosives. Instead they falter, fracture, double back, and yo-yo; and in that temporal stutter people yet must live their lives.

Heine's birthdate is contested. Düsseldorf's circumcision

roster was destroyed, and Heine sometimes leveraged that un-certainty to date his arrival in the world to the very end of 1799, so it would crisscross past and future. "The last moonbeams of the eighteenth century, and the red dawn of the nineteenth century played about my cradle," he wrote. But there's enough evidence to indicate that his birth probably happened in mid-December 1797, two years after the bombardment reduced many of Düsseldorf's principal buildings to not especially romantic ruins. The Napoleonic wars had made the study of geography futile during his youth, Heine claimed. He defended his poor marks in the subject on the grounds that the French were al-ways shuffling frontiers until the Devil himself couldn't keep the borders straight, and he himself was permanently disadvan-taged at finding his way around the world.

In 1801, control of Düsseldorf reverted to the Rhenish Pa-latinate, a territorial jurisdiction whose origins could be traced to the dark ages of the Frankish Court, and whose feudal over-lords acquired the title of prince-electors in the thirteenth cen-tury. A huge bronze equestrian statue of the Elector Jan Wil-helm stood in the middle of the town square. Though Wilhelm ruled in the seventeenth century, with his rigid glower and martial baton he could have galloped straight out from the older, denser Teutonic forests that made a fecund womb for German folk creatures.

Heine was always tantalized by the legendary past of his home region, and many of its nightmare marvels were resusci-tated in only lightly ironized form in his writings. The Wild Huntsman, who sweeps the skies for departing souls. Dwarves, nixies, and the Lorelei, an elusive siren water spirit that would make Heine's fortune as a poet. He liked to say that in his child-hood he breathed the air of France, but the old *Volk* mythos also lingered in the local atmosphere and swarmed beneath the surface of the Rhine. For all Heine's criticism of Germany's stagnant narrow-mindedness, his feelings about Palatinate rule were ambivalent because its foundations were sunk in that richly storied mire. When he waxes sentimental about his core identity as a *German* poet, it's often this older mass of material, which his acquaintances the Brothers Grimm were then beginning to refurbish for bourgeois consumption, that Heine had in mind.

The true revolutionization of Düsseldorf began, anyway, not in 1795 but in 1806, when the French reoccupied the city under the command of Napoleon's brother-in-law, Joachim Murat. Instead of firing projectiles at the place, Murat treated its foremost citizens to dinner at the Grand Ducal Palace. Dubbed the Dandy King for costumes like the one he wore when painted by François Gérard, in which the combination of gold festoons, silky white, and plumes suggests a swan mating with a treasure chest, Murat knew how to win a crowd by projecting genial candor. Though he was the standard bearer for systemic change—making dogma of the principle of Égalité by enforcing the Napoleonic Code with its novel legal protections for all citizens—Murat stressed continuity in his speech. The day after his arrival, he issued a decree announcing his decision not to replace a single person in authority or to reform any aspect of municipal administration until time should indicate which changes would be indisputably advantageous to the country. Then he effectively withdrew for the duration of his tenure to a luxurious estate six miles out of town.

When Heine later recalled the transfer of power in Düsseldorf from his eight-year-old perspective, he tapped the collective unconscious of the occasion. In Heine's account, one morning he woke to find the city sunk in a funereal atmosphere. People drifted silently through the market square, pausing to study a long poster plastered to the town hall façade. The lips of the bony tailor trembled, while his blue wool stockings drooped, giving elegiac glimpses of his naked legs. An old soldier in the uniform of the Palatinate read the notice out loud, tears plopping down his battered face. Heine began to weep with him, and eventually asked why they were crying.

"The Elector thanks his subjects," replied the veteran.

As Heine pondered this announcement, the coat of arms was being pried off the building. The sky was overcast. Everyone appeared so gripped by foreboding they might have been awaiting an eclipse. The sight of the town's omnipotent policeman, inert and apathetic in the square, as if henceforth there would simply be no more commands to issue, added to the eeriness. The town lunatic, Alouisius, stood nearby balancing on one leg while grimacing wildly and chattering the names of Napoleon's generals. Gumpertz, the drunken hunchback, was rolling in the gutter, singing a revolutionary song about hanging the nobility from lampposts. Yet the policeman never made a move to silence them.

Heine wandered home, sobbing to his mother, "The Elector thanks his subjects."

She couldn't solace him. He went to sleep crying and dreamt the end of the world. Gardens and pastures peeled off the ground and rolled up like carpets. The policeman scaling a high ladder and taking down the sun. The tailor mumbling to himself that he had to go home and put on respectable clothes because he was dead and due to be buried that day. It grew darker. Stars pattered down like autumn leaves and Heine was left alone stumbling about in terror. He came upon a man spading up the earth. Beside him a horrific woman clutched what appeared to be a human head but turned out to be the moon. She lowered it into the gaping hole with nervous care. At Heine's back, the old soldier kept sobbing, "The Elector thanks his subjects."

"I dream with open eyes," Heine once said, "and my eyes see." One would be hard-pressed to find a writer from any period who refers to dreams more frequently. But except for the occasional erotic narcotic, his dreams rarely offer escape. Rather, they tend to serve as glaring illuminations of the delusional waking world. Heine defined the great poet as "absolute monarch in the kingdom of dreams." He never said where the boundaries of that kingdom lay.

Stendhal remarked of the Milanese that before the French turned up, the people had been bored for a hundred years. In Düsseldorf, the ennui went back too far to register. With Murat's official entry the morning after Heine's dream, things began to get exciting. He watched the troops march by his front door, enchanted by the music and finery: bearskin caps, tricolor cockades, shining bayonets, and the mighty drum major in silver regalia, flinging his gilt-knobbed stick up past the first story of the houses, and casting his gaze higher still, to pretty girls leaning out between the shutters of second-story windows.

Heine pressed his way back through the crowd to the main square. Someone mentioned that school was canceled. He clambered onto the enormous bronze horse supporting the elector to get a better view. The town councilors below were wearing fancy clothes and practicing saying *Bon jour* to one another. Imperial flags were draped about. Pickpockets worked the assembly. Horns blew. The mayor delivered a windy speech. Heine heard that the new authorities wanted to make the citizenry happy. He shouted "Vivat!" with all the others when the drums began to beat, then was overwhelmed by vertigo and clutched for the elector's neck. The world spun upside down. *Hold tight,* the statue whispered. Only the boom of jubilant cannon fire restored his senses to where he could eventually dismount the horse.

Reaching his mother Heine announced, "They want to make us happy so there is no school today"—a nicely drawn child's pinhole view on world upheaval. But the next day he was somehow back in class, squirming once more through endless Latin declensions. Even if school hadn't been abolished, more had altered than people first realized. Although Murat's wife,

Caroline, Napoleon's sister, stayed in Paris, demoralizing the high society of Düsseldorf who had thought her chic might prove infectious, and Murat's ruling touch was light enough to qualify as derelict, the town did acquire a fresh glaze of tolerance. And for Jews, the inauguration of the "rational dictatorship" held far-reaching implications.

Before Napoleon's constitution began to be enforced, the circumscription of Jewish life in Germany was penal and vindictive. In Frankfurt, no Jew was allowed to enter a public park. Jews couldn't walk down the street more than two abreast. After 4 P.M. on Sunday afternoons, they were forbidden from setting foot outside the ghetto. Opportunities for employment were severely limited. Spontaneous assaults were always a hazard.

Even if Napoleon's motivations for granting equal civil rights to Jews had been self-interested—he wanted their money, and to dilute their troublesome idiosyncrasies in the larger population—he had dissolved the ghettos and removed restrictions on marriage. Did it matter whether his professed dedication to establishing "a universal liberty of conscience" was heartfelt?

Heine never wrote about Napoleon's particular significance for Jews. Some think that's just because his family never suffered much prejudice. But the omission also reflected Heine's qualms about owning up to any fixed trait, a discomfort with inherited identity as such, which the unique liabilities of Jewishness compounded. He once called Jewishness his "unlucky genealogical communication." Elsewhere he characterized it as a cosmic taint, exclaiming upon the indestructability of "that mummy of a people which roams the earth . . . a petrified piece of world history, a ghost that makes its living by peddling bills of exchange and cast-off trousers." Yet the sheer scale and persistence of Jewish affliction also imbued Heine with a certain aghast loyalty. Nor did the Jewish stigma burnish the appeal of

Christianity. In one poem he characterized Jesus as his "poor cousin, poor dreamer." But he also summarized his own relation to the Savior in a quip: "No Jew can ever believe in the divinity of any other Jew."

And notwithstanding all his criticisms, Heine also evinced a kind of savage awe at the Jews' capacity for survival in the face of unremitting persecution. Over and over in his writing Death appears as humanity's archnemesis. "Even if I am only the shadowy image in a dream, that is still better than the cold, black obliteration of death," he declared, citing with approval Achilles' famous remark to Odysseus in the underworld that he would prefer to be a landless, destitute servant following another man's plough than to be king of all the perished souls. The Jewish people in Heine's writing are Death's own most galling adversary.

Chapter Four

IF THE FIRST APPEARANCE of Napoleon's armies in Düsseldorf brought fears of unrelenting warfare and triggered Betty's nostalgia for an age "when Germany was still Germany," the advent of Murat aroused her own imperial enthusiasm. This had more to do with a sense of expanded opportunities for the family enterprise, however, than with fervor for the extension of the Rights of Man. Under the new administration perhaps her husband would finally prosper, or at least scrape his way to solvency.

For a time, Betty's hopes for a French windfall seemed justified. The pace of Samson's trade in fabrics quickened. His specialty was velveteen. He loved the velvety cotton with an affection that went beyond mercantile calculation. Indeed, Heine said, his father treated the stuff less as goods for sale than a favorite toy to caress and roll about in.

Samson's best suppliers were based in Manchester and Liverpool, to which he traveled, boasting of the fruits of his commercial pilgrimage in local papers. "In response to persistent enquiries whether the goods I have ordered from England have arrived, I hereby notify my friends and patrons that they are indeed to hand," began one advertisement he placed in 1809.

One connection Samson forged among the fabric dealers there was so intimate that he anglicized his son's name to honor it. At least Heine said he'd done so. In family circles, among neighbors and schoolmates, the name Heinrich recorded at his baptism anyway became Harry—quite a testament to his father's affection for a faraway companion he referred to only as someone expert at buying velveteen for resale.

Even though his father's looks had something "excessively soft . . . almost womanish about them," Heine assured his readers that Samson gave abundant evidence of his manliness, especially when he himself was young. "I, after all, am living proof of it," he bragged. Much of his father's virility seemed to manifest in his predilection for strutting around town in the tight-fitting costume with sky-blue velvet tracings of his home guard unit. Did Heine ever wonder about the nature of his father's attachment to the mystery Harry? Was it entirely a factor of his love affair with velveteen? Could the link also have some bearing on the bouts of homophobic jeering Heine indulged in, which mark the ugliest exercise of his wit? And if, as some suggest, Heine invented his father's beloved English partner in velveteen, what made him do that?

His tirades against the English nation were in any case more extensive than his jibes against homosexuality. A poet should never be sent to London, Heine maintained. "Exaggerated London," with its "colossal uniformity," mechanistic rhythms, and pinched spirit even in the midst of pleasures, smothered the imagination and tore the heart. Some of Heine's indictments of the country's ice-cold solipsism still bite. "Egoistic England," he remarked, less resembled the "well-to-do fat man with a beer-swollen belly" of classic caricatures than "a long, thin, bony bachelor who sews on a button that has come off his trousers with a piece of thread whose end-knot is our terrestrial globe. When he no longer needs the thread he cuts it and calmly allows the whole world to tumble into the abyss."

English domestic liberty, nonetheless, remained a lifelong touchstone for Heine, just as Shakespeare was his ultimate artistic hero: "At once Jew and Greek," he wrote, Shakespeare enabled spiritualism and art to permeate each other "in a conciliatory way and develop into a higher whole." Heine told friends that he also felt more kinship with Byron than any other contemporary poet—so much so that he rarely read him, for "we prefer to associate with people whose characters are different from our own."

In truth, the passions evoked by the English version of his name went beyond anxieties about his father's masculinity, or disgust with England's selfish, bourgeois mind-set. Heine asserted that the springtime of his life was in fact ruined by his having to answer to "Harry." When he was young there lived in Düsseldorf a character known as Mucky Mick, the refuse man. Each morning Mucky Mick passed through town with his donkey hitched to a wagon, collecting all the filth that Düsseldorf's housemaids had swept into little heaps up and down their streets. Mucky Mick's ass would stand patiently while a fresh load got forked onto the cart, or would trot on to the next house, depending on the pitch of his master's voice as he called out *Haarüh!* Heine never knew whether this word was actually the donkey's name or some conventional command, but either way, when issuing from the mouth of Mucky Mick, "Haarüh" bore a dreadful semblance to "Harry."

Heine's schoolmates seized on the echo, pronouncing his name with all the tonal variations Mucky Mick himself employed when addressing his donkey, and they'd do so at moments designed to maximize the shame of Heine's homonymic kinship. Big children taunted Heine to his face. Little ones derided him at a distance. Whenever a donkey got mentioned in class all eyes would swivel to Heine. Street urchins flung horse dung at Heine's head while chanting *Haarüh, Haarüh.*

Heine's spirited narration of the scene shows his reflexive admiration for the children's satire. Even when he tells a story involving his own persecution, he can't help relishing the music of inventive mockery. But the bullying also rings true and hurtful. What did it mean for a man whose vocation derived from hypersensitivity to the sounds of words to be plagued by the sound of his own name? Once again, the world had tried to brand him with an identity over which he had no say, imposing destiny by way of the past. Since the donkey's signal curse was the abrasive, senseless *hee-haw* of its voice, his mother told him there was no choice but to become so clever that no one could ever confuse him with an ass. At the time, it didn't stop the teasing, but Heine took her counsel to heart, to wit—to song.

The figure of the donkey remained a fixture in his writing to the end of his life. Heine rhapsodized over Napoleon's white pony. He waxed nostalgic over the mailed war mounts of German legend—memorializing the bronze horse in Düsseldorf's town square as a world-stabilizing axis. He exalted his own muse "Pegasus, beloved steed," flying and galloping, full of joy. But he always came back to the braying ass. Ultimately, that creature proved more potent in his vision than the lyric stallion with wings and gold-shod hooves.

$$\blacklozenge\!\!\cdot\!\!\blacklozenge\!\!\cdot\!\!\blacklozenge$$

Chapter Five

BETTY HAD A FRIEND named Louise, the undistinguished daughter of a local swordsmith, who married one of Napoleon's generals and overnight became Duchess of Dalmatia. Thereafter the possibilities of the new world order flashed in Betty's eyes more brilliantly than her prize jewels. If her own consort wasn't destined to rise above the realm of regal fabrics, there was yet her firstborn son. Betty resolved that with her goading the boy would manage to scale the French bureaucratic ladder to some plum administrative post. She dreamt of him wearing the goldest of gold epaulettes, presiding over some majestically embellished office.

To realize her plan, she made sure Heine was schooled in all the essential subjects for empire building: geometry, mechanics, hydraulics. He came close to drowning, he later said, in logarithms and algebra. In none of the practical fields did he shine. His aptitude was greater when it came to natural history.

He pored over engravings of monkeys, kangaroos, and rhinoceroses for hours, until their features were etched in his memory. Later in life he encountered people he felt sure he'd met before—only to realize belatedly that he'd confused them with some character from his zoological gallery. He did best in mythology, however, reveling in the cheerful nudity of the gods. "I don't believe there was a schoolboy in ancient Rome who knew the principal points of his catechism—that is the love affairs of Venus—better than I," he testified.

Betty's ambitions for her child became yet more aggressive when Napoleon tightened his continental blockade, halting German trade with Manchester and Liverpool. The disruption wrecked Samson's business. Before long he went bankrupt, cementing his dependence on his banker brother Salomon, whose coffers would prove alluring and corrosive to the poet also. Meanwhile, Betty did her best to train Heine for a career as a high strategist at court, or at least a supervisory post in some distant province. The French Empire had taken away and now the French Empire must surely pay, ideally with interest.

At first, the expectations dramatized in a play at Düsseldorf's National Theater staged to mark the start of the French occupation seemed on the verge of being realized: Minerva floated down to the boards from painted clouds. The Goddess of Wisdom declared Napoleon the epoch's greatest son, the beloved of Olympus, guardian of humanity. Europa appeared in the portico of Fame's splendid temple, supporting a giant bust of Napoleon on her shoulders. She extended her great arm to embrace the whole of the eastern hemisphere, whereupon a star flamed up in the branches of the laurel. Heine wanted to be part of all of it, and he applied himself to his mother's program.

Then France invaded Russia.

Caulaincourt, Duc de Vicence, personal aide to the emperor, tried repeatedly to discourage the project. Formerly ambassador to Russia, well acquainted with the tsar, Caulaincourt knew the country's domineering winter and underlying political resolve. Napoleon scoffed at Caulaincourt's foreboding: "A single victory, and the Tsar will come crawling toward me," Napoleon vowed. "The great landowners will rise against him; I shall emancipate the serfs." To his former police chief, Joseph Fouché, Napoleon remarked, "I must make all the people of Europe into one people, and Paris the capital of the world."

He rode out of France with more than 600,000 soldiers. When the army reached Moscow, in September 1812, Napoleon strode into the Kremlin accompanied by his entourage, completely unopposed, and discovered the clocks all ticking softly in the grand, deserted halls. He pivoted to Caulaincourt. "Well, my Lord Duke, what about this Russian climate of yours? It is as mild as a September day at Fontainebleau." Then having silenced his Cassandra, Napoleon began dictating a set of complex new regulations for the Comédie-Française. His capacious spirit could attend to everything simultaneously.

At the end of the first week in November, one of the officers in Napoleon's inner council reported that the sky had undergone a sudden change. Its azure tint had simply vanished. All at once, the men were marching through an icy mist, and all at once again that vapor became opaque. "It seemed as if the heavens were falling and joining with the earth . . . in one common league for our utter destruction," recalled Napoleon's subordinate.

Less than three months after his victory lap around the Kremlin, Napoleon stood in the middle of nowhere, stamping his feet, trying to keep the blood flowing while staring out at fields in which the snow-covered bodies of his fallen soldiers lay in huddles resembling enormous flocks of sheep. In the midst of a calamitous retreat, he finally handed off his decimated army to Murat and rode on with his escort for Paris. By the time the Grande Armée found its way once more into France, it had suffered more than half a million casualties.

Although in later years Heine became more willing to criticize the boundless self-regard that undermined Napoleon's potential for becoming, as he wrote, "the George Washington of Europe," he yet saw the general's downfall as a tragedy. The loss of the universal ideal Napoleon championed was a blow to all humanity. That his defeat could elevate a mediocrity like Wellington ("a stupid ghost with an ash-grey soul in a body of stiff linen") was sheer desecration. Heine predicted proud England's eventual collapse: Westminster in ruins, the royal dust within its tombs untended.

Heine did have a prophetic gift. But as is often true with oracles, he was weakest when it came to anticipating the form in which salvation would manifest. More than once, he got his messiahs wrong. When it came to charting the winds of the apocalypse, however, Heine earned his seer's stars.

Chapter Six

THE CONGRESS OF VIENNA, convened in 1814 to arrange Europe's post-Napoleonic future, had a simple premise: put everything back on the shelf where it had been before the Revolution, only now bolted fast with new antinationalist alliances. Instead of nurturing the more worldly aspects of German identity that the French had played off, the agreements forged in Vienna rewarded a parochial military culture. Düsseldorf went to Prussia. The Napoleonic Code went out the window. Jews were to be reclassified as a separate, inferior category of humanity.

Betty dropped her Empire-born ambitions and began to dream a second dazzling future for her son, this one hatched under the sign of Rothschild. For though Klemens von Metternich, Austria's representative at the congress, might have wanted to reinstate the old royal balance of powers, the throne occupied by Capital had begun to shine fairer than them all.

The Rothschild clan exemplified the new prospects enjoyed by families at the upper echelon of banking. Not long before, Heine noted, when a king wanted a loan from one of their tribe, he'd simply pull the man's teeth out molar by molar until the fellow coughed up, but such medieval customs had grown unfashionable, and now these bankers could amble blithely in the Tuileries. Despite Heine's disdain for money chasing, his feelings about the new breed of speculators were divided. For these "princely pursemasters" enacted a revolutionary program: they were destroyers of the old aristocracy based on landed privileges, and hence among Europe's "most terrible levellers." (Heine skirts the fact that the Rothschild name was partly made by establishing the pipeline of gold and silver that enabled Wellington to keep paying troops throughout the campaign, steeling anti-Napoleonic resolve with precious metals convertible to local currency.) One thing Heine despised more than Mammon was hereditary privilege.

The path to fortune changed direction, but Betty still aimed high: Heine was now to be a mighty financier. She reconfigured his program of study: in place of hydraulics, bookkeeping; instead of geometry, geography and the mechanics of commerce by land and sea. He was to become fluent in all major European languages, with English the first priority. "Under the archways of the London Exchange every nation has its allotted place," Heine observed. The Exchange taught the world that the old, stereotypical hierarchy of races was no longer profitable and simply led to dreary errors.

He was shipped out to the countinghouse of one of his father's bankers, then to the warehouse of a spice dealer. He learned to draft bills of trade and to know his nutmeg. Eventually, he chose a famous millionaire to apprentice with. On presenting himself and volunteering his services, Heine found that the man, instead of embracing him, suggested that there was no sign he'd ever shown the least aptitude for making money.

Heine laughed in agreement. Several months into his new curriculum, he purportedly confessed that he still wasn't quite sure of the difference between debits and credits. Then a business crisis struck Germany. His father's savings were erased, and the whole plan fell apart. It was too bad, Heine told his brother, since he'd gleaned early on that bankers would rule the new world.

Betty now devised a third career for her son. She resolved that the boy must turn his energies to law, the influence of which had grown exponentially under the French regime. Even after the Empire's defeat, advocates in Germany were ascending to the country's most prestigious offices. At Betty's urgings, Heine applied to study jurisprudence at the University of Bonn.

From the moment he strode into the amphitheater to find his place among the youths squeaking pens across the page while a moribund instructor droned away in clouds of chalk, Heine discovered in himself a disgust for law exceeding his distaste for business. Roman law and the principles of property ownership extrapolated from it were the basis for all the institutions of the modern state most inimical to our humanity, he decided. The corpus juris itself, the foundation of German jurisprudence, he named the "Bible of selfishness."

But with Samson's livelihood in shambles, his mother had grown desperate. She'd sold her precious necklace and earrings to pay for his studies. Heine had to honor her sacrifice. It took him more than ten years to extricate himself from this profession. By the time he'd done so, the world had begun to recognize him as a writer.

Betty's attempts to realize her ambitions through the career of her firstborn son evoke the labors of some doomed striver in Balzac. Yet they also evince a striking optimism about the malleability of their family stature, notwithstanding the limitations imposed by race and social circumstances.

And in truth, Betty's faith that her offspring could rise above their station was misplaced only in Heine's case. Though there's no evidence that she dedicated herself so assiduously to advancing the careers of her other children, all of them ended up making real money and two out of three acquired titles.

Heine's younger brother Gustav initially pursued a career in agronomy. Farming, Heine pointed out to a Jewish friend who he hoped might help his brother, was not traditionally a goldmine for the circumcised. Agriculture didn't take, but Gustav changed pace and enlisted in the Austrian army, where he quickly turned reactionary. His portrait depicts him in spanking white dress uniform, narrow gaze limpid and supercilious, his hair swept to one side in a fussy bunch of black curls, like a funeral rosette. Service in the Habsburg corps, where Gustav proved reliably conformist, became a stepping-stone to a post editing a Viennese newspaper that chirruped the government line. In 1870 he was knighted for that journalistic sycophancy and thenceforth signed himself Baron von Heine-Geldern. Uptight and temperamental, he tried to help Heine out from time to time, but the meddling mostly made things worse.

Their brother Max was more stable, but earned a reputation for being thick, degree in medicine notwithstanding. He became a military surgeon with the Russian army, and drifted right politically. The tsarist circles he now moved in opened conjugal routes to power. Max married the titled widow of Nicholas I's court physician, who added a "von" of her own to the Heine surname. In his portrait, Max is thick-jawed and small eyed, his heavy walrus moustache snuffling down below his chin, just one neck fold above a high, stiff collar, while gilt epaulettes spray his shoulders with all the swag his mother once fantasized for Heinrich. After the poet's death, Max circulated cute anecdotes about their youth while doing everything he could to cover up the family's Jewishness.

Charlotte, amused and amiable looking, with long clusters of dark bell-pull ringlets, was the only sibling Heine felt close to, although her gossiping chafed him. He called her *Plapperlotte:* Blabber Lotte. She married Moritz Embden, a stodgy Hamburg businessman. Heine was cordial to him at first, although the terms in which he excused his brother-in-law's conservativism have an edge if one is inclined to spot the glint. "It is good to know that the future husband of my sister is no revolutionary," he wrote on the announcement of their betrothal. "I always find it quite natural that the man who lives in comfort and is a happy bridegroom should not desire to overthrow the *status quo*, and should be greatly concerned for his own and Europe's tranquility." In his own case, Heine continued, things were different: "I experience a strange sort of feeling when I chance to read in the newspapers that people freeze to death in the streets of London, and that others are starving in the streets of Naples." Forgive my instinct for basic human compassion, he hovers on the brink of saying. But Heine also acknowledges that he's unable to count himself among the new radicals in Germany since he is well aware that if they gain power, "a couple of thousand Jewish heads—and those the very best—would roll."

Charlotte and Moritz lived comfortably enough together, and Charlotte remained one of Heine's principal supports. But Moritz became increasingly hostile to Heine over time, ultimately making it impossible for Heine to share a roof with him. This couple's son became another baron, and their daughter, through sleight-of-marriage, turned into the Princess della Rocca.

Two barons plus a princess within a generation. Not bad for one middling Jewish family in early-nineteenth-century Germany. Only the son with real gifts to lavish on humanity failed to flourish materially, through either business or matrimony. Perhaps the other children's greatest blessing was that their mother's worldly ambitions were focused on the son who had no ability as an administrator, a businessman, or a lawyer. And who knows—maybe all that overwrought maternal drive to make a conventional career for her firstborn played some role in goading Heine himself to swerve off into literature.

Chapter Seven

It wasn't that Betty ignored the aesthetic disciplines proper to a bourgeois education. She got Heine violin lessons. After nearly a year of them, she happened to be strolling in the garden and was moved to hear the melodious tones of a well-played violin wafting from the music room. She swept inside to commend the teacher for his accomplishment, only to discover Heine lolling on the sofa while the teacher fiddled for the boy's amusement. Thus matters had proceeded for the entire tutorial: Heine couldn't even play the scales. Though Heine's verses would be set to music more frequently than those of any other German poet—his scored lyrics number in the thousands—he seemed to have no aptitude for any instrument but language. Just as telling, however, is Heine's purported response to his mother's intrusion: he bewailed the fact that she'd broken the stream of beautiful thoughts conjured by the music. The teacher's violin *had* provided instruction, he protested—in unleashing his imagination. (Lest one overrefine the scene, Heine also spent the session drawing pictures of donkeys, which he secretly pinned to the poor man's coattails.)

Betty next bought Heine dancing lessons. When the little martinet who taught him bopped him for some bit of clumsiness, Heine tossed him out the window into a manure heap. So went the family legend anyway, and there's no evidence that Heine ever resumed these classes, although dancing is everywhere in Heine's poetry. Not only people, but linden trees, clouds, books, and animals begin swaying, snapping, and spinning at the first opportunity. The language of folk dances might foreshadow new revolutions, Heine suggested. He described the motions of one expressive performer carrying "an eerie premonition of rebirth, the pregnant breeze of new spring." Napoleon had but to whistle for the entire Holy Roman Empire to break into dance, he declared elsewhere.

Drawing was another field in which he was expected to acquire conventional proficiency, and the brother of a famous Nazarene painter gave Heine classes in fine art. His early biographers sometimes claim he showed more talent in drawing than in other mediums; but there's no surviving proof of this, or even any funny stories.

What else could Betty have done to set her son on the standard path to fortune? Late in life she made a confession that shocked Heine: she wished she had consecrated him to service in the Catholic Church. The jolt was double since she'd neither renounced her Judaism nor expressed religious sentiments of any sort other than the pristine deism consistent with her faith in Reason. But the theological element in Heine's education was continually in flux.

There was a local *heder* that Heine could have attended, run by Rabbi Scheuer, a well-known Jewish educator, but Betty was embroiled in a feud with him. Heine briefly attended a Jewish school administered by a distant relation, but not much

Heine learned there stuck. He could decipher noncursive H‐
brew letters, and had a rough understanding of major holiday
but allusions to Jewish ritual in his writings are error-strewn
Nor did he have much perspective on the overall significance
of his ancestry. After he'd moved on to a Christian school
Heine asked his father who his grandfather had been. Samson
gave his son an amused, defiant look and answered "a little Jew
with a long beard." The next morning in school Heine eager
announced, *My grandfather was a little Jew with a long beard*
The room exploded in a riot, with his schoolmates chanting
back the sentence while jumping onto desks, tipping over ink
wells, bleating, grunting, barking, crowing. When the teacher
Father Dickerscheit, entered and learned how the ruckus h‐
begun, Heine was severely beaten. Jewish identity as such
seemed a cue for comedy—but comedy as bloodsport.

For most of his early education, Heine was enrolled
Catholic schools, since for the most part that's what Düsseldorf
had to offer. Heine's unremarkable transition into an institu‐
staffed by clergy, based in a former Franciscan cloister, serv‐
as a reminder that Jews and Gentiles still mingled regular
then. When legal rights were more firmly established late
the nineteenth century, and the trappings of assimilation we
more self-consciously affected by successful bourgeois Jews, th
actual segregation of social worlds was often more hermetic.

Heine's main teacher at the Catholic Lyceum, the recto
Agidius Jakob Schallmeyer, introduced him to the works
important secular philosophers. Heine never mentions wheth
he was bar mitzvahed. But he reports that in his thirteenth
year he'd already been given training in all the systems of fr
thought. His father was skeptical of these studies—"As a mer
chant I need my head for my business," he said—but ultimate
Samson washed his hands of the matter, as of much else, by d
claring his son's education to be his wife's affair.

Heine portrays Schallmeyer as exemplary for his ability

teach the writings of secular thinkers without feeling undermined in his personal faith. Schallmeyer, for his part, spotted talents in the boy that he thought likely to prosper under proper church instruction. He advised Betty to send Heine to Rome to study at a Catholic seminary, and promised to use his influence to advance Heine's standing among prelates at the Vatican. Heine wisecracked late in life that although he was not ambitious by nature, he wouldn't have declined a nomination to the papacy. But his mother couldn't bear the thought of him going around in one of those leaden cassocks that German priests wore so unbecomingly, Heine explained. If she'd only been aware of the panache with which Roman abbots shrugged their shoulders in their neat silk mantles, his whole life story might have turned out differently.

The idea of Betty plotting a theological future for Heine is not altogether farcical. Studies that nurtured this vocation might have been more in tune with the poet's character than the courses she did promote. Heine thought a lot about God in his youth, he tells us. What's more, he'd not yet come to see Our Lord as a delirious inebriate.

Chapter Eight

As a child, Heine spent whole days gazing up at the sky, wondering about God's nature and hoping for a glimpse of him. By evening time he'd invariably be disappointed to have seen only the foolish grimaces of the clouds. But he kept wondering how it was that with all the splendors people said were up there, not one item ever tumbled down to earth. Not a single "diamond earring, or a string of pearls, or, at the very least, a small slice of pineapple cake."

Once he dreamt of seeing God in the far-off firmament. The Holy One was staring contentedly out some window in the sky, a pious being with a Jewish beard, scattering seed-corns from his little aperture. As they fell, the kernels "burst open in the infinitude of space, and expanded to vast dimensions, till they became actual, radiant blossoming, peopled worlds, each one as large as our own globe." Heine could never forget the face of that cheerful old man, "sprinkling forth the world seeds from his little window in the sky." Through all the different turns of his theological speculations, it appears the world's deity would be literally nothing if not lavish.

The imperative of generosity was a consuming principle in Heine's life. He makes a point of saying that though Betty could be frugal, she was so only with respect to herself, and could be munificent on behalf of others, especially her children. She didn't love money but only valued it, Heine wrote. The praise is tepid compared to his remarks about his father's charity. Samson oversaw a poor relief fund in Düsseldorf. When distributing alms, Samson would put away his costly silver candlestick with its wax taper, substituting a copper one with a tallow candle that threw off a dismal flicker but was less intimidating to the poor who queued before him. Some of them received two bags, and in these instances the larger bag was always filled from Samson's own purse, Heine reported. "Many people whose hearts are in the right place do not know how to give," he noted. "My father's heart and his pocket, however, seemed to be linked by a railway line."

Old women adored his father. He was "charm personified" in his dealings with them, no less than with the younger ladies. Everyone who approached him received words of sympathetic counsel along with their sacks of coin. Heine's description of his father's grace is moving, though even here he cannot resist a little tweak at the mask of self-regard: since handsome men whose specialty consists in being handsome have great need for flattery, no matter the source, so long as the incense billowed forth in great clouds, it could be understood how his dear father, "without any deliberate speculation, nevertheless profited from his dealings with old ladies," Heine wrote. "Flatter me a bit, even a bit too much," his father seemed always to insinuate.

Away from his father's gallantries, Heine read voraciously from the older troubadours. Records from Düsseldorf's public library show that he checked out books constantly, and when he went to Bonn for his doctorate in law, only one other student at the university borrowed more volumes than he did. *Don Quixote* was the first substantial book he read, devouring it over a series of spring mornings in the Hofgarten on a mossy bench beside the Avenue of Sighs, while listening to nightingales and glancing up from the page to an orgy of buds and sunbeams. The story's comedy was completely lost on him then, Heine wrote, for he didn't yet know "the irony with which God has permeated the world"—and which the great writer replicates. The sufferings of the noble knight just made him weep. The birds that heard him shared his sentiments, Heine insisted. "We despised the base mob that treated the poor hero so roughly, but even more that mob of nobles decked in gay silken cloaks, who with their fine powers of speech and great titles made mock of a man so vastly their superior in intellect and nobility of temper."

He kept returning to the book throughout his life, feeling shadowed at every crossroad by the curious phantoms of "the haggard knight and the fat squire." In time he came to understand that Cervantes had taken the old chivalric romance and used that foundation to create "a new species of poetry which we call the modern novel" by incorporating a faithful description of the lower classes—"by giving the life of the people a place in it." In so saying, Heine anticipated Walter Benjamin's dictum that "all great works of literature either dissolve a genre or invent one," but went yet further by suggesting that the greatest masterpieces do both. "They found something new while they destroy the old. They never deny without affirming something." Cervantes' openhearted attention to the full spectrum of humanity made the author kin to the painter Bartolomé Esteban Murillo, who "stole the divinest colors from heaven" to paint his glorious Madonnas, even while depicting with equal love "the filthiest beings on earth." But the ability to embrace the spectacle of a beggar child delousing himself, which made art modern, also cast into relief a politically unsustainable disparity of fortunes, foreshadowing the collapse of the artist's contrasting subjects in the muddy palette of mass rectitude. This conundrum highlights the ambivalence of Heine's post-Romantic, revolutionary viewpoint, which recognized the need for a radical redistribution of the world's material goods, while wavering as to whether the real beauties of the past would survive their more equable allotment.

The key to Cervantes' allegory—like the rationale for retaining the idea of God—was bound up for Heine with the tricky relationship between humanity's corporeal needs and the yearnings of exalted dreamers. Perhaps, Heine mused, the gaunt knight was meant to caricature idealistic enthusiasm, while the roly-poly squire was intended as a parody of reason. In that scenario, reason held the more ludicrous position since the squire, "with all of his traditional and useful sayings, must nevertheless trot around on his calm donkey following behind enthusiasm." So material understanding would always plod in the footsteps of fantastical passion, Heine wrote. In middle age Heine came to see the book as "a great Mystery in which the question of spirit and matter is discussed in ghastliest authenticity." In truth, he opined, "the body seems often to have more insight than the spirit, and thinking with one's back and belly is often far more correct than thinking with one's head." It's with the gnawing stomach of the people that justice makes its home.

Only justice, in Heine's schema, is not the repository of mercy, imagination or love. And, notwithstanding everything, he confesses elsewhere that in the depths of night his neighbors could yet sometimes hear him crying, "Dulcinea is the fairest lady in the world; and I the most luckless knight upon the earth."

Chapter Nine

HEINE'S READING ranged widely, but books were not the only vehicle transporting his imagination. Betty had a brother named Simon, a small, plump man whose clothes were French, genteel, and out of date: breeches, white silk stockings, and shoes with giant buckles, complemented by a pigtail that flew and danced behind him. When Simon was lost in thought, or in the pages of his newspaper, Heine became possessed by an irresistible urge to jerk that pigtail. This drove his uncle crazy. The man would exclaim over the younger generation's woeful deficit of respect, which Heine owned to without apologizing. He always took a little excess pride in his inability to contain himself.

But if his uncle's look was silly, Heine continued, the man's heart was golden, the finest he ever encountered. Simon's sense of honor had a rigor out of old Spanish chivalry, which did not preclude his indulgence of earthier appetites, especially at one local wine house that served up steamy platters of field fare sprinkled with fragrant juniper berries.

A failed humanist scholar whose parents had bequeathed him enough so that he didn't have to worry about earning a living, Simon spent most days at home in "Noah's Ark," the little house his father had left him, pursuing his erudite hobbies, fads, and bibliomania.

For all the disparities in their ambitions, Heine maintained that this uncle might have been the person who inspired him to become an author. Simon gave him exquisite, costly books to read, along with topical pamphlets, and permitted Heine to explore the attic of his Ark. Full of dust, with giant cobwebs spun across old lumber stacks, the space objectively was rather frightening. But Heine was eager to spend his days up there exploring in the company of a fat Angora cat that was its only other occupant. Everything seemed to be steeped in the light of fantasy. The attic became a magnificent palace, Heine wrote, where even the old cat was transformed into an enchanted princess who, freed from her animal form, could now reveal herself in her beauty and splendor.

A mysterious pleasure came over him as he climbed into that arcane room, which he also called, less loftily, an old-age home for decrepit household items. There he found his mother's dilapidated cradle, which now held only his grandfather's moldy wig. A rusty dress sword hung on the wall alongside a set of fire tongs. Heine chanced upon a green china pug dog and his dead grandmother's stuffed parrot. (It had lost one eye, along with all its feathers, while changing tone from emerald to cinder gray.) There were globes and charts of the planets, and chests full of books on occult sciences, in addition to quack medicinal tracts, and works of that archrationalist Descartes.

But his most tantalizing discovery was a notebook kept by one of his grandfather's brothers, another Simon, filled with what Heine took to be Arabic, Syriac, and Coptic characters.

(They were actually cursive Hebrew letters—another reminder of the limitations of his Jewish schooling.) It contained citations in French as well, which he navigated more successfully. *Où l'innocence périt c'est un crime de vivre*—where innocence dies it is a crime to live—was scrawled over and over across the journal's pages: a haunting remnant of some penitential discipline.

Between the notebook and interviews he conducted with his elderly aunts, Heine learned a good deal about his great-uncle, who had been known as "the Easterner" on account of his prodigious travels through the Levant, and his insistence on wearing Oriental costume even after he returned to Europe. He led one of those eccentric lives possible only in the first half of the eighteenth century, Heine wrote. "Partly an enthusiast who propagated cosmopolitan, utopian ideas intended to benefit humanity, partly a soldier of fortune," the Easterner knew his strengths and took advantage of the weakness of a moldering society to vault across its rotten barriers.

Born in 1720, Simon van Geldern fled the study of Talmud in Frankfurt and began wandering across Germany while still an adolescent. On returning to his parents' house, he took up a position as a "shop-Jew" in his father's business; then tried his luck selling lottery tickets and rambled farther afield, first to a rich uncle in Vienna, eventually to London. When his lottery enterprise flagged, he survived by giving language lessons to the aristocracy, and by finagling allowances from relatives. He always set aside a tenth of his income for buying books—later hawking many of those same books for a profit. Nights he spent cultivating a passion for opera, cafés, cards, and courtesans.

At some point he was seized by the longing to make a pilgrimage to Palestine. Traveling inland from Acco, he rode an ass up the stony hills to the famed mystical city of Safed, where he studied with Kabbalists. In Jerusalem, he went into an ecstatic trance on top of Mount Moriah and experienced a vision, the contents of which he never divulged. Soon afterward, he secured an appointment gathering alms for the Holy Land and began journeying along the North African coast, where he learned the trade of an armorer from Portuguese artisans in Morocco. Holy business notwithstanding, he often reverted to gambling for his living. Eventually, he reached an oasis where he got himself elected sheik of an independent Bedouin tribe—which meant he became a robber baron, Heine explained. (Though some said he just became the bandits' victim.) Among the nomads, he learned the art of horse breeding before striking out on another adventure involving a ship back to Palestine that was commandeered by pirates. As hostage to the corsairs, the Easterner spent his nights lost in hallucinations of his mother, and the Germany of his youth. Days were taken up with maddening religious disputations forced on him by the theologically obsessed ship's captain, who happened to be deaf, and whose arguments were echoed by a pair of priests who continually flanked him. In spare moments, Simon played with a young wolf the captain had picked up in Barbary. But the wolf began biting, and one night someone heaved it overboard.

In time, the Easterner returned to Europe, where he went on a spree of faro playing and lost all the charitable funds he'd collected. He got to know Voltaire—then tried to cadge a loan off Voltaire's banker. When this plan didn't work, he went back to gambling and book dealing, sojourning in a string of courts where he won regard for his dignity and erudition, until a liaison with a high-born lady put his life at risk. (The Easterner's story evokes the progress of a Jewish Casanova—and in fact, the two men's paths crossed on several occasions.) Some of the more outrageous adventures of Heine's relative are the best corroborated: at the age of fifty-seven, having been enlisted in a scam to dupe a bunch of ruling princes, the Easterner got himself hired as an oracle to the Prince of Hesse—then was ordered to use his Kabbalistic skills to find the mastermind behind the crime he himself had helped to perpetrate. The Easterner got out of that bind but was soon thrown in prison for a different transgression. In Paris, the police kept a special file in their dossiers on "Samuel van Geldern, Rabbi and Adventurer." Periodically, he set off on new pilgrimages to Palestine that involved him in fresh signs and wonders—as well as dramatic encounters with marauders and rulers. In the final decade of his life, the Easterner became Court Kabbalist, Secret Magic Councilor, and Court Factor to his Serene Majesty in Hesse-Darmstadt—a position that entitled him to lodging in a castle.

Much of the story of Heine's great-uncle is the stuff of penny ballads, but there's a twist at the end that swings him onto the grand stage of history. The Easterner somehow became an adviser to the Abbé Grégoire, providing the influential liberal cleric with material for an essay he wrote before the fall of the Bastille in support of the Jews' emancipation. The document served as one blueprint for that project in the Revolution's aftermath—Heine's great-uncle thus helping to bring justice to his people while himself enjoying a racy thrill ride through the world.

It's a life pitched to capture the imagination of any child with a grain of pluck, suggesting that if you cast yourself head-first in fortune's way you might live your days the way you dream a dream. Or compose a romance. Given sufficient wits and derring-do, you could make up the song of your own existence.

At least once upon a time you could, Heine qualified. But his observation that the hour when such boundless self-creation was possible had passed by the middle of the eighteenth century doesn't jibe with Simon's history, which carried on at a rollicking pace until 1788, or with Heine's own self-appointed role as a colorful bridge between cultures and eras. The temporal parentheses Heine places around the story may represent an attempt to confine it. Indeed, on closer view, none of the ways Heine would have been expected to regard his great-uncle's story mesh with the reality, just as the typical read of his fascination—that Simon's dramatic history helped inspire Heine's future, adventurous path—should almost be reversed. For the true significance of Heine's encounter with his great-uncle came from the lesson it supplied about the dread suck of the ancestral tide.

Chapter Ten

One September, Heine paid a visit to Norderney, a stormy island off the northern German coast where the dirt-poor locals lived by fishing. The people loved their seafaring, though the men were often gone for years or lost for good in shipwrecks. But deeper than their passion for the ocean was the men's longing to be home again, huddled in their bitter huts, sipping tea that reeked of boiled seaweed. What drew them back, Heine decided, wasn't so much love as shared traditions and a kind of infinite familiarity. Outside such temporal cul-de-sacs, we've become so strange to one another that the ability to make a tiny gesture that sparks laughter or tears among old intimates who complete the chain of associations for us seems marvelous. Yet Heine refused to idealize the quiet consolations that derive from communities of habit. The Roman Catholic Church had tried to inculcate a similar like-mindedness, he argued. But the fantasy of our lost collective life remains impoverished next to an individual's joy in moments of true liberation.

While strolling the white sands, he mused on the question of what binds the world's residual tight-knit communities together. The Jews were one such people, known for sharing a mass of history and attitudes. For Jews, however, intertwined survival was less a result of bundling together against the elements in some godforsaken place than of contending jointly with the savagery of other people, often at the centers of civilization. This complicated their relationship to time-hallowed Gentile traditions that were seen as bolstering camaraderie. If one's ancestors going back for generations have always killed roebucks, then one might well tingle at the prospect of a chase. Personally, his ancestors had belonged not to the hunters but to the hunted, and if he were to take aim at some poor animal, his blood would curdle. Indeed, he'd find it far easier to turn his firearm on the huntsman, "who is himself inclined to dream back to the days when hunting people was fair game and good sport."

But his contempt for the descendants of those who had once stalked human beings and now shot wild animals for recreation didn't quell a deep unease with the implications of his heritage. Jewish history appeared to be a remarkable but maddeningly repetitive tragedy—and the most tragic aspect of all, he declared, was that if one tried to write about the calamity of Jews in modern times, "one would be laughed at for one's pains." This tribe—*his* people—who'd come out of Egypt, "the homeland of crocodiles and priests," carrying "skin diseases and stolen vessels of gold and silver," while wrapped in "ancient lettered mummy-cloth," had been damned centuries ago, and now dragged its misery through the ages. What could be more excruciating, or risible, than the sight of some old Jew sitting mumbling eerie prayers in which he cursed nations that had long ago disappeared from the face of the earth—a man who hardly registered that he was sitting on the gravestones of the adversaries whom he was even then beseeching heaven to annihilate?

His great-uncle's story at least contained surprises. The stories that billowed around the Easterner like the folds of his outlandish kaftan weren't entirely true; but as opposed to castigating his relative for the fabrications, Heine mounts a defense of charlatanism. Simon was not one of those common mountebanks who pull peasants' teeth at fairs, he noted, but rather one of the exceptional deceivers who boldly push their way into palaces and extract the giant molars of the great. (Again with the dental metaphor.) You must advertise your goods if you want to sell them, says the proverb, and life is a matter of flogging one's goods. When God himself delivered the Law from Sinai, he accompanied his commandments with thunder and lightning. *The Lord knew his public*, Heine wrote.

Yet though he exonerates Simon's trickery, Heine sounds less proud than shaken when he invokes his memory. Instead of liberating his imagination, the Easterner's flamboyant experiences held young Heine in thrall. He wrote of being so absorbed by these adventures that he was periodically gripped by conviction that he'd actually *become* the man. Over the daylight hours, he seemed merely to be living a continuation of his dead great-uncle's story. At night, this identification was projected through his dreams. Heine compared himself during this time to "a great newspaper, the upper section of which contained the present, the day with its daily news and debates, while in the lower section the poetic past was fantastically proclaimed in continuous nocturnal dreams, like the episodes of a serialized novel." In that image of a verbal chimera flapping and streaming with different registers of speech, half prosaic broadsheet, half lyric history, Heine revealed the degree to which he saw himself as a being composed entirely of language—a modern iteration of those forebears swaddled in "lettered mummy cloth." In his dreams, he'd altogether merged with his great-uncle. He walked confidently through places he'd never seen, and met people with peculiar faces whose hands he shook as if he knew them. When these weird figures opened their mouths they spoke an idiom he'd never heard, yet Heine understood them perfectly, and when he answered back, to his amazement, the same language left his own lips, while he gesticulated with unfamiliar violence.

So far from constituting some classic schoolboy reverie of swashbuckling escape, Heine records the horror he experienced on realizing he was not himself—that his identity could be interrupted any moment by the intrusion of another. And since that character was the Easterner it too was fractured—between west and east, free wanderer and court flunky, huckster and hero.

Heine's state of uncanny self-division continued about a year, but left permanent tracks in his soul, he averred. Numerous idiosyncrasies, desires, and antipathies that diverged from his true nature emerged at this time. Whenever he made errors for reasons he couldn't fathom, he blamed them on his Eastern double. Key passages of his youth mimicked Simon's life course. In different words at different times, Heine kept returning to the fateful question: what if we simply can't escape the shadow of our predecessors?

He came of age with the notion of the *Doppelgänger*, a term coined by Jean Paul Richter in his novel *Siebenkäs*, published the year before Heine's birth. In Richter's work, the doppelgänger (literally "double-goer") functioned mostly as a comic device: the protagonist flees an unhappy marriage by following the suggestion of a friend to whom he bears a striking resemblance that he fake his suicide, then start up life anew in the guise of this obliging comrade. Amorous complications proliferate.

Over the next several decades, the doppelgänger became a fixture of Romanticism in Germany and England, often in the guise of a darker, menacing double who reveals the limitations of the conscious self: the figure of madness haunting a Capuchin monk in E. T. A. Hoffman's *The Devil's Elixirs;* the underworld shade whom the Magus Zoroaster meets while striding through a garden in Percy Bysshe Shelley's *Prometheus Unbound;* and the monster Frankenstein in Mary Shelley's novel who exposes the abysses in his maker's character. But Heine gave the trope a special Jewish twist by linking it to the specter of memory, personal and collective, as well as to the question of what action Jews qua Jews were really capable of in contemporary Europe.

At the conclusion of his chronicle, Heine recounts a scene in which he sought to excuse himself to his father for some peccadillo by citing the doppelgänger's influence—a gambit that prompts Samson to tease that he hopes the Easterner hasn't signed any bills of exchange which will one day need to be repaid. Later, Heine reported that he'd never yet been served with an Oriental claim—Occidental ones had caused enough trouble—but added that our ancestors have saddled us with worse debts than monetary ones. "The fathers have eaten sour grapes, and the children's teeth are set on edge," he wrote—a truncated quotation from Ezekiel, to which he tacked a prophetic rumination of his own: "There is a solidarity among successive generations; indeed, the nations that succeed one another in the arena share such a solidarity, and in the end the whole of mankind will liquidate the assets of the past—perhaps through a universal bankruptcy."

While many doppelgängers subvert the respectable self-image of their originals, this disillusionment is typically achieved by exposing the instinct-driven underside of the person shadowed, not by revealing the vertiginous depths of our shared ancestral identity. The Gothic device of exposing the skull behind the maiden's face was one thing. Heine saw through the countenance of the present to an immeasurable mountain of bones that formed the backdrop to civilization as such. How to maintain the sheen of any future-oriented utopia in view of that? Simon epitomized the radical autonomy Heine forever hankered after. But if the form of freedom that concerned him most was the freedom to realize his own *sui generis* nature, the feeling of being possessed by his great uncle's story could only redouble his sense of disorientation.

Once Heine began to write, doppelgängers start popping up everywhere: hovering over the poet's shoulder, pale and silent, while he pens letters to friends; manifesting as a murderous "mist man" whose terrifyingly tender embrace threatens to transform his lover into a phantom herself. Most famous is one from his cycle *The Homecoming* that Schubert set to music in the last year of his life, and which has been called the single greatest pairing of a poet's verse and music: "The night is still, the streets are dumb / This is the house where dwelt my dear." As the narrator approaches the building from which his lover departed long ago, he finds another man standing before the façade, wringing his hands, with his gaze turned to the sky. A shudder passes through him as he realizes that the figure in the moonlight is himself. "Pale ghost, twin phantom, hell-begot! / Why do you ape the pain and woe / That racked my heart on this same spot / So many nights, so long ago?" the poet cries.

Yet how does this figure mock the narrator other than by embodying his own memory?

"True dreaming began with the Jews," Heine once said. "Our descendants will shudder when they come to read what a ghostly life we led, how our humanity was cleft in two and only one half had a *real* life."

But it's the dream half in Heine that often feels most vividly alive since when it acts things happen.

Chapter Eleven

SAMSON HAD A BROTHER named Salomon with a well-buffed brow, sealed lips, and eyes like hard, dark coins. His steady gaze peering out from portraits conveys the will to do right by others, along with perfect assurance that what he does will be just that. Here is a rich man who, if he can't fit through the eye of a needle, will simply gobble up the steel that surrounds it.

All six brothers from that generation of Heines went into business. Two died young; the others, excepting Heine's father, prospered. Disproportionate financial acumen wasn't the Jews' fault, Heine observed. It could be traced back to the medieval lunacy that stigmatized money dealings, pushed the most lucrative part of the business over to the benighted Jews—then reviled Jews all the more for making the best of their shameful lot. But Salomon was a case unto himself.

Born in Hanover in 1767, he got a job when still in adolescence at a Hamburg banking house run by relatives, shot up the ranks, and did a little money changing on the side. By the time Heine was born, he had launched a small bank of his own. Ten years later, he'd made his first million. Deftly juggling government bonds, Uncle Salomon managed to keep his fortune growing steadily through all the upheavals of the era. He soon became the richest man in Hamburg and, eventually, one of the most successful bankers in all Europe.

The scale of his riches made for a scenario Heine's second-favorite dramatist, Molière, might have relished: arrange for a free-spirited, cheekily improvident poet to know that a portion of one of the most colossal fortunes of the age lies waiting in time's wings for him. Only don't let him discover just how great a sum he might safely bet on, or how late in life the inheritance will actually come. And hold in reserve just the nagging flicker of a possibility that his benefactor might, at the last moment—miffed at something the poet scribbled under the spell of his reckless muse—decide to cut him dead.

Heine got along fine with Salomon when he was growing up, and they managed adequately thereafter. Salomon liked chaffing Heine about his fiscal ignorance, and writing mildly sadistic letters that described the scrumptious delicacies served at family dinners his nephew had been obliged to miss. The fact that Salomon contributed something to Heine's maintenance into middle age helped tame Heine's comebacks. Indeed, he respected his uncle's strength of will and self-made character. In strained ruminations he sometimes overdressed their similarities. To one friend he wrote, "I love him to an extraordinary degree, almost more than I am myself aware of." Almost, but not quite. They were incredibly alike in character, Heine continued. Both of them combined impulsive bravery "with an unfathomable softness of sentiment and incalculable caprice." One looks in vain for other testimonies to Salomon's mushy side, let alone his whimsy. The only difference between them, Heine concluded, was that fortune had made Salomon a millionaire while he himself was the opposite: a poet. This man, too, it seems, is Heine's doppelgänger, only distinguishable in consequence of a random fork in their vocational paths.

The evidence suggests that Salomon would have found his nephew's views on their resemblance unhinged. He took the trouble to consult one Professor Zimmerman, a recognized Hamburg literary expert, on the question of whether his nephew had any marketable talent, since he couldn't make it out himself. Zimmerman assured him—yes, Heine had the goods. But the professional endorsement didn't much affect the banker's attitude toward his nephew. Salomon took Heine's gifts most seriously with respect to the havoc he might wreak should he choose to pen something scurrilous about a family member.

When Betty was trying to set Heine up as a shop-Jew, she asked Salomon to find a post for him. Salomon apprenticed Heine at M. Heckscher & Co., his own bank. Of course he would expect the same diligence from his relative he'd demand of any other young man, but he saw the logic of providing his nephew a leg up. There was nothing to be gained from watching Heinrich founder alongside his shiftless father. So in 1816 Betty packed him off to Hamburg.

Fields filled with waving bean, clover, and buckwheat blossoms spread behind the poplars that lined the road Heine traveled. But nature never much interested Heine in and of itself; its purpose in his work is to counterpoint or emulate our inner landscapes. Since people were influenced by their natural surroundings, nature might grow to reflect the character of its human inhabitants, he speculated. Perhaps that was why nature in Italy appeared passionate, while in Germany it was solemn, broody, and phlegmatic. Surely nature wanted to express itself as much as people did. Summer lightning represented nature's attempts at speech, Heine wrote. Those electric scrawlings across her lovely countenance were stammerings in light. The vain gesture made him weep in sympathy, and his compassion, in turn, moved nature to laughter. He understood her stars. She got his tears. They traded pantheistic consolations, like the hieroglyphic secrets contained in the patterning on lizard skins.

From several miles away, Hamburg's copper-sheathed bell towers came flashing into sight, followed by the ramparts Napoleon had erected at colossal expense, which were now being converted into boulevards and gardens. Notwithstanding its grand new avenues, the town was still riddled with narrow, dirty lanes, hemmed in by tall houses. The spiderweb of older streets exacerbated the threat from Hamburg's coachmen, who were constantly running over poor people. The murderous drivers were given a wrist-slap fine for leaving the unlucky ones behind in pieces, and the fortunate paid the accidents no further notice. The indifference of Hamburg's moneyed citizenry to these victims struck visitors as downright "Vandalic." And no less appalling in tourists' eyes were the throngs of deformed children and hunchbacked adults, suffering from diseases such as rickets that the city's administrators could have alleviated had they invested in the public's health.

The tightfisted coldness of the officials infuriated Heine—but also burnished his uncle's reputation as one of Hamburg's principal philanthropists. Salomon gave liberally to Jewish and non-Jewish charities alike—even helping to fund the Orthodox-Evangelical domestic mission, which intended eventually to convert all Jews. Religion as such meant nothing to him, except when prejudice obstructed business. This ecumenical charity might have helped protect him three years later when antisemitic violence swept over Germany.

Theoretically driven by efforts of the Jewish community to recover civil rights that had been rolled back after Waterloo, popular fury was ignited by immediate food shortages and timeless economic jealousy. *Hep, Hep, Jude Verreck!*—Hep, Hep, Jew, die like a beast—was one of the chants roared out by rioters as they burst into the coffeehouses where Jews were congregating. Though the etymology is uncertain, "Hep" might have been an acronym for the old Crusader standard: *Hierosolyma est Perdita*—Jerusalem is lost—and in any case the cryptic cry gave its name to these disturbances, which became known as the Hep-Hep Riots. Local governments took a two-birds-with-one-stone approach to the disturbances. On the one hand they defended the Jews against physical harm by thrashing the rabble—always a worthy exercise in that period when French revolutionary notions were still circulating among the lower classes. On the other hand, they cited the risk of further carnage as an argument for refusing to grant the Jews the basic liberties they had lost.

The generous attention Salomon paid to Hamburg's social ills almost certainly provided him some cover against anti-semitic rage, and his standing opened the city's doors to his nephew. At first, the unfamiliar sense of possibility made Heine giddy. A young man, full of fresh ideas and musical words, plunging into a new metropolis, bigger and more affluent than his hometown—a self-described "free and unpretentious bard" entering society at the top, eager to make his mark (or at least itching to graffiti everything), bursting with confidence about how awesome his signature would appear to everyone—how could he not be exhilarated? "The nephew of the great (??) Heine is everywhere popular," he wrote a friend in Düsseldorf, adding that "pretty girls ogle him, their bosom-kerchiefs rise and fall, and their mothers calculate."

But delight at his instant popularity couldn't blind him for long to the narrow, niggling sensibility beneath the city's business dynamism. When he looked more closely at the city's residents, their costly raiment fell away and he saw that they were nothing more than numbers: "Here a crooked-legged Two was walking alongside a fatal Three, its pregnant and big-bosomed consort; behind them came Mr. Four on crutches." Yes, Hamburg was a good city full of sound, respectable houses—one governed not by the notorious Macbeth, but instead by *Banko*. The spirit of Banko reigned everywhere in that bustling town where people might have differences of opinion on matters of religion, politics, and science but all agreed on padding their coffers and eating gluttonously. "What is the art of printing or the Reformation compared to smoked beef!" Heine expostulated. The local men were mostly coolly reasoning characters with low foreheads and heavy red cheeks that reflected their exceptionally developed eating mechanisms. Their hats looked nailed to their heads, and their hands stayed deep inside their pockets, as if their owners were constantly on the verge of asking, "How much do I have to pay then?" The Hamburg women, for their part, tended to be charming in their abundance, Heine wrote. Though it was also true that they didn't demonstrate much dreamy idealism in their approach to romance. Cupid often shot his sharpest arrows at these ladies, but, whether from a prankster's instinct or mere clumsiness, the winged child, missing the heart, pierced the Hamburg women with his appetite-inducing darts smack in the belly.

For hours on end, having nowhere else to go, he would haunt the Alster Basin watching pretty girls pass by the calm, blue waters on which swans floated, "so proud, and beautiful, and secure." Some fellows exclaimed on The Female's angelic qualities. Others licked their lips at the thought of what delicious morsels the girls would make. But Heine just sank down in a café opposite the Swiss pavilion thinking sweet nothings, one after the next. *Aut Caesar aut nihil* became his motto: Either Caesar or nothing. He had barely settled in, yet already all the city's bounties seemed fixed beyond his reach.

Chapter Twelve

IT WASN'T ONLY that Uncle Salomon was rich, but also that he had two pretty daughters. The older one, Amalie, might just have been Heine's soulmate. Why not? Or even knowing all the reasons, who knew what would happen until he had tried—then tried again, repeatedly? He couldn't know for certain that the part of him that believed completely in his charms was more fallible than the part that questioned everything. He'd been thrust into an environment at once antipathetic to his lyric side and gleaming with enticements. How could Heine help thinking about Salomon's money together with his offspring? His ducats, his daughter. All those millions and Amalie, whom he'd met one time two years before. (Therese, the younger girl, had similar charms, just less mature.)

The family had a bust made of Amalie looking gently melancholy, gracefully attenuated. Her eyes aren't so big. Her mouth is more petulant than lush. Yet everything about her draws the viewer in, from her fluted throat to the cool etched gaze—the whole display cresting in an empress coif that ripples back in gentle Alster waves from her classical, smooth forehead. Heine found her intoxicating. When decades later he wrote a poem for Amalie's daughter, inspired by the similarity he detected between mother and child, he described the girl's attributes reincarnating the enchantments of "that beloved siren," the "springtime dream of youth!"

The settings where he saw her surely added to her luster: the family's massive five-story townhouse, and the villa in suburban Ottensen, the jewel in Salomon's domain. The house was set on an elevation above the Elbe in a stately park adorned with monumental trees and winding walks. Near the entrance stood an elegant, cream stone garden house with a sloping darktiled roof where Heine tried to buttonhole his uncle for a loan. At the edge of the property, successive views unfolded: high-masted sailing ships, steamboats, and smaller skiffs lifting smoke and color from the smear of water. In the distance, on a gauzy spit of low, green land, stood a windmill twirling gently, untroubled by Quixotes or even snoozing Panzas. And beyond the windmill's modest arms another copse of trees, then more water, and beyond this liquid swath, yet more bosky ground.

Heine's uncle's home took in everything.

Other fancy houses belonging to assimilated German-Jewish merchants of the era had elaborate parquet floors and giant chandeliers, dripping with glass icicles. Couches with smart, striped upholstery. Music stands. Family portraits. Daisies and hyacinths in ornamental urns on pedestals. Scooped, maroon valences trailing lacy fringe down long, diaphanous white curtains. Big heavy desks with polished column borders. Light drawing room chairs with dove-gray velvet seats angled in tight constellations about gigantic rooms. Glass-doored bookcases topped by statuettes of Roman orators. Round polished tables inlaid with floral borders set on massive black wood bases like inverted octopi. A colored print of a colossal, orientalist synagogue. Gilt candelabras held aloft by winged nymphs. A bronze dog's head paperweight. Pink geraniums on window ledges. A white stone mermaid waving from another desk. A Pan. A stag. A bedside crucifix. (Some family members went whole hog with the assimilation business. Sometimes whole families converted.) A huge bell jar clamped over a precious clock as if time might otherwise fly off.

Periodically, the rooms filled with muted voices and careful steps. Elaborate dresses rustling; the scent of heavy perfumes, pipe smoke, sweat. Heels stepping from carpet to plank. Silver tinkling. Scraping chairs. Heavy bodies in stiff costumes shifting the close atmosphere.

Heine didn't know how to behave. He talked too much about himself, then complained to friends about the bores parading through his uncle's chambers. "Diplomatic cocks-of-the-walk, millionaires, sage senators, etc. etc." The complaints seem aimed at justifying his own lack of finish. Everything at his uncle's place was "prim and curled," "decked out and lick-spittle." Naturally, the uninhibited manner of a poet "very frequently sins against etiquette," he explained to Christian Sethe, his best pal from Düsseldorf. What could you expect? Hamburg was a town of swindlers, without the tiniest instinct for poetry. All marriages there were strictly cash-on-delivery pasquinades, just like the baptisms and burials.

Nobody knows the details of what happened; but Heine made clear the main stations in his passion. Amalie was lovely. He decided that he loved her. She chatted with him nonchalantly. She listened up to a point. She smiled casually when he spoke. Her cajoling eyes were seas and emeralds. Objectively speaking, what was the objection? Indeed, wasn't there a clannish rightness to the alliance? Amalie kept allowing her cousin to keep her company. But the very ease of their exchange betrayed its lack of gravity. Notwithstanding gusts of self-esteem, he soon deduced that his feelings were not reciprocated. And still, he told Sethe, he chose to build himself a beautiful house of cards on top of which he balanced, holding her in his arms while knowing better all the while.

"I am a mad chess player," Heine announced, a feverish gamester who lost his queen on the very first move and yet continues to "play and play—for the queen."

How exactly did he play and play? He wrote poem after poem to her. He couldn't stop. Before the move to Hamburg, Heine seems to have written little more than routine ditties for family celebrations and national anniversaries. But the occasion now was unrequited love, which could be observed continually.

The financial work his uncle assigned didn't take much time, at least not the way Heine did it. The rest of his hours were filled with poetry. He didn't know whether the poems he was writing under Salomon's roof were any better than those he'd written before, he confessed to Sethe, but they were certainly more tender and sweet. They overflow with moony knights, castles, dreams, and blossoms—and maiden cheeks damp, flushed, and shiny. Harps and smiles and wild self-sacrifices, along with mystery bridegrooms standing where he should have been, and blood, and more blood: foaming cataracts of frustration. There's irony from the beginning also, but initially that key is less convincing than the straight-up lamentations of his lonely singers.

Yet along with the courtly content drawn from the archaizing register of German Romanticism, there are also weirder flashes, mingling a terror and elation conjured from more remote antiquity—and too many dreams swimming through the verses in too unstable a relation to waking life to fit snugly inside the conventions of any genre. Moreover, from the beginning Heine's poetry exhibited a striking technical fluency, a pure-lined beauty that gave composers spacious openings for their musical interpolations. His language was often hypnotically melodious, while his strophic meters carried infectious momentum. Heine himself once ascribed the onset of his lyric revelations to a French drummer bivouacked with the family during the Napoleonic period. This man made Heine understand the great historic moments of the era by drumming out the marches that accompanied them: you couldn't really get a feel for the beheading of their majesties until you heard the roll of the red Guillotine March, he opined. Even if this drummer was apocryphal, there's no end of allusions to actual drums and marches in his poems, along with percussive cadences.

Heine told friends that his Madonna didn't like his lovely lines—that in fact she hated them. It was truly terrible behavior on her part. Nonetheless, "the Muse is dearer to me than ever before," he wrote. Amalie's indifference kept blowing on the fires of his fancy. He notes in one poem that while a poet can imagine basilisks, dragons, and vampires, no poet could invent real female beauty; just as no poet could invent a face so innocent as his beloved's—specifically, "your false looks and artless smiles, dear." The poet needs an actual person in order to know the human ideal and the *ne plus ultra* of mendacity alike. But once the loved one has supplied that knowledge, the poet has no more need for her. The artist's task then becomes to chart the inner ripples made by the weight of that understanding as it sinks deeper through the psyche, shattering sequential layers of illusion as it drops.

Even in his youthful verses, Heine wove together moods of intense intimacy with depersonalized poses: the woman he's addressing might not even be Amalie. But he has made a compact with the idea of her: the notion of a woman who can engender such a vital inner conversation by definition never really being there.

If the first crop of his verses resembled pain dipped in honey, the second batch was pain dipped in honey, then infused with a reduction of black bile. And by the third set he was serving up whole flights of conflicting emotions in a single poem: acid next to tears beside a spreading leer.

The heart's inconsistent attitudes toward a love object don't cancel one another out in Heine's verses, any more than in the Talmud the voices of dissenting rabbis on a legal question are excluded from the final judgment. And this *is* original in a manner that the Romantic gambit of making the loved one more or less imaginary—a metaphysical excuse for poetry—is not. Here the *lover's* lack of a persuasively fixed identity is poeticized as well. Heine caught the sound of our strongest, purest emotions cracking against their contradictions, and left the different stages of that collision all legibly juxtaposed. He became known for swerves and splits, the famous Heine *Stimmungsbrechung*—breaks in tone that happen often at the ends of poems when the speaker veers off suddenly in a fresh direction, addressing someone or something unexpected, coinciding with shifts in verb tenses so that, as critics noted, readers find themselves abruptly entering a new poetic time zone. The nineteenth-century American writer Kate Hillard, who grew up reading Heine, described the transitions as "a sort of touch-and-go effect," which proved "inexpressibly charming. . . . It is like a bird that lights on a bending branch, shakes out one burst of melody and is gone before you fairly realize its presence."

Within a few years of his arrival in Hamburg, Heine began to shape a poetry that broke through the plaster molding of standard lyric passion to expose the scaffolding of the poem and the poet's mind. In offering up a kind of exploded-view psychology, Heine revealed as well that our integrity is always partly a reflection of porosity to other selves. "My songs are filled with poison—" begins one early verse.

> Why shouldn't that be true?
> Into my budding manhood
> You poured your poison through.

My songs are filled with poison—
Why shouldn't that be true?
My heart bears a nest of serpents
And also, darling, you.

But the particular strain of self-consciousness that finds expression in his verses isn't a factor only of the way his lover, his adversary, takes possession of his voice. It's also attributable to the way she unconsciously becomes conjunctive with the entire tradition of idealizing love poetry. Heine's unlucky lovers are tormented by knowledge of their literary precedents in tandem with that of the punishment delivered firsthand by their sweethearts. What's more, they're mocked for being haunted, since their consciousness of enacting a cliché proves no prophylactic against pain. (The lover in this sense pairing with the eternal suffering of the Jew.) One of the most powerful poems from his early years taxonomizes the situation in a stark equation:

A young man loves a maiden
Who chooses another instead;
The other loves still another
And these two haply wed.

. . . It is so old a story,
Yet somehow always new;
And he that has just lived it,
It breaks his heart in two.

The age-old tragedy that remains evergreen to the participants—and that the writer will experience both from inside and out—crops up repeatedly in Heine's writing. The second chapter of his fictional memoir, *Ideas: The Book of Le Grand*, begins with an epigraph: " 'She was lovable, and he loved her; but he was not lovable, and she did not love him.' (Old Play.)" The history of poetry itself here plays the part of phantom doppelgänger contemplating the agony of its own repetition—and finding the misery compounded by this doubling. For it encompasses not just the failure of private passion but the breakdown of the old Romantic model—which poetry can't transcend, since the fragments left behind by the collapse of that edifice still trip up each successive person, who must reexperience the fall individually. When Heine thought back on his love for Amalie, what drove him to distraction was not the idea that he couldn't make her happy, but that he couldn't ruffle her enough to make her feel *anything*. It's an old story, he concluded, once again.

> They filled my cup with poison,
> They poisoned the bread I ate—
> Some of them with their love, and
> The others with their hate.
>
> But she who hurt me more than
> The others I am thinking of,
> She felt for me no hatred
> And felt for me no love.

How closely Heine's deepening recognition that he couldn't touch Amalie tracked his declining status at Salomon's bank isn't certain; but clearly he began to feel he was being humiliated whichever way he turned. In time, he nicknamed his uncle's home *Schloss Affrontenburg*, the Castle of Effrontery. In its "accursed garden" not a single tree grew under whose shadow an insult hadn't been cast at him, "by tongues / Refined or crude, and suave or blunt." All the seductive roses there soon got sick and died; so did the nightingale. An eavesdropping toad passed the story of his gross humiliation to the rat, who promptly scuttled off to tell his aunt, the snake. Everything around Heine babbled and croaked the news of his pathetic suit.

The interconnected realm of Heine's animal detractors evokes the interconnection between his private anguish and the malformation of society. For the materialistic prejudices of Amalie's class, which contorted all natural feeling, were responsible for dividing them, Heine decided; just as the fragmentation of his inner life was a consequence of greater sociopolitical fractures of the age. His romantic harmony couldn't be consummated until a solution was found for the defects and dissonances of the larger civilization.

When next Heine walked along the Jungfernstieg, it was winter. The lime trees were dead; their branches trembled wraithlike in the bitter wind. A hearse passed, followed by a procession of smug civic mourners with red, mercenary faces, wearing absurd, old-fashioned Burgundian costumes. As the silent cortege trudged along, his ears were struck by a shrill metallic shrieking coming from the waters beyond the promenade. It was a lunatic cry, accompanied by frantic splashing and gasping.

Turning, Heine saw that the Alster basin was entirely frozen except for one square pool inside which all the swans of summer were thrashing round and round. The dreadful screeches had come from these pitiable white creatures, who had once swum the basin's wide expanse so gracefully. Oh the lovely, white swans! Heine exclaimed. Their wing bones had been snapped to stop them flying south, and now they'd never fly again.

Despite the agony, Heine reported to friends how much Amalie's indifference had given him as a writer. (She later married one John Friedlander, a conservative estate owner. "The world is stupid and insipid and unpleasant and smells of dried violets," Heine wrote in reference to their union.) He quipped that if he could only arrange another unhappy love affair it would be the making of him.

Yet this may overstate the case for his muse of amorous disappointment. In truth, if another romance held the secret to Heine's artistic maturation, that affair came earlier, and hadn't been unhappy. Rather, it was weird, sexual, and spellbinding. In the course of this relationship, instead of being martyred to a fruitless passion for a queen, Heine reached down the social ladder to the *Volk*. Whatever distance prevailed between Heine and this woman derived not from her inaccessible elevation, but from her elemental mystery.

The autobiographical fragment that became known post-humously as his *Memoirs* closes with ruminations on this for-mer attachment, which occurred while Heine was still in ado-lescence. And though Heine wrote of this love that it would prove but a prelude to the great tragedies of his majority—that just as Romeo was first infatuated with another lady, he himself had yet to meet his Juliet—he seems to forget that the hero-ines of Shakespeare's comedies and romances are often greater than his tragic females—at least they have more play and pluck. While Amalie was his Juliet, he calls Red Sefchen his Rosalind.

Chapter Thirteen

Frau Flader, an aged charity case, the picture of indigence and misery, with "a big, trembling body, a white leathery face," and colorless, frightened eyes, depended on Heine's father's alms. The last time she came to see him, she was so feeble she had to be propped up by her grandson Jupp, who happened to be the lead bully among those who shouted *Haarüh!* at Heine. On this occasion, Samson presented her with an especially large money bag, whereupon Frau Flader broke down weeping, saying what a lovely child his boy was, and counting off the many prayers she'd offer the Virgin on his behalf. She ordered Jupp to kiss him. Jupp made a face but complied, planting his lips on Heine's hand. Heine felt that kiss like a viper's fangs. Without knowing why, he then dug into his pocket and gave Jupp all his money.

The next day Jupp chucked horse manure at Heine's head and whacked him with his fishing rod, just as he always did. But if Jupp didn't take his grandmother seriously, Heine's nurse-maid Zippel did. Zippel, who was in the room when Frau Flader praised the boy, realized that he was being cursed by the evil eye—especially dangerous since Frau Flader was a witch.

Heine didn't believe the accusation, but Zippel did her best to counter the wicked spell anyway by spitting on him three times, according to a popular remedy. However, she knew the curse could be broken only by another witch, so Zippel hustled Heine away to visit a widow known as the Mistress of Göcherin, who cut several hairs from the top of Heine's head, then spat on her thumb and rubbed it into the bald place, while mumbling abracadabras.

Perhaps that ceremony initiated him into the Devil's ministry, Heine speculated. He kept in touch with the woman, and over time she taught him the occult arts she was proficient in. Her husband had been an executioner, and everyone knew the man had passed his profession's dark secrets onto her. One of her most lucrative sidelines was with publicans. The fingers of hanged thieves were said to enrich the flavor of beer and boost its volume. Most taste-enhancing of all were the fingers of men who'd been unjustly hung. The Mistress of Göcherin kept plenty of these digits in stock, and she would sell them to tavern keepers so that they could float them by strings inside their beer barrels and improve business.

Along with her trade in fingers, she also dealt in all sorts of love potions, along with magical articles that allowed a woman who had been cheated of her man to get back at him or his new darling. For example, the Mistress had special locks for sale. If a woman's former suitor was getting married, the jilted lover simply had to go into the church where the ceremony was taking place with one of these locks hidden under her apron. At the moment the priest was concluding the nuptials, the woman merely had to snap the lock shut: the bride's womb would be sealed for good.

There were also alarming ways of making a bridegroom impotent, which Heine detailed after saying they were too awful to reveal. One involved removing the offending man's genitals, then placing them high up in a leafy tree. At first, the organs would be so despondent (perhaps from homesickness, Heine speculated) that they would just hang there listlessly. But all the fresh air they got up in the branches had a tonic influence, and gradually the genitals would begin chirping away like cicadas, thereby attracting the attention of local birds. Mistaking the noise for hungry fledglings, these creatures would feed the squirmy flesh, which grew strong and fat in consequence, twittering ever more loudly. Witches just loved that sound. On cool summer nights they liked nothing better than lounging beneath the trees listening to the singing of amputated male organs, which they called their nightingales.

Around the time Heine turned sixteen, he began to visit the Mistress of Göcherin's cottage more often, drawn by a spell more powerful than any philter. This woman had a niece around his age who had suddenly transformed, grown tall and slender with a figure her tight clothing enunciated, like wet drapery on a sculpture. But more beautiful than any marble statue, the girl in Heine's recollection was "a revelation of life itself." Her large dark eyes appeared to be forever awaiting the answer to some riddle she'd just posed, while her small, pursed mouth seemed to say there was no point in even trying to guess the answer because you were too dull. She had abundant red hair that swirled down below her shoulders. When she gathered it up beneath her chin, it looked as if she'd just slit her throat.

She didn't have a lovely, musical voice. In fact, it was husky. But when passion seized her, Red Sefchen's tone resonated in a manner that uncannily resembled his own, Heine felt. At those moments, he would have the disconcerting sense that he was hearing himself speak; her voice reminded him of how he sang in dreams. If Amalie's silence later nurtured his inborn creativity, inspiring him to make poems of sorrow and sarcasm in the void she left behind, the sound of Red Sefchen was so communicable that her words and inflections left his lips. While his uncle's daughter in the big stone house on manicured grounds launched him on a voyage of self-discovery, Red Sefchen had opened him to the voices of the people—initiating his exploration of the subterranean rivers of the popular imagination. Amalie and Red Sefchen were complementary muses—and perhaps, as they've come down to us, filtered through his writing, were equally Heine's invention.

One of Red Sefchen's songs concerned a malefactor named Tragig, who serenaded his beloved Otilje with speculations that she wouldn't be his final lover. Would she hang on the lofty tree or swim in the blue sea—or, Tragig wonders, would Otilje agree to "kiss the naked sword,/Decreed by the almighty Lord"? Otilje answers that she will not hang from a tree or fall into the sea, but will kiss that naked sword. Once when Red Sefchen sang this song, Heine watched her becoming overwrought by emotions he couldn't understand but that drove the pair weeping and wordless into each other's arms for the next hour. Heine asked her to write down the verses. She did so, using her blood for ink.

Red Sefchen's father had also been an executioner. He died young, which was how she'd ended up living with the Mistress of Göcherin. Then at some point she lived at her grandfather's house—he too was an executioner. Three ancient female relatives shared that domicile. They sat at spinning wheels, bickering and swigging from a brandy bottle while they spun. On stormy nights, when flames flickered in the hearth and wind raged in the chimney, Red Sefchen heard knocking at the windows and knew that dead thieves had descended on the house demanding to retrieve their chopped-off fingers.

One night, more than a dozen shrunken old men marched into the cottage, clutching swords under their scarlet cloaks.

These were the most senior executioners in the realm. Having all gathered, the men went outside again to a clearing beneath some oak trees. Her grandfather made Red Sefchen fetch a special silver cup embossed with dolphins and sea gods. She was supposed to go to bed at this point, but instead she hid and watched the executioners drink from the goblet and mutter prayers. Red Sefchen's grandfather made a speech she couldn't hear. Then the old men wept. One kept howling, "Oh God! Our misery has already gone on so long we can no longer bear it!" On hearing this, they all rose from their seats, and walked two by two toward a certain tree. Someone took out an iron spade, and began digging a pit. Red Sefchen's grandfather walked up to the hole and drew a thin, cloth-wrapped package from beneath his mantle. He lay this package carefully into the hole. Then the men quickly filled it with dirt.

Horrified, Red Sefchen rushed back into the house, and buried herself beneath her bedsheets, then passed out. The next day, she thought the scene must have been a dream. But on going outside, she saw that the earth under the tree where the ceremony took place was indeed freshly turned over. What had been concealed there? Treasure? An animal? A dead child? She was too frightened to tell anyone what she'd witnessed, let alone to try and excavate the thing. It wasn't until five years later, when her grandfather was dead, that she dared describe to her aunt what she'd seen that night.

The Mistress of Göcherin was completely unfazed by her story. No, she told Red Sefchen, it wasn't gold, a cat, or a baby that the men had buried there. It was a sword. For the executioners maintained that after a sword had sliced off the heads of a hundred men, it acquired an independent consciousness. Having shed so much blood, the blade gained an appetite for butchery that made it unsafe to keep around. In fact, you could hear these hundred-head swords rattling about in cupboards where they were stored; one of them had recently driven someone to slash his brother to death. Even so, she said, these swords also possessed magical powers, which was why after the burial of this particular sword she had immediately dug it up and had kept it to this day.

Heine asked to see the dread weapon. Red Sefchen went to fetch it from the lumber room and returned, swinging the enormous blade while chanting in a teasing, menacing voice, *Will you kiss the naked sword/Decreed by the Almighty Lord?* Heine answered that he would *not* kiss the naked sword, he would instead kiss Red Sefchen! And he rushed straight for her. Afraid of accidentally cutting him, she had to lower the blade, which left her defenseless. He seized the opportunity—embraced her and pressed his lips to hers.

Yes! Heine exulted. Notwithstanding all the curses, he had kissed the executioner's lovely daughter! "I kissed her, not merely because I was fond of her, but also to mock the old order of society and all its obscure prejudices," he wrote, adding that when he did so, there flared up in him the twin passions to which he would dedicate the remainder of his life: a love for beautiful women, and for the French Revolution.

It's a dizzying tale, from start to finish, made more remarkable by the matter-of-fact tone in which Heine narrates its jolting details. Lips to the naked sword. A hundred severed heads. Singing genitals. The self-reflection at once bends past the analytic frame and lends itself to endless excavating. Who knows what the executioners really buried that night? Heine's politico-aesthetic explanation for the kiss gives as much insight into his motivations as anything he ever wrote—and also sounds no less contrived than the fantastical events he's just narrated. Liberation *was* his cause, and just as he came to conflate Amalie's inaccessibility with the impregnable castle of great wealth, the French Revolution was an emblem for society's release from the tyranny of hereditary stature as such. But while Heine battled for a more just society, free of supernatural palliatives, what would his writing be without its fecund loam of folk belief? Even as he claims to be passionately invested in exposing the folly of occult practices, his obvious delight in describing the bizarre rites and carnal enchantments conjured by Red Sefchen undermines his pose as a freedom fighter for the Enlightenment.

This ambivalence becomes only more striking if, as some suspect, the executioner's daughter did not in fact exist, if Heine himself created the living vessel for these old legends. Parts of Red Sefchen story were unquestionably lifted from traditional tales. Other elements of her story are so finely textured, and consistent with better corroborated reminiscences from Heine's autobiographical writings, that it seems likely there's some real-life model for her. Regardless, since he's writing about people who are themselves steeped in myth and magic the line between Heine's narration of the world they believe themselves to inhabit and the one that objectively surrounds them blurs. The imaginative verve of the story has a revolutionary quality of its own that challenges the status quo.

A few years after the end of his nonaffair with Amalie, Heine found a way of merging the voice he'd developed in resistance to her—the sophisticated, perplexed, and omniscient interrogatory tone in which he presented the state of unrequited love—with his neofolklore style. In that idiom, he wrote the verses that made him a famous poet. And when he found a way of applying this hybrid, urbane form to the nightmare farce of contemporary politics, he produced the work that won him not only honor among champions of liberty, but also an arrest warrant from the Prussian government.

◆┃◆┃◆

Chapter Fourteen

TRAVELERS FROM OTHER NATIONS chattered on about Bonn's elegance and charm—the soulful beginning of the picturesque Rhine country—a spired town, with Roman ruins and a lovely double avenue of chestnuts that flanked one's passage to the Chateau of Poppelsdorf: home to a museum of natural history containing a collection of fossil frogs that illustrated the entire life cycle, from squiggly tadpole to old bubble-skinned jumper; and the site of a church with a trapdoor in its pavement that opened onto a vault filled with rows of open coffins in which the bodies of twenty-five monks lay grimacing up at visitors, still in cowl and cassock, fraying flesh shriveled to the consistency of stockfish. Sightseeing in Germany, Heine indicated, was most rewarding for those with a taste for the primordial macabre.

However, Bonn was best known for its university, where eminent faculty enlarged on grave questions of history and higher destiny. August Wilhelm Schlegel was the place's most esteemed professor, and perhaps the foremost German critic of the age. Schlegel was so pale and ethereal by 1819, the year Heine met him, that he appeared translucent: Spirit personified. Heine also said that Schlegel was the first great man he ever met, though in giving him that title Heine made clear he referred to the scale of Schlegel's influence, rather than inherent merit.

When Heine came to Bonn, August and his brother, Friedrich, were leading lights of the German Romantic school, a movement with a hallowed intellectual pedigree, which was now mutating into something its founders would have spurned. Between its inception near the end of the eighteenth century, and the period of Heine's higher education, the project's philosophical premises had been gradually adapted to the changing times until the political implications turned inside out.

Conditions in Germany were favorable to Romanticism after the country's humiliation by Napoleon, Heine commented. At a certain point in that conflict, the Germans lost all self-respect and its rulers sought to promulgate a philosophical outlook that would restore pride and fealty simultaneously. The Romantic school that Heine encountered was intended to forge a national-religious aesthetic such as had prevailed in the Middle Ages. "Need teaches prayer," says the proverb, and never was the need greater in Germany than at that time, he wrote. All at once even the high commanders began speaking of German customs, the common German fatherland, and the reunion of old Germanic tribes.

The Schlegel brothers took over Romanticism's mantle from the philosopher and theologian Johann Gottfried Herder, who had died in 1803. But Herder's version of nationalism had been culturally magnanimous, directed toward the ultimate unity of all humanity. "Herder did not sit in judgement over the diverse nations like a literary grand inquisitor, damning or absolving them according to the degree of their faith," Heine asserted. Instead, he saw all the earth's peoples as individual strings in a great harp, "tuned in a distinctive manner, and he understood the universal harmony of the different sounds." For Herder's successors, the German Romantic school still composed the upper atmosphere of thought, but somehow their patch of heaven had been snipped off from the rest of the world's sky, and irradiated with special Teutonic luster, while life beneath that shrunken canopy got musty, dim, and sanctimonious.

When Schlegel delivered addresses in his delicate treble, sipping all the while from a glass of sugar water, he quoted the classics in three languages and the public listened avidly, just as they did to their princes. For "no people is more loyally attached to its rulers than the Germans," Heine stated. The problem with the devoted attention the people gave to Schlegel was that in their thirst to bloom again they drank with crazy greediness at the springs he conjured, like an aged waiting-maid who—discovering her mistress has a rejuvenating potion—gulps down the whole bottle when she should have confined herself to a few drops, and so ends up regressing all the way to bawling infancy.

Not long after Heine enrolled at the university, Schlegel chanced upon his poetry and invited Heine home for coffee. Heine was trembling when he approached the man whom at that point he considered a genius, conscious of the fact that while he himself wore coarse student's garb, Schlegel exuded *eau de mille fleurs* and was dressed in the most refined Parisian manner, right down to his kid gloves. His servant donned baronial livery to trim the tapers in the silver candelabra. Schlegel referred to "my friend, the Lord Chancellor of England." Everything he did was garnished. And this splendor changed Heine's sense of what it meant to be a poet: never had he known the vocation could be so exorbitantly graceful. Farewell to the old model of the miserable German poet lying in the gutter, threadbare, drunk, and licked by moonbeams after a lifetime scrawling lyrics for weddings and christenings.

When Heine's poems began appearing in magazines, Schlegel made some metrical corrections to his work. Heine benefited from these edits and repaid Schlegel by composing panegyric sonnets to counter the lampoons being circulated against the scholar's conservative pontificating. For Schlegel, Heine wrote, embodied the school of literature that "floated with the stream of the times; that is to say with the stream that floated backward to its source."

Heine's first poetic submission, to the publisher F. A. Brockhaus, in 1820, was rejected despite Schlegel's endorsement. But Heine continued to cultivate him, not yet having resolved that technical expertise was really all he had to offer. He still appreciated Schlegel's translations of Shakespeare, which he hadn't yet proclaimed a trifle slippery, like superpolished mahogany, falling into the whipped cream category of writing: you could never be quite sure whether the lines in question were intended to be slurped or eaten. And even if his reservations were already gestating, Heine meant to profit from the professor's erudition while he could.

Compared with students at English universities, where it was considered honorable to drain one's thirst for spirits and women, undergraduates at Bonn had a reputation for earnest devotion to their studies. But in the eyes of local authorities searching for signs of political delinquency, these same young men were perpetually suspect. The explanation for this mistrust goes back to contradictions that Schlegel's Romanticism was implicated in, and which reverberated with Heine's own self-divided state: the interests of the broader liberal movement and of Germany's jingoistic factions had gotten muddled after Waterloo.

Established in 1818, the year before Heine's arrival, on the fifth anniversary of the Battle of Leipzig, the University of Bonn was designed to provide an academic inoculation against the Napoleonic spirit. After the Wars of Liberation, Metternich, the master diplomat who served as foreign minister of Austria, exploited the competing ambitions of Germany's different states to oversee the formation of an illiberal confederation. Not only might a united Germany threaten the balance of power calibrated at the Congress of Vienna, it would also be more likely to nurture pan-European revolutionary impulses than would a messy jigsaw of sovereign interests. Real unity should be confined to the councils of Europe's ruling powers, these same powers decided, while busily reactivating their old networks of privilege. France and revolution became bywords for terror, with total stasis the ideal. Heine defined himself in opposition to such principles, which became axiomatic for the restored Prussian Kingdom.

Germany was to be maintained as an alliance of thirty-five states and four free cities. Members of the ruling houses of these entities would meet periodically in a Diet that made no pretense to popular representation and lacked executive authority, though it was the only organ of central governance. While the Diet had the ability to develop policy in certain areas, it couldn't impinge on the sovereignty of different member states by mandating adoption of any regulations. Most German principalities, Prussia chief among them, were absolutist states without a constitution. Though in 1815 the Prussian king had assured his people that such a document would be forthcoming, four years later he was still waffling on whether to fulfill his promise.

In this climate, protests kept erupting at institutions of higher learning as students and liberal-minded faculty lobbied for basic civil rights and a document to enshrine them. Frustrations turned violent just months before Heine started university. August Friedrich Ferdinand von Kotzbue, a popular dramatist with eighteen children and a spiteful, reactionary streak, ran afoul of the rising generation when he began to slander key figures of the German enlightenment with charges of extreme sexual adventuring. After he started publishing a weekly periodical that belittled liberal aspirations, he became the bane of young believers in reform. In March 1819, Karl Ludwig Sand, a theology student who supported the cause of German unification, burst into Kotzebue's house and stabbed him repeatedly in the chest while crying out, "Here, you traitor to the Fatherland!" When Kotzebue's six-year-old daughter came into the room and burst out sobbing at the sight of her father's wounds, the student, heart-stricken, plunged the blade into himself. Bleeding profusely, he handed a servant a manifesto justifying Kotzebue's murder, then staggered out into the street, where he stabbed himself again before collapsing.

That might have been the end of the affair, but Sand survived, was arrested, and resumed his political activities from prison with redoubled zeal. Passionately defending the struggle for German emancipation, he denounced Kotzbue in his grave as an enemy of the German people. Sand's indictment of his victim didn't move his judges, but his paean to liberty stirred the populace. By the time Sand was carted off to the place of execution in Mannheim, a huge crowd was following his progress. Sand mounted a wooden scaffold with hands bound and a red sash tied around his eyes. The executioner cut a few curls off the top of his head for his mother. The rest of his long black hair was tied back with a ribbon. Then the executioner swung his giant sword. The neck snapped. But it took a second stroke before the head detached. Once that fell, the spectators rushed forward, daubing up the blood with handkerchiefs. They broke up the chair he'd been seated on and divided the pieces to make fresh relics. When they ran out of chair, they started ripping up the scaffold. Sand became a holy martyr to German nationalism.

Anxious about the risk of insurrection spreading, the German Diet passed a set of regulations, known as the Carlsbad Decrees, that shut down every forum for political conversation liable to promote reform. University lectures were vetted in advance. Newspapers and magazines were subject to stringent censorship. In a student songbook published in Bonn the summer before Heine started taking classes, even individual words that raised official eyebrows had to be expunged. Thus the refrain of a patriotic song that ran "And this last, to whom shall I bring it in the wine? / Sweetest of all things—Freedom—to thee will I bring it in the wine," had to be amended to read, "Sweetest of all things, to thee will I bring it secretly." The word "Freedom" had itself become seditious.

Such was the atmosphere in which Heine began his higher education. He was a natural ally of the liberal movement; but taking that position also meant embracing Germany unity—which in turn was associated with a holistic Christian-German identity that excluded Jews. Heine may have been the first Jewish writer to explicitly grapple with the dilemma of a forward-looking, freedom-oriented political movement that boosted solidarity among its participants by regressively vilifying his own people.

Among undergraduate agitators the situation was especially confused. The *Burschenschaften*, student fraternities, which evolved after the Napoleonic wars from sleepy medieval corporations into vanguard advocates of the nationalist cause, sought to bar all foreigners from German campuses—French and Jewish students in particular. Their first major action, in October 1817, before Heine got to Bonn, involved staging one of the largest popular demonstrations ever seen in Europe: a mass procession to the fortress of Wartburg, where Luther had taken refuge from his Catholic persecutors. Ostensibly the gathering was meant to celebrate the three hundredth anniversary of Luther's nailing of his Ninety-five Theses to the door, and the fourth anniversary of the Battle of Leipzig. In fact its aim was to promulgate the fraternities' message of German national and racial unity—which implicitly entailed a protest against the current order. Hundreds of students from all over the country climbed the steep, woody hill to the fortress, waving black, red, and gold flags, dressed in chalky blue uniforms, and singing chauvinistic hymns. Karl Ludwig Sand (still two years away from turning assassin) marched proudly among them. Atop the hill, there were speeches and a torchlight parade, at the end of which they tossed their torches into a pyre and began shoveling books into the flames. First to go was the Napoleonic Code. In as well went a history of Germany by Auguste von Kotzbue, along with the best-known work by Heine's future acquaintance, Saul Ascher, an indictment of "Germano-mania."

The Wartburg Festival, as it became known, was in Heine's thoughts when he wrote the line for which he is best remembered: "Where they have burned books, they will end up burning people." More than a decade later he was still pondering this ominous event, lambasting the "narrow-minded Teutonic spirit" that had reigned there, with crowds of students speaking "loftily of love and faith, but anchored in a hate of foreigners and their religion."

The fact that Sand—who epitomized the young, idealistic German revolutionary—was at the forefront of this barbaric ceremony, while Kotzbue was among its targets, makes clear the challenge Heine faced in trying to honor both the spirit of political progress and the sanctity of his own skin. In France, Heine observed, patriotism worked very differently. In France, the heart gets warm; through warmth it begins to swell; it keeps on expanding until eventually it encircles not only those nearest and dearest, but all France—all civilization—with embracing love. In Germany, on the other hand, patriotism was expressed through a vascular contraction, the way leather contracts in cold weather. It consisted "in hating foreigners; in ceasing to be European and cosmopolitan, and in adopting a narrow-minded and exclusive Germanism."

Heine was seeking to turn the project of German self-realization away from nationalistic retrenchment toward a greater European identity, even as that enterprise was being shaped by autocratic bureaucracies empowered at the Council of Vienna. Seeds of the wavering right-left political connotation of notions like globalism began to be sown in this period.

How could Heine help feeling inwardly fractured? Between the draconian interventions of the government and the righteously intolerant protests of the liberal youth, it was natural that Heine's real allegiance should be to the cause of his own divine comedy. After all, as he noted in his epic malediction, *Germany: A Winter's Tale*, the poet's power exceeded even that of the Redeemer. There were hells, Heine wrote, from which no liberation was possible. Don't you know the inferno Dante created? he asked his readers.

> Those whom the poet imprisoned there,
> No God can ever free them—
>
> No God, no Saviour can deliver them
> From these singing flames—no, never!
> Beware lest we condemn you too
> To such a hell forever.

Chapter Fifteen

HEINE'S LEGAL STUDIES were dense and dull, and he imme diately began leavening them by writing a drama, *Almanso* His first verse tragedy projected the core dilemmas faced b nineteenth-century Jews in Germany onto the Muslims i sixteenth-century Spain, who were forced by Ferdinand an Isabella's edicts to convert to Christianity. All its major charac ters struggle with a different aspect of the injunction to chang faiths. Some perceive the integral beauties of the new religio while failing to reckon with how Christian practice diverg from its theology. Others, unwilling to abandon their hom or the advantages that might accrue to them by conforming t the dogma of the new regime, accept conversion in the hope some eventual sublimation of all beliefs. One fiercely uphol the dictates of his fathers' religion and condemns the conver as traitors. Almansor, the eponymous protagonist, has no dee relationship to Islam but feels loyal to his people's heritage-

and is made furious by the external pressure to renounce his born identity. "For all my hat and coat I have remained a Muslim:/I wear my turban here, in my heart," he declares. In Almansor's eyes, Christianity's political enforcers are themselves guilty of converting the religion of mercy and love into a coercive weapon.

Ultimately Almansor commits suicide, after which his father, Ali—who has strained to justify his own conversion, both in terms of worldly benefits and in the hope that his Christian faith will one day provide true solace—appeals to Jesus directly. The Almighty's will is opaque to him, he says. Yet even in the midst of his petition for deliverance, Ali expresses a heretical foreboding that, whatever else might happen, the lily and myrtle will be torn from the roadway when the Lord's triumphant gold chariot comes rolling in. That note ends the play. It offers an early iteration of Heine's abiding doubts as to whether the world's loveliest creations can withstand the onslaught of a higher justice.

In a letter to a pair of literary friends from Bonn, Heine wrote of laboring with all his powers on the drama, injecting the historical framework with his "own self, with my paradoxes, my wisdom, my love, my hatred, and all my craziness." Startling poetic images glitter through the verses, he added, as if the whole tragedy were coated "with a film of diamonds." But *Almansor* was something of a turgid mess as well: he couldn't claim it rose above the level of a "pretty puppet show." He dedicated the play to his Uncle Salomon.

Heine made few lasting friendships at university. One pal, Johann Baptist Rousseau, sketched the freshman poet as a small, wiry figure, with a high forehead, light hair and a good-humored ironic smile. Heine tended to clasp his hands behind him and waddle forward, like a duck, Rousseau wrote. He thought himself good-looking and surreptitiously peeped at his reflection whenever possible. He liked the sound of himself speaking—always laughing loudly at his own jokes. When this happened, his features which "normally are not particularly oriental, assume a wholly Jewish expression and his eyes, at all times small, practically disappear." (The pair fell out over Rousseau's escalating nationalism.)

Another fellow student described him as the kindest hearted, most loyal person he knew, but added that Heine seemed embarrassed by his own affability, and sought to show himself in the worst possible light. Certainly Heine wanted to appear more of a roguish libertine than the evidence supports. In his student days he occasionally visited prostitutes and had several affairs. It has long been thought that he contracted a syphilitic infection in this period, which finally killed him, though some recent efforts at retrospective diagnosis have blamed toxins in the water pipes. In any case, he always remained affectingly consumed by his own family's domestic concerns. His deepest amorous dreams were monogamous, and once married he revealed a shamelessly uxorious streak.

Still, not all Heine's Byronesque swagger was spurious. At Bonn, he also fought a duel, apparently over an antisemitic slight. It was the first of at least ten he fought—some drawing blood. Soon he began wearing his student's red cap pushed back to show the scars on his forehead resulting from these encounters, which he called, disconcertingly, "a flower of beautiful humanity." Perhaps Heine really did find some form of grace in these elemental contests, which evoked the martial glory he'd thrilled to in childhood. All the ideological convolutions of the era dissolved in their pure physicality. It might also be the case that Heine's attachment to dueling stemmed from the writer's perennial longing for the moment when words turn into deeds—a yearning with special resonance for Jews, who were regularly accused of physical cowardice.

Heine carried on his legal studies without disgracing himself, and his own writing developed considerably in this period.

Nonetheless, later recalling his state of mind at Bonn, Heine remarked that his heart would have died for lack of sunshine had it not already been annihilated by a winter gale (his experience with Amalie). A year after enrolling, he moved on to study at Göttingen. It was unremarkable then for students to switch universities regularly; Göttingen was also considered the foremost institute of higher learning in Germany, and law was one of its top faculties. The decision to change schools may have come at the urging of his family, who hoped that Göttingen would inspire more diligence in him. Betty must have guessed how much of her son's time was now occupied in extramural labors—he gave the family almost everything he wrote, so they knew the scale of his output. After passing along *Almansor* to them, he observed to a friend that his mother had read his tragedies and songs but didn't really like them. His sister just tolerated the work. His brothers made clear that they couldn't understand his writing, and his father didn't even try to read a word.

Not that Samson was absorbing much of anything by this time. In Heine's first year of university, his father suffered some type of mental collapse. Doctors tried to rally him through solar treatments, but therapy didn't help. Salomon and another brother became Samson's legal guardians. They yanked the remnants of his beloved velveteen business from his frail, scented hands. Heine's family was now entirely dependent on Salomon, who arranged for them to move to Lüneburg, a small Hanseatic town close—but not too close—to Hamburg. Heine never ceased to be stunned by the deficit of basic human sensitivity his uncle displayed as he exercised his almighty beneficence. It made the charitable virtues of his poor father, who lived for eight more years, seem all the more poignant. "He was the person I loved more than anyone else on this earth," Heine wrote.

In the last days of Heine's own life he dreamt his father was alive again. Samson was having his hair dressed, and Heine saw him through clouds of powder. Overjoyed, he rushed to his father's arms. But as he came nearer things became confused. When he tried to kiss his father's hands, he found himself forced to draw back, shivering with cold. The soft fingers had turned to dry branches. His father had become a bare tree, covered in winter frost.

Chapter Sixteen

EN ROUTE TO GÖTTINGEN, Heine made a brief retreat to Düsseldorf, which served to remind him how politics could make time leap backward into a semblance of the past that excluded one's own history. Even the houses seemed startled to see him. Exhausted sparrows fluttered about old chimneys. Everything appeared at once dead and fresh, like lettuce sprouting in a churchyard. When he was young, everyone had talked French; now they exclusively "spoke Prussian," Heine wrote. A Prussian court in miniature had assembled there, and people were fabricating titles appropriate to their doll's house dignity. His mother's old hairdresser had become the "Hairdresser Royal," and there were "Haberdashers Royal," and "Shoemakers Royal," "Exterminators Royal," and "Liquor Stores Royal"—the whole town seemed to have become an "Asylum Royal" for "Crackpots Royal," Heine wrote.

He rambled on foot from Düsseldorf through pastoral

Westphalia, the expedition giving him opportunity to explore the literary potential of the walking tour, which he'd cultivated until then mostly through reading Laurence Sterne's *A Sentimental Journey.* Scholars have tabulated the rhetorical devices shared by the writers: a preference for launching narratives midstream, the careful deployment of an apparently informal, fluid conversational tone, frequent shifts between humor and sentiment, direct appeals to an elusive female reader, and heavy reliance on double entendres. Sometimes Heine simply poaches or riffs off the older writer's techniques. Other times it seems that, inhabiting a parallel emotional-philosophical universe, his style just serendipitously aligns with that of his predecessor. Either way, Heine's voice invariably conduces to the sense that he is accompanying his readers on the walk: not only engaging them in conversation, but traveling into their thought processes.

While enjoying the hospitality of country pastors and farmworkers, Heine experienced a fleeting affection for the virtues of German character. But from the moment of arriving in Göttingen near the end of October, he was complaining to friends about being bored silly. The town's atmosphere was "stiff, priggish, disdainful." The students were "dandies, flops, éditions de luxe of prose writers." Its teachers were unmovable as Egyptian pyramids—but pyramids in which nothing of any value had been entombed. Everywhere Heine encountered a "dry, parochial vanity."

If the distance weren't so great, Heine swore he'd head straight back to Bonn. He felt great need of "soothing, healing and exalting!" The only thing one could do in this place was to be "a good ox." So he would play the ox and "play the ox horribly, since it was only for the ox's sake that I came here," he swore to a friend.

In later years, Heine wrote a tour de force send-up of this hallowed place of study. "The town of Göttingen, famous for its sausages and university, belongs to the King of Hanover, and contains 999 hearths, sundry churches, a lying-in hospital, an observatory, a lock-up, a library, and beer-cellar, where the beer is very good," he observed at the outset of his travel memoir, *The Harz Journey*. There, the fraternities proudly carried on all the customs of the Dark Ages and the town's residents could be divided into four categories—students, professors, philistines, and cattle—"which four classes are by no means sharply distinct," with cattle being the most important. His pen darted like a fencing foil, pricking Göttingen's pretenses in telegraphic flashes. (Mention of the "lying-in hospital," for example cues readers to the students' notoriety as seducers of local servant girls.) But for all the nimble humor of his descriptions, Heine was miserable there, and the violent headaches with which he began to be afflicted never fully left him.

Göttingen was swarming with young men in exactly his position, cramming mechanically for their law degrees: the congested jumble of German states ratified at the Council of Vienna had been a boon for the legal sector, at least. Copious legislation was introduced to restore old economic and social entitlements of the feudal squirearchy, along with endless regulations to constrain the masses and manage Germany's multiple administrative fiefdoms. Landed proprietors were required to maintain a judge to oversee the workings of the law on each of their estates. If properties were not contiguous, one landowner might be obliged to support several different judges. (Sometimes this condition proved logistically unfeasible, and reputedly judges responsible for more than one estate had to write and answer letters to themselves in order to collect the fees pertaining to each jurisdiction.) In terms of tracking the tides of economic opportunity, Betty had been right to steer her son toward law. But the lackeys of the old Roman legislation who taught the subject were, in Heine's opinion, concerned

solely with "dusting the wardrobe" that spirit had left behind—
"cleaning it of moth, or botching it up for modern use": they
codified humanity's most brutal instincts.

Even more appalling than the courses Göttingen promoted
were the subjects it allowed to languish. Heine was stunned to
discover that the university had only a single professor lecturing on old German literature—and even more astonished that
he himself was one of just nine students to attend those courses.
The absurd notion that he might be considered less German
than his peers because of his Jewish ancestry when he was more
interested than they were in cherishing the cultural heritage of
the German language revolted him.

Heine couldn't foresee the toxic repercussions of the Romantic definition of German as an *Ursprache*—a primal language
that circulated through the *Volk* like blood, carrying linguistic
vitality allied with elemental Nature. In 1807, when Johann
Gottlieb Fichte, another founding thinker of German Romanticism, began articulating his mystical theory of language—
claiming German as one of civilization's original languages, on
a par with ancient Greek—his intention had been to distinguish it from the superficial French tongue, thereby elevating
the German people over Napoleon's soldiers, then occupying
Prussia. Yet his work undergirded the reasoning of later anti-
semites, who charged that however fluent a Jew's German might
be, the language was never *really* his or hers; linguistic facility
merely disguised the Jew's true role as contaminating inter-
loper, capable only of a parasitic relation to the German nation.
These arguments would eventually be projected backward in
time to condemn the works of Heine himself, whose books
were hurled into the Nazi bonfires. (It's an abiding source of
controversy that substantial spadework for this derogation was
performed by the Viennese Jewish satirist Karl Kraus, who in
1910 charged Heine with having "so loosened the corset on the

German language that today every salesclerk can finger her breasts.")

The deficit of broader cultural interests at Göttingen was compounded by the ethical apathy of its student organizations. Though they had taken part in Wartburg's torchlight festival along with the *Burschenschaften* of other major German universities, once the students had had their outing, they promptly settled back into their colored caps and tasseled pipes. Indeed, Göttingen's reputation for passivity was one reason that enrollment spiked there after Wartburg, when many other institutions were being brought to heel, or even, as in the case of one neighboring university, shuttered altogether.

From Heine's viewpoint, this was the worst of all possible scenarios: a hive of boorish fraternities that could be easily pacified with respect to aspirations for civil liberties, but were quick to embrace the lowest prejudices associated with the nationalistic movement. Göttingen's narrow-minded quiescence reflected the high proportion of students from noble families in residence, and their displays of tribalism clinched Heine's loathing for the place. The scions of Hanover's nobility, who presumed they'd one day rule the state, were invariably sent to Göttingen, Heine observed. They lolled about in packs, blabbing endlessly about horses, dogs, and ancestry. Since they never bothered to learn anything about current affairs, their conversation grew ever more akin to starchy linen. The delusions they entertained were identical to those nurtured by their fathers: they were the flowers of the earth—everyone else was grass. And just like their progenitors, the current crop of students sought to cover over their own worthlessness by exalting their ancestors without bothering to inquire whether those characters might actually be marred by some fatal blemish, such as chronic disregard for true virtue, together with a habit of bestowing endless titles on panderers.

The lot of them cared nothing for individual ability. (Heine's only secure asset.) Their cultivated ignorance made him sick. How often had he burst out laughing at the significance they ascribed to some flouncing swish of etiquette! As if there were any challenge involved in mastering those empty protocols of representing and presenting: that grinning without saying anything, that talking without thinking—all the petty arts that ordinary good citizens gawked at as they might some wonder risen from beyond the sea.

One scene stood out above all others from his time at Göttingen. On a broiling summer day Heine came upon an impoverished athlete who, having worn himself out running a strenuous training course, was spotted by several young bloods of Hanover—pedigreed students of ethnography. They offered him a few thalers if he'd run back over the entire distance he'd just traveled. The man desperately needed the money and, notwithstanding his exhaustion, he ran. Heine saw him struggling not to fall while, right behind him, the well-fed noble youths galloped on their high horses. Every so often the hoofs of these steeds cracked the desperate runner's back as he gasped for breath.

"And he was a man!" Heine exclaimed.

The outrageous indifference of the aristocrats to a human life they deemed inferior to their own is given extra shading by Heine's note about their field of study. Perhaps the most famous professor at Göttingen was Johann Friedrich Blumenbach, who taught anthropology and ethnography while surrounded, as visitors noted, by "a chaos of skulls, skeletons, mummies and other materials of his art." Blumenbach developed a comprehensive taxonomy of the races, and was the first person to popularize the term Caucasian for light-skinned European peoples, a classification incorporating his assessment that the people of the Caucasus were the most beautiful on earth.

He also explored the role played by environment in shaping physical appearance and cultural opportunity. While the moral objective of his research was to demonstrate a universal aptitude for contributing to the larger project of civilization, that message tended to get lost in the visually suggestive constellations of material he assembled. (Next to a drawing of Amazonian Indians pummeling each other—their faces likened to baboons by one contemporary—Blumenbach hung the placid portrait of the celebrated sixteenth-century aristocratic beauty the Countess of Mansfeld.) In this freighted pastiche the only definite ordered sequence was a "very complete collection of skulls" intended to diagram the progression of the species up to its Caucasian apogee.

Blumenbach was trying to bring scientific method to the study of racial difference. He made a point of praising the "capacity for scientific culture" of different African peoples, together with their possession of attributes demonstrating parity with white Europeans. But the crude spectrums he developed to illustrate his theses about ethnic variation proved easily manipulable by those who sought to make exactly the racist arguments he rejected; while his elevation of the idea of Caucasian beauty to the pinnacle of the hierarchy compromised the case he made about the equal distribution of human aptitude. Indeed, aspects of his research were eventually adopted into the arsenals of pseudoscientific racists. Perhaps in labeling the aristocratic hunters of other men in Göttingen as ethnography students, Heine intuited that when a belief in genealogical superiority received even a veneer of biological affirmation, the consequence would be murderous dehumanization.

Barely three months after Heine arrived at Göttingen, a Hanoverian student who overheard him make fun of the petty rules of the fraternities declared his comment to be a violation of the students' code of honor. Heine shot back that the code belonged to the *leges barbarum*. An undergraduate by the name of Wilhelm Wiebel contested Heine's assertion and threw in a personal insult. Heine challenged Wiebel to a duel with pistols. He accepted and they fixed their seconds. The pro-rector was informed and confined both students to their dorm rooms. Apologies were demanded, grudgingly offered, then retracted. There were further inquiries and more half-hearted reconciliations. Although Heine was mostly accounted the injured party, the governing body of the university concluded that he should be expelled for six months.

"Wonder of wonders! I have received the *consolium abeundi*" (advice to go), Heine told a friend in the midst of jubilantly reporting the progress he'd been making on *Almansor*. Rather than return to Göttingen after his suspension, Heine now enrolled at the University of Berlin. Law didn't become more interesting to him there. But unlike the turgid atmosphere of Göttingen, Berlin was dancing when Heine got there, and he plunged headlong into the whirl.

"I dance and run, and joke, and nod to everyone, and laugh and chatter whatever comes into my head," he wrote in reference to the fetes he began attending. His favorites were the costume balls. "What does it matter who's behind a mask?" Heine asked. One wants to enjoy oneself, and for pleasure's sake disguise is all that's necessary. Humanity is at its purest and most simple at a ball where the mask of wax covers the mask of flesh, he continued. The former reestablished the "beautiful equality" and "familiarity of primitive societies."

Even were he to encounter his most deadly adversary at a ball, he'd just say to him, *Tomorrow, we shoot each other, but today I'll kiss you.* Whoever he encountered there, he instinctively kept saying, "I adore you, my beautiful one." He doffed his hat right and left, marveling at the politeness his overtures engendered. All those men in silken dominos and opera hats. All those ladies peering out from behind black, lacy face coverings! Oh the glory of *Maskenfreiheit*—the freedom bestowed by masks!

Suddenly, Heine twists from the exaltation of self-concealment to the hazards of positing any integral identity. For at that joyous gathering, there was one German youth who began thundering at him in his "ancient Teutonic beer-bass": "At a German mummery, Germans should speak German!'"

Heine protested: How foolish and blasphemous the words sounded when his soul was embracing the whole world with love. With overwhelming joy he "would embrace both Turks and Russians, would throw myself weeping on the breast of my brother, the enchained African! I love Germany and Germans, but I love none the less the inhabitants of other portions of the earth, whose number is forty times greater than that of the Germans. Love gives mankind his true worth. . . . I am worth forty times more than those who cannot extricate themselves from the swamp of national egotism, who love Germany and Germans only."

Perhaps Heine's searing indictment of racial bias in the midst of a rhapsody to the equality-conferring mask harks back to Almansor, who is forced to wear a Christian mask in order to survive that kingdom's anti-Muslim prejudices. By invoking the enslaved African in his speech, Heine signals that the freedom of all the world's peoples rises or falls together. Jews and Muslims are interchangeable in Heine's historical writing since, from the perspective of the majority culture, they are politically indistinguishable: the outsider French could be switched with the outsider Jew whenever doing so became expedient. Just as the Romance tongues, with their "shallow Latin roots," which the French had sought to introduce, could be replaced by synthetic Jewish-German, which camouflaged the alien Semite. The subhuman is a fungible category for those promoting their own supremacy. In response, Heine declared the human spirit as such to be infinitely various. Beneath the mask, we're all offspring of Proteus.

Chapter Seventeen

THE THING ABOUT BERLIN, Heine wrote, was that it wasn't actually a town—it was just a place were lots of people happened to be cooped up together. Neither its identical houses nor its long streets—"built by the line and level"—evolved naturally from the people's consciousness. Rather, they grew from the vision of a single man: "Fritz the Great," who exemplified "the extraordinary Philistinism and the freedom of understanding, the shallowness and the uprightness of his age." All Berlin's music, art, and witty conversation coexisted with an ever-widening network of surveillance and censors tasked with choking off the slightest hint of dissidence. The city demonstrated how free you could be in many areas of life while not being free where it most counted. Certain forms of social liberty might even serve the state, substituting erotic license for access to the body politic.

Heine's first publisher understood the system.

Friedrich Wilhelm Gubitz had an unruly pouf, and penetrating eyes. He tied his cravat with loose panache over a rumpled shirt that added to his air of studied negligence. His father had been a modest typesetter. After apprenticing in that trade, Gubitz moved on to woodcuts and engravings, building a name for himself with landscapes, portraits, and allegorical figures. One depicts a skeptically amused young lady on tiptoes, holding out her robes at odd, dramatic angles to expose her jutting breasts, between which beams a brilliant sun. Arrayed around her delicate feet are a sphinx, a mask, an owl, and a beehive. Beneath this tableau a luminous oval radiates a single word, *Wahrheit*—Truth. Gubitz liked his wahrheit to appear classically knowing, and just a little saucy.

By the early 1820s, when he was in his mid-thirties, Gubitz was established as a convivial professor at the Academy of Arts, who found time to compose dramas, poems, and criticism, in addition to editing the *Gesellschafter,* one of Berlin's most prestigious literary periodicals.

One day in the spring of 1821, he later recalled, a young man turned up in his chambers, announcing, "I'm completely unknown to you, but I *will* get known—through you."

Gubitz was tickled, if dubious. He took the sheaf of poems, and skimmed through the verses—churchyard ballads of madness, midnight horrors—genre stuff. Even so, the extremity of their macabre imagery caught his attention. When he glanced back up at the author, the fellow's gaunt, sickly frame added to the poems' effect. His features showed evidence of "premature pleasures," Gubitz decided.

When Heine finally gave his name, Gubitz commented favorably on his verses, but said the lines would never pass the censors without some changes. Heine resisted, but soon made the emendations. Certain poems were then accepted for the *Gesellschafter*—marking Heine's first appearance in print. An ongoing exchange started between Heine and Gubitz, who always mixed his admiration with admonitions about the improprieties in Heine's work, which Heine would then grudgingly revise in a process he dubbed "Gubitzing."

Once he had published a handful of individual pieces by Heine, Gubitz helped arrange for a collection to come out with a book publisher. Though the author was paid only with forty copies of the volume, *Gedichte* (Poems) received mostly positive reviews. Critics for and against his verses grasped that he was doing something unusual by crisscrossing genres: melding folk songs with the high lyric tradition, and restlessly tacking between emotional registers. Detractors complained that the "shattering experiences" his work produced contravened the mission of poetry, which was to solace the bruised spirit with quasi-religious verbal balm. They also cluck-clucked at what they saw as the absence of any overarching principle of composition; instead of aspiring to harmony, Heine seemed bent on dissonance. He "tears up all the flowers of life and never allows the palm of peace to take root," one critic wrote. At the same time, an anonymous review that has been attributed to the enlightened theologian Friedrich Schleiermacher contended that the dissonance served a higher purpose. Never before in the history of Germany literature had a poet "set forth his entire subjectivity, his individuality, his inward life, with such boldness and such astonishing ruthlessness as Mr. Heine has done," this critic wrote.

In part, the impression of Heine's inner self being projected onto the page was achieved through formal innovations that kept running readers' expectations off the rails. The unpredictability of his lines seemed to signal authenticity. One way to think about Heine's work as it began to mature would be to say that he took the conventional forms in which he'd precociously developed great fluency, employed them traditionally up to a point, and then just at the last moment, when you were expecting his lines to conclude a certain way—

Chapter Eighteen

UPSET THE SENSE of everything preceding with peremptory silence, an ironical epiphany, or an outburst of sincerity. Or introduced a word like *Weltkuddelmuddel* to characterize a world-engulfing mess. "Only genius has a new word for a new thought," Heine declared.

Although often, also, at the very last moment he would rein his lines back in for a polished finish, instead of further tweaking them. And frequently his twists were metrical—freeing his verses by employing nonstrophic lines of disparate lengths. As if where the beat should fall, some chunk of private life burst through the writing at just the wrong, or right time. Almost, but not quite, rhyming.

Most people, anyway, liked the shocks Heine's poetry conveyed, and he liked shocking them. A second collection came out, *Tragedies with a Lyrical Intermezzo*, which included *Almansor* and another play called *William Ratcliff*. Of the two dramas

Heine told a friend, "I will confess to you in confidence that they are very good, better than my collection of poems, which are not worth a shot." Posterity has disputed that appraisal, but it's worth considering why Heine made the claim. Perhaps it was a factor of ambition: *Almansor* engaged with profound issues of ethnonational identity, while *William Ratcliff* at least touched on what Heine labeled *die Grosse Suppenfrage*—the great Soup Question—the ongoing war between poor and rich.

Heine still subscribed to the commonplace that lyric poetry should treat of Love and Nature, refracted through the lenses of the poet's own experience. But Heine's personal experience of the world was changing, its political features becoming more intrusive. "Songs and stars and flowers by the ton,/Or eyes and moons and springtime sun,/No matter how much you like such stuff,/To make a world they're just not enough," he declared in one verse. When he told a friend that poetry was "a beautiful irrelevancy," he didn't intend the comment entirely as critical. Yet social observations that his poems could not accommodate were becoming too importunate to ignore.

In an effort to be more topical, he resolved to publish several chatty letters to a friend on scenes he'd witnessed in Berlin. In the first of these, Heine laid out the project's context as a familiar, touching paradigm: a young man from the provinces who has left behind a large group of loved ones and friends so that he can pursue his fortune's star resolves to show that he has not really abandoned those back home by promising to faithfully share with them all his discoveries. "I have no lack of notes," Heine promises. "The only question is, what shall I not write about?" Since each of his well-wishers will be interested in another facet of the metropolis, he resolves to let his pen dance among subjects from one day to the next. Heine's self-appointed contract with the public is not with some abstract monotype of the Reader but with a variety of individuals with eclectic temperaments. "Require nothing systematic from me, for that is the exterminating angel of all correspondence," Heine proclaims, before embarking on his role as epistolary cicerone.

But in truth, no one was soliciting his opinion about anything: Heine invented the distant addressee, and his own circumstances at the axis of a gregarious, cultivated society. The entire form intended to underscore the experiential truth of the news he relayed from Berlin was make-believe. Given the reality of his situation then, his decision to conjure that adoring multitude, along with his consummate man-about-town persona, seems more sad than playful. At the same time as his correspondence was appearing, Heine was telling Christian Sethe, "Everywhere I hear my name, followed by derisive laughter." Before many months had passed, he confessed that his situation was dire, "Sick, alone, persecuted, unable to enjoy life—that's how I live here. . . . I require shower-baths. I have almost no friends."

What were the *Briefe aus Berlin* about, then?

Perhaps it's simple: an invented correspondence would allow Heine to paint the world around him in a manner that showed off his quicksilver wit and keen descriptive powers. Newspapers had been publishing epistolary reports from far-off places for some time. On top of which, by crafting a narrator who was closer to the man he wanted to be—missed by everyone he used to know and welcome nearly everywhere he wished to go—Heine would be able to indulge in a bit of happy daydreaming. If the letters became a success, they might even bring his fantasy self a little closer.

He first hoped to get the letters published in a prestigious Berlin paper, but an agent provocateur working with the Prussian secret police sabotaged that plan. The snub may have sharpened his inclination to peer more coldly at the city's novelties. He took the project instead to the *Rheinisch-Westfälischer Anzeiger*, an ambitious regional newspaper, published just fifty miles from his native Düsseldorf. The editors there embraced

Heine's scheme. What's more, they gave his letters far more space and prominence than *Korrespondenzen* typically received. As a rule such letters were fine-print lists of news items stuck into the journal's last pages; Heine's *Korrespondenzen* appeared as the lead or second article for weeks, the three letters broken into ten installments. That extra room was part of what inspired Heine to stretch the conventions of the genre, scattering poetry, fiction, digressive reflections, and extended narrative set pieces through his reportage.

"We are standing on the Long Bridge," he announces at the outset of the series, immersing his readers in Berlin's famous sites—and the buffeting distractions brought on by the frenetic immediacy of city life. "You murmur to yourself, 'It is not so very long!' Pure irony, my dear friend. Let us stand here a moment and examine the statue of the great Elector. He sits proudly on his horse, while chained slaves surround the pedestal. . . . But I see you are being hustled on all sides." Part of what Heine is pointing out about the spectacle of modern society is the absence of any Archimedean point from which to study that spectacle, while also splitting his consciousness between chaperone and traveler to foreshadow the responses he hopes to elicit from his readers.

One thing he seems to discover in practicing this mobile, panoramic form of observation is that its conclusion will always be political. Heine urges readers to contemplate not just the grandeur of the Elector but also the shackled slaves that support this figure: the provocative conjunction is there for anyone to scrutinize who takes in the whole group and not just its central subject. If we keep turning to the end of the scroll reality presents us with, we'll eventually perceive the glaring inequities and forced labor on which magnificence depends. Heine reflects at last that the splendid bronze ensemble can at least be *freely* contemplated, since it stands on a bridge—reminding his readers of all those Prussian treasures hidden from public view inside the bastions of privilege.

He moves on to Berlin's cathedral and, hard by the church, the Stock Exchange, where "the upholders of the Old and New Testament Traffic." One doesn't want to approach that place too closely, he cautions. "Oh God what faces!" Greed pulsing in every muscle. "The richest must certainly be those whose pasty faces show the deepest imprint of discontent and ill-humor." He proceeds to describe a prostitute, decorated military officers, and a café. Side by side, these become functionally equivalent attractions—the soldiers' medals another form of seductive accessory akin to the adornment of the lady, or the newly printed cards listing delicacies at a restaurant. Heine is most of all a guide not to any particular facet of Berlin but to a way of seeing—one that uncovers the incriminating juxtapositions which the world itself displays for us.

But his sheer verve of consciousness also brings to light more venial afflictions of the age. Heine may have been the first person in history to record the way a hit tune echoes around town, until its ubiquity drives anyone really listening crazy. In this instance it was a song by the Romantic composer Carl Maria von Weber with the richly quavering refrain *I weave for thee a virgin crown.* Heine heard it from the barrel organist at one street corner, then a blind fiddler across the road. It leaked from every door and window. Even the dogs seemed to have begun barking the dreaded chorus. Finally, he took refuge at his lover's house. "Like a hunted roebuck, I lay my head in the lap of the prettiest of the Prussians," Heine sighed. She stroked his rough hair, and lisped, "I love you. I love you." He felt himself at last relaxing, whereupon his dreams were shattered by the words, *I weave for thee a virgin crown.* She'd taken up the chorus! He tore himself from her embrace, flew home, rushed inside his room and threw himself on the bed, gnashing his teeth. Suddenly he heard a sound—a song—the warble of his aged cook, *I weave for thee a virgin crown.*

Even this spirited vignette carries a political inflection, however: von Weber's rival, Gaspare Spontini, known for his thunderously martial music, was a court favorite, whom the king had recently made it illegal to criticize. The story of the song's omnipresence may well be meant to tweak Spontini's nose, and by extension the royal's dignity, by showing that Weber remained the people's darling.

What's certain, anyway, is that the more Heine saw of Berlin, the more the city's restrictive aspects impressed themselves on him. His way of seeing fed upon itself. "My appetite clamors, and I would fain turn in at the *Café Royal*. Will you drive?" he asks his tourist alter ego. While that imaginary companion takes the reins, Heine carries on his madcap patter. "Quick, driver! What a moving stream under the Lindens! How many loiterers there, confident of their dinner today! Do you thoroughly comprehend the word *dinner*, my friend? Whoever grasps the full meaning of that word knows the secret of all the agitation of human life. Quick, driver! What do you think of the immortality of the soul? Of a truth it is a great discovery, greater than that of powder. What is your opinion of Love? Quick, driver! Is it not true that it is the law of attraction and nothing more? Do you like Berlin?"

The fusillade of sights and exclamations at last throws light on what it would mean to have no dinner, no soul, no capacity for genuine attachment to another person. *Do you like Berlin?* (In the contemporary idiom, "Are we having fun yet?") Though Heine perseveres in his character as irrepressible escort-raconteur, a note of disgust recurs. He starts enthusiastic, only to see through each bright façade into a moral void. The only place that proves truly free in Berlin is the masked ball, where everyone is someone else—except the rabid nationalist, who takes pride in flaunting his small-mindedness.

When Heine turned up in Berlin he had thought to prove his worthiness to Germany's arbiters of literary talent. Any biases against him—whether based on blood or his own behavior—should have been surmountable in that cultured metropolis by a display of virtuosity on the page. Instead the city brought Heine's misgivings about German character to a head.

By the time Heine's second brief appeared in print, one passage had been replaced by the black dashes that indicated where censors had slashed text. Parts of the third letter was rendered completely incoherent by the officials. Heine was incensed. By treating the royal family delicately and confining his criticism to social conditions rather than overtly political matters, he had sought to spare his work governmental defacement. Still, he got away with more than might have been expected, and aspects of his feint-and-skewer strategy proved gainfully stimulating. Indeed, the artful dodging that he began to practice at this time to outwit the censors helped shape Heine's mature prose style.

But Heine finally ran more dangerously afoul of the authorities, and the letters break off suddenly. Between the passages written against nationalism and Heine's naming of individuals in contexts they found offensive, he had provoked enough official animus that there was talk of having him expelled from Berlin. Hence, although the letters excited substantial interest among the general public and helped build his popularity, the trouble they caused also exacerbated his sense of persecution. It's fair to say that Heine was further radicalized by the reception of his own work.

At the outset of the letters he had proclaimed that instead of developing an overarching structure for his narrative, he would always work by way of the association of ideas. He had the gift of making a compositional virtue of his natural proclivity toward a kind of cascade of consciousness—and the inspiration to then use this retroactively identified aesthetic principle to mask a political judgment. (Prostitute, soldier, café, et cetera.) Heine's free association of ideas offers embodied evidence for how society comports itself, regardless of its pretenses to efficiency and rectitude.

While Heine is often thought of in this period as experimenting with techniques of collage, counterpoint, and superimposition that he will hone in later prose, no less important is the flair with which he begins to create a theoretical defense of the position he found himself historically consigned to. Rather than a systemic argument, he reveals a continuity of ideals and antipathies, which combine to shape recurrent themes. The array of discontinuous mosaic bits he works with enables him to assemble a more genuinely heterogeneous sampling of the world, he suggests. You can hold the mirror up to nature whole, but a broken mirror is best for showing civilization. Civilization came broken to begin with.

"Do you hear God's voice in the dark ocean? / He speaks with a thousand voices," Heine declared in one poem. This too can be understood as a revolutionary conceit. Absent a just social order, Heine set about writing the politically dominant, monolithic worldview to pieces.

Chapter Nineteen

THEN AGAIN, part of Heine longed just for acceptance. There were moments when he thought back on the period he'd spent with his uncle in Hamburg at Schloss Affronten-burg, wishing only that he had managed to fit in, to be one of those who have an image of what life should look like: the placid spouse, the spotted pug, brittle china, linen, Turkey carpets, a dependable profession that required one to check a fob watch frequently—to have *some* such picture in one's mind would, after all, be something.

He'd been in no real state to judge the place when he was there, he confessed to a friend. His inner life had consisted of "brooding and immersion in the gloomy pits of a dream world," while his outer life was "mad, dissipated, cynical, repulsive." Amalie didn't love him; the others found him bothersome. He'd tried to make his outward being as different as possible from his inner one lest the latter destroy him, he confessed. If only the two would integrate, and that merged pair could synchronize with the surrounding world!

Sometime after publication of his Berlin letters, relations with his uncle began deteriorating again. Heine kept complaining to his intimates that this man with millions had to be squeezed to part with a penny. All he was asking for was the support he'd been assured of to finish his studies, he wrote. "Lack of money or excess of it has not the slightest effect on my principles, but all the more on my actions," he concluded, somewhat incoherently.

Heine knew about the shimmery gatherings of Prussian elite in grand halls festooned with chandeliers, some hanging overhead like flame-crowned angels in a cloud of glass, others blossoming from the hands of sculpted Nubian attendants who stood against black columns with golden cornices. How could such pictures not be enticing? All those Prussian officers bending smartly at the waist over smiling ladies in décolletage who lent admirers half an ear while fingering their jewels or twirling champagne flutes. He longed for entrée. "I dreamed: I am the dear Lord God / Enthroned in Heaven's palace:" one of his lyrics from this time began.

> I ask for costly cakes and sweets,
> And nibble them all day,
> And drink them down with rare old wine,
> And have no debts to pay.

But ultimately the stiff phlegmatic life up there would make him sick, he acknowledges, and were he not God, he might have been Old Nick.

The song goes on to fantasize about bringing democratic access to heaven's treats:

> I'll work new wonders every day:
> They'll make your senses spin
> . . . .

The paving-stones along the street
Shall suddenly be splitting.
And fresh and clear, in every stone
You'll see an oyster sitting.
A rain of lemon juice shall fall
And sprinkle them like dew.

The gutters would carry the best Rhine wine down every avenue in town.

How happy all the poets are
At such a godly scene!
The ensigns and lieutenant-lads,
They lick the gutters clean.

But where was he now? He had no money. Family pressures to make good were mounting. His studies were a mortal bore. Year by year, new regulations kept being ratified to limit the options for those of Jewish birth. All the ways that his German citizenship was circumscribed made him think nostalgically of the time when his homeland had been part of France. How anguishing, to have grown up in an era when your small-minded, inward-looking country became part of a larger continental enterprise, and then to have to watch that greater European identity being peeled away to nothing. Why, in the name of honoring some trumped-up conceit of sovereignty, would a nation bellicosely, inanely, hurl itself back toward the Dark Ages? What choice did Heine have but to cultivate a revolutionary imagination?

Sometimes he lost track of what the great difference between long-settled German Jews and their Christian compatriots was supposed to consist of. To begin with, hadn't Germans in truth absorbed a great deal from Jews with respect to their own Protestant religion?

But disgust with the vacuous hypocrisies of German nationalism didn't mean that Heine could take comfort in the fantasy that those judged inferior by the majority population were civilization's true elite. Whatever else Jewishness meant to Heine, he never simply flipped the value set to find refuge there for his self-respect. Repeatedly, he labeled himself the born adversary of *all* positive religions. Just because he believed that all people deserved civil rights didn't make him more inclined to "champion a religion that first thought of discriminating between man and man." If sometimes he seemed to be such a champion, this, he specified in one letter, was due to "sentimental attachment, obstinacy, and a calculated desire to have an antidote ready."

The liberating, chameleon nature of the human spirit he'd exalted at the masked ball had a darker aspect. In "To Edom," an unpublished poem written a few semesters after his arrival in Berlin, Heine declared that for thousands of years his people and the Christians had managed to put up with each other. "Graciously you tolerate my breathing,/I bear with your raging fury." While it was true, he continued, that now and then some passing fit seized the Gentiles, whereupon their meekly loving claws dyed themselves red in his blood, as everyone could see, their kinship nonetheless grew daily deeper: "I too have started raving, murdering/Now I'm almost just like you."

The poem is partly a reminder of the unequal burden of forbearance placed on minority populations—and partly a reminder to his coreligionists not to forget how to hate. It had the quality Nietzsche later celebrated in Heine: "That divine malice without which I cannot imagine perfection."

Heine was barely out of adolescence when he began arguing that the traditional divisions of people by way of faith and heritage should be replaced by a classification based on vocation and temperament. In later years this evolved into a more philosophically considered effort to categorize everyone as either Nazarene or Hellene. The former were persons with ascetic, iconoclastic impulses who hungered for ever more spiritualization: Orthodox Jews and puritanical revolutionaries like Robespierre epitomized this paradigm. The latter were life-loving champions of both art and the real world who gave the glad eye to all forms of human development. The breakdown was reductive, but not biologically determined. "Thus there have been Hellenes in the families of German preachers, and Jews who were born in Athens and perhaps descendants of Theseus," Heine wrote, hinting that he himself, whatever else, knew his way around a labyrinth. And despite his instinctive Hellenistic allegiances, in hours of distress his self-identification sometimes swung the other way. Ultimately, his dream was of merging the two character types.

All Heine's reflections on how he did and didn't fit in German society were shadowed in the first half of the 1820s by his recognition that the day kept drawing nearer when he might have to get baptized. While a legal career was the only way he could hope to attain financial independence, new regulations meant the only way he would be able actually to practice law would be as a Christian. This requirement had its own implications for Heine's self-respect, though fully half of Berlin's Jewish community were said to have converted in the period. No similar case of "apostasy en masse" (as some nineteenth-century German-Jewish historians labeled it) had occurred among the Jews since fifteenth-century Spain.

He was the only member of his family who harbored the smallest objection to the step, he told friends. For Uncle Salomon and his mother, the whole question of belonging was economic. If your livelihood depended on reeling off the holy singsong about blessed Jesus—well, then, that was the form in which redemption, here on earth, was bound to come. Just get your Gentile ticket and be done with it.

Heine agreed with his relatives in principle—and still he kept equivocating. It wasn't that he had an objection to baptism because of an attachment to Judaism, he repeatedly insisted.

But nonetheless he rankled at the notion of being *compelled* to jump religions just to get a job in "dear old Prussia." Perhaps the way he kept protracting his studies by going to lectures that had little or nothing to do with law was partly a tactic for deferring conversion. So long as he didn't have a law degree, there was no point in acquiring the Christian faith that would allow him to practice. But even if he had been panting for a career in the courts, Heine would have dropped his books on jurisprudence to go hear the Berlin professor whose reputation was surging as the most significant German thinker since Kant.

Chapter Twenty

IN HIS PORTRAIT, Hegel's eyes are blue and bright—narrow, red-rimmed, and looped below with leaden half-moons. His forehead could not be higher, nor the strands of pale hair feathering that luminous convexity more wintery. His thin mouth turns down at the corners, while the deep folds at his cheekbones where his long face tautens accentuate a look of mistrust, disapproval, or perhaps just cosmic apprehension. Even with a lush fur mantle drawn to his ears, Hegel's countenance gives off a chill that frosts as you step nearer.

Yet Hegel was known for being amiable enough to students. Preserving an air of "kind yet ironical courtesy," as one recalled, he let them accompany him on his walks while passing along reading recommendations. He enjoyed his snuff and games of chess, some said in imitation of Kant's amusements. When his protégés got involved in the political reform movement and became known to the authorities, Hegel kept on trying to hire them. After one was arrested and locked in a jail cell on the river Spree, Hegel rowed out in a boat with several other pupils at midnight to buoy the prisoner's spirits, discoursing with him in Latin so the guards wouldn't understand. And in 1820, when police actions against the youth movement were at their height, he met with students at a tavern in Dresden, where he insisted on buying the most expensive champagne, filling the youngsters' glasses himself and tossing back his drink with them, announcing, "This glass is for the 14th of July, 1789—to the storming of the Bastille."

By the time Heine began sitting in on his lectures about the philosophy of history, Hegel was recognized as one of Germany's foremost public personalities. Students hung on Hegel's every word—no matter how many syllables each one contained, and even though he constantly fumbled with his pages. Outside the classroom, when a new painting by a well-known artist appeared, or a fresh invention emerged from some industrial workshop, contemporaries remarked that all Berlin asked: "What does Hegel think about it?"

Heine could tell that he was in the presence of a phenomenon when Hegel spoke, even while he suspected its real implications had less to do with philosophy, or even culture, than with faith. Hegel was Heine's first great man of ideas, and Heine wanted to learn what the philosopher's vision signified for his own predicament.

Hegel always talked in a monologue, Heine said, "sighed forth by starts in a noiseless voice" and strewn about with oddly rough phrases. Tremendous future events—the upheaval of the social order consequent on the dethronement of Christianity's moral authority—could be prophesied from his ruminations, Heine asserted in his reminiscences, adding that he could see Hegel's "serio-comic visage, like a setting hen, brooding over the fatal eggs; and I heard his cackling."

Heine also confessed that while Hegel was lecturing he

rarely felt certain what the professor was pattering on about, only later making any sense of the presentations. He became convinced that Hegel was "purposely obscure." Nonetheless, they did strike up a friendly relationship of sorts, Heine reported, and one beautiful clear evening, after they had eaten well and drunk their fill of coffee, they stood together in a window contemplating the sky. Heine broke out in raptures over the sublimity of the stars. "They are the home of the blessed!" he cried.

"They're only a brilliant leprosy on the face of the heavens," Hegel muttered.

Heine protested: "Is there no happy dwelling place above to reward virtue after death?" Hegel fixed Heine with a wilting gaze. "So you want a tip for having taken care of your sick mother and for not having poisoned your dear brother?"

Yet however much Heine might have puzzled over in Hegel's exegeses, some large ideas stuck and resonated with his own intuitive sense of the universe's construction. Hegel's notion that history had a purpose—a destiny toward which all life was tending—accorded with Heine's incorrigible belief that for all the misery of the present, and notwithstanding the long roll of humanity's miscarried ideals, better, indeed joyous times would eventually arrive. For the universe was alive. This infinitely variegated and interconnected organism was in the process of fulfilling its true nature. Against the empiricist's mechanical vision of how cause and effect operate in history, styled on the workings of scientific law with its prerequisite of uniform repeatability, Hegel contended that events and eras live in dynamic relationship with each other—rather like the dancing, polymorphous bodies at Berlin's masked balls that gave Heine his image of incarnate freedom.

The principle of development through time, which Hegel defined as necessarily rationally intelligible, both sanctioned the unique character of individual being (personal, national, and epochal) and revealed that nothing could be truly understood except in its largest context. Past and future, west and east, were vitally linked as partial representations of the drive toward self-realization of Hegel's Absolute Spirit. This wasn't exactly God or Nature; was partly Mind, but only partly; always actively advancing history, inextricably bound up with freedom's actualization, it was immanent in each phase of the world development, yet forever transcending any particular iteration of its own measureless identity.

Stepping back from the imponderable, it's not hard to see why the concept of everything at once possessing a singular integrity, *and* being a fragment in some larger, unfolding revelation, would have resonated for the author of the Berlin letters.

Critically, moreover, Hegel's picture of the motion of history, despite its unidirectional course, was hardly a linear slide. To the contrary, development was all by way of smash and collapse. Revolution, war, devastation, and mortal struggle between irreconcilable forces were the means whereby the unsustainable inconsistencies of a given age found expression and were finally brought down, whereupon a new, more evolved set of forces emerged and began to accumulate fertile tensions of their own. (The ABCs of dialectics: thesis, antithesis, and synthesis, provide the familiar abbreviation of this process.) Heine's expositions through contrast, and the deployment of irony as a device for exhibiting deep-rooted social incompatibilities, are lightly correlative with these principles. He tried to teach stiff Prussians how to play, or at least to make a little mischief with their own reflections in ways that freed them up a bit.

In Hegel's philosophy, it wasn't that either of the two ideas entering into a historically determinative clash should prove superior. Each was valuable, but fractional, requiring fusion with another to complete its purpose. By the same token, each civilization had a singular mission that furthered the advance of Absolute Spirit's self-consciousness, toward which all history was tending—furthered, without being able to autonomously complete the process. The essential identity of a people could thus be perfectly consummated, and made obsolete by the forward lurch of history.

Parallels in this model between the fate of individual cultures and persons were intentional. Hegel criticized the work of earlier historians who had scissored out a single epoch from the annals to build their theses with. In Hegel's schema, traditions of architecture, law, ritual, costume, language, and folklore were complementary, connected features of humanity's organic being. Each one merited study as a manifestation of the society's drive toward self-mastery, which had an institutional history coinciding with its pursuit of freedom.

Encountering Hegel's approach to the association of phenomena, Heine might have felt that he glimpsed elements of his own creative methodology in a mirror where everything fit seamlessly together in exactly the kind of all-enveloping system he himself had cockily eschewed. It left him blinking. He had pined for acceptance, and Hegel's dialectic framework found a place for nearly anything. The image in the glass was awesomely embracing, but got somewhat lost in condensation as he went deeper. So Heine mostly picked magpie-style from the surface of Hegel's disquisitions for the shiny filaments that could best adorn his poetic nest: human progress and historical purpose. Freedom and the inevitability of conflict in the course of Spirit's advance through the forms of different civilizations.

With his own attachment to the notion of the great man as a galvanic index of humanity's potential, Heine was bound to be attracted by Hegel's conceit of the "world-historical individual," who was personally responsible for catapulting history from one culture to the next by destroying an outmoded paradigm and heralding its successor. (Napoleon and the French Revolution were both examples upon which Hegel drew repeatedly.) Yet at the same time, Hegel often seemed to subordinate the needs of corporeal beings to the larger cause of a transcendent union between the human mind, the universe, and history. Was the philosopher on the right side politically or not?

As his fame grew, Hegel's professional implication in the state that sponsored his academic chair became more suspect in the eyes of young people. What accommodations with the forces of repression had he made when he put on "the gleaming livery of power," Heine wondered. Along with listening to his lectures on history, Heine heard Hegel introduce his *Philosophy of Right*. In its preface, Hegel declared, *Was vernünftig ist, das ist wirklich; und was wirklich ist, das ist vernünftig*: The rational is actual and the actual is rational. Rational in Hegel's program meant ethically fulfilled. This elliptical statement—which became known as Hegel's *Doppelsatz*, double dictum—immediately sent Heine's hand waving.

Hold on, he demanded, more or less. Are you saying that the Prussian state, since it is real, is already by definition as it should be? Are you endorsing the status quo?

Hegel gave him a peculiar smile and answered that the proposition could also be expressed, "All that is rational must be."

The minigloss made Heine conclude that Hegel was doubling down on his conservatism. Since the rational boasted the awesome engine of History behind it, the rational would necessarily be that which existed. Prussia was *just*, by virtue just of being. Whatever liberal political aspirations might once have accompanied the philosopher's program, Hegel had been so spooked by the Revolutionary Terror that he'd suppressed those energies, leaving behind just the billowy abstractions that Heine came to describe as Hegel's "dialectic cobwebs."

More than twenty years later, Heine recanted this interpretation with a somewhat chastened head-slap, acknowledging that another way of understanding Hegel's *Doppelsatz* would be to take from the portentous formula a message that the rational—the ethical and righteous—must one day conspire to overthrow the cruel, inherited forms of governance we suffer under now. The world was made to pivot over time toward freedom, even by means of violent revolution. Perhaps other abstractions Heine attributed to Hegel were also consequences of points he didn't fully understand, while those phrasings of Hegel's theories that were genuinely abstruse might have been elaborated obliquely to prevent the incendiary aspects of his thought from being focused on before the time was ripe.

The whole business made Heine dizzy. "Life in this world's a fragmented business!" he exclaimed in one verse from this period.

> Our German professor will give me assistance.
> He knows how to whip the whole thing into order,
> He'll make a neat System and keep it in line.
> With scraps from his nightcap and dressing-gown's border
> He'd fill all the gaps in Creation's design.

Around this time, Heine told his friend the banker-mathematician Moses Moser that he'd dreamt about a crowd of people jeering at him. He had run from them to Moser for comfort, and Moser had opened his kind arms, telling Heine not to worry about the mocking throng because, after all, he was only an Idea. To prove his point, Moser took down Hegel's *Logic* and showed him a particularly obscure passage, just as another companion under Hegel's spell knocked at Heine's window, spouting philosophy yet more fulsomely, while Heine ran around the room like a madman crying, "I am no Idea. I know nothing of an Idea. I never had an Idea in my life!"

He woke up in a panic.

It was *life* that Hegel gave short shrift to—claiming that reason in itself could justify existence. "Life for life's sake" became Heine's motto.

Chapter Twenty-one

THE PERSON RAPPING on the glass in Heine's nightmare was Eduard Gans, and Gans was yelling loudest of them all, while on his shoulder hunched their tiny friend Ludwig Marcus, shouting in his own peculiar, raspy voice from the vast table of quotations that padded Gans's speech. German scholars were notoriously fond of pedantic references in their conversation, but Gans was a regular Rothschild in the business of citations, Heine wrote.

Awake or sleeping, when Heine thought of Gans, this fervent disciple of Hegel was always noisy—roaring with laughter, booming out the inner meaning of a knotty concept, or amplifying a bit of gossip. Born, like Heine, in 1797, Gans had a big head and a bumbling, oversize body. The daughter of one Berlin salon grand dame found him strikingly handsome, suggesting that with his "proudly arched eyebrows" he resembled a "spiritual Antinous." Others noted his protuberant blue eyes, portliness, and ruddy skin, which might have been symptoms of the condition that triggered his fatal stroke at the age of forty-two, midsentence over lunch—a martyr to his passion for discussion, one newspaper declared (though those who knew Gans's appetite probably wondered what was on the menu). Many illustrious Berliners found him brilliant and welcomed his gregariousness. He was a tireless leader and a joiner both, yet he fit no better professionally into his surroundings than Heine did.

At the time Heine met him, in August 1822, Gans had completed his program of legal studies and was already gaining acclaim for sharp analyses of the rules of inheritance. Instead of securing his future, however, Gans's skills made him even less employable: his talent pinned a warning to his brow. When he had first applied for a position on the faculty of the University of Berlin several years before, the 1812 Law of Emancipation was still in effect, and regulations on hiring Jews hadn't yet been codified. But though qualified Jews could technically be appointed to academic positions, the authorities also had the right to pronounce upon their moral fitness for specific posts. This stipulation had been interpreted by the restored Prussian bureaucracy to mean Jews should be banned altogether from a wide range of offices, theological and administrative. Since teaching in particular involved shaping character, the education ministry resolved that Jewish participation in any pedagogical activity would be severely restricted.

Gans's suitability for public service was challenged on these capacious grounds; he protested his exclusion. "I belong to that unfortunate class of human beings which is hated because it is uneducated, and persecuted because it tries to educate itself," he lamented to one official. The case churned slowly through the bureaucratic mill until, in February 1822, after the intervention of a sympathetic minister, the education authorities finally agreed that if Gans confined himself to obscure research in the legal systems of Oriental nations—Persians, Hindus, and Arabs, for instance—he could become a professor. Gans accepted the humiliating terms; he had to earn a living somehow. Yet the compromise only provoked some members of the faculty to balk yet harder at the notion of so incorrigibly avid a Jew working anywhere in their vicinity, while others saw his case as an opportunity to clarify regulations regarding the stiff-necked people generally. That same month Gans met Heine, the king was persuaded to issue a special cabinet order formally revoking the emancipation edict. Dubbed the *lex Gans*, this act demonstrated the lengths that Prussian authorities would go to safeguard the status quo. Proscribe an entire people to block the hire of a single irksome candidate—why not? The state was still compact and homogenous enough that it could afford to be extravagantly petty.

Through all this, Gans continued to impress more gifted teachers at the university with his intellectual fortitude. Hegel was his foremost champion. For Gans, Hegel's dialectics seemed to trace a path out of the professional vacuum into which he'd been cast by regressive state policies. Hegel maintained that the vitalizing power of ideas could elevate men's spirits beyond their inherited prejudices. So if Jewishness itself could be represented as integral to the process whereby Absolute Spirit was achieving self-consciousness, then the Jews' failure to accept Christ might be understood not as having dammed up their development altogether, but rather as having diverted them along a separate channel that flanked the Gentile track. Moreover, it stood to reason that Christianity itself was an evolving proposition, trending away from its doctrinal niceties toward greater universalism. All Gans had to do was teach his fellow Jews to live up to the forward-looking aspects of their true historical character, and induce Christians to welcome a continual influx of Jewish blood. That was it. No problem.

At the time he met Gans, Heine was feeling particularly disgruntled. He'd gotten in a spat with his last remaining friends back home, fed by his increasingly envenomed pronouncements against German character. His headaches were becoming worse, no matter how many medicinal baths he took. And now he had discovered that—thanks to Gans's drama—he'd been rendered ineligible for *any* academic post until he went through with his conversion.

The two young men struck up a voluble exchange, inflected by parallels in their plights and passions. Little, dapper Heine with his long, wavy auburn hair, and big, ungainly Gans striding over the flat ground between the huge columned buildings of the university, dark frock coats flapping, white cravats flashing, voices ricocheting off the stones. Gans shook his noble head. He shrugged his ample shoulders. He didn't dance, Heine later jested: Gans loved humanity too much for that, knowing that if he began to caper he might set off an earthquake.

From the first Heine made out Gans's robust brilliance, and Gans acknowledged Heine's dexterous wit. Heine communicated his frustrations with all their groveling in the moldy archives of Roman law. Gans agreed: the real spirit of history— forward motion!—had to be injected into German jurisprudence. Gans let Heine know, however, that disputing Hegel was misguided. Their situation might be radiant with future hope; but the present moment, unfortunately, was somewhat retrograde. They needed every ally they could get. The two of them had become extra-special nuisances to guardians of the status quo: Heine for his Berlin letters, Gans for going after blind vigilantes of tradition who blocked every effort to rationalize the law. It might seem that they were only dodging *droshkies* as they crisscrossed Berlin's streets, but Heine must know they were marked characters, threading a passage between the steely eyes of the Prussian state police.

The balustrade of Berlin's arsenal, hard by the Royal Palace, was decorated with a cavalcade of trophies: bronze helmets jutting from the keystones of each basement window; sculpted heroes making elaborate muscles all along the architrave. Inside, in one direction were endless guns and field pieces, along with tumbrils and caissons. The other way—bombs, mortars, howitzers, and blunderbusses. This was not a state they could afford to leave to its own devices, Gans warned. ("All the instruments of destruction that have been devised by man to injure, maim, and annihilate his fellow-creatures, are here systematically and beautifully arranged," explained contemporary guidebooks.) One could just imagine the fearsome double-headed eagles carved above official portals flapping their stone wings, cracking free of heavy pediments beneath wrought iron crowns—diving down to peck away the livers of such troublemakers!

There was no doubt that Hegel was right about the direction of history. The underpinning of the Idea was no more perishable than the substratum of Nature itself, Gans promised. But meantime, if they didn't make some progress soon, Prussia would obliterate them. They were Jews, and hatred of their people was surprisingly invigorated, despite history's ever-onward motion.

Heine knew this; but was sick of being made to run around the clock wheel of his tainted birthright. There were moments—many, actually—when he felt uncertain what precisely they were holding on to in their Jewishness.

Gans agreed. He'd suffered plenty in his youth under what he called the Jewish "double aristocracy" of rabbis and money. But that didn't make it acceptable that Christianity, with all its prejudices, should be reinforced throughout the vast Prussian administrative state. Why should they be compelled to make peace with the resurgent forces of reaction?

Heine agreed with this as well.

Then plainly they must do whatever they could to nurture Higher Understanding, so that Christian dogma would finally be transcended altogether! Gans could enumerate a dozen ways that Hegel's ideas might be drafted in support of liberal causes: he meant to show Heine how Hegel could be *used*. (In his approach, Gans was not unlike the Russian democratic writer Alexander Herzen, who found in Hegel's categories "the algebra of revolution.") What mattered, Gans said, was Hegel's argument that freedom was the principal idea at work in modern life, and was gaining ever greater influence because all earlier iterations of European identity had so spectacularly failed. Hegel, moreover, understood the most salient aspect of freedom's operation in society: it wasn't enough for individuals to espouse an ideal; there had to be an institutional framework through which to concretize the principle. Law, politics, the market economy, and other aspects of civic life were like garments that Spirit needed to pull on in order to become visible.

The question they confronted was how any small nation with a long, distinguished history could find a place within the hegemonic culture of the modern state. Gans said that Hegel had revealed how, if a minority people identified itself with the cause of freedom as it developed, they could be integrated into the living fabric of European culture without sacrificing their essential attributes. Hitherto, Gans argued, educated Jews like themselves who'd left behind the old "solid texture of Jewish life" had stumbled into lonely individualism—"the complete negation of the earlier condition." While "the enthusiasm for religion and the genuineness of the old relationships had vanished," no compensatory passion had emerged. They were "stuck fast in a Negative Enlightenment" that scorned tradition without laboring "to give that empty abstraction content."

Such a thesis would make sense to Heine—even if it too seemed a trifle abstract—but what were they supposed to do in practice?

The time had come for Jews to assume the role of the State themselves, Gans contended. This meant completing Napoleon's unfinished business—elevating the Jewish community en masse to a level parallel with the rest of European civilization, thereby inspiring the government to reemancipate them. "Neither can the Jews become extinct, nor Judaism undergo dissolution; but in the great movement of the whole shall it appear to pass away and yet live on, as the stream lives on in the ocean," he thundered—adding that Hegel had made all this clear. "Absorption is not vanishing," Gans insisted.

He became swept away by the majesty of his arguments as he talked. Heine took note of this, darting along beside him, while Gans clomped over the cobblestones beneath puddly flames of pendant oil lamps and the waving silhouettes of leafy trees. The pair had so much to talk about they might have continued their exchange all across Berlin, down streets thick with summer dust, stinking of the sewage that clotted the gutters from people dumping their night's wastewater, and excreting more or less in place. (Public toilets were notoriously rare in the city. Heine's zest for scatological humor had a corollary in sensorial realities.) Here and there a dark brick church jutted out unevenly into a narrow backstreet where older, lower houses still brushed streaks of rose and lime pastel behind new, monumental, sallow edifices. Metal signs embossed with trade symbols hung overhead on chains attached to iron mounts projecting from façades of shop buildings. Dogs loped right and left, yapping at boot heels and horses as circumstances required. Raw surroundings always colored Heine's impressions of lofty talk— making it hard for him to swallow any purely philosophical conclusions. And just as had been true in his perception of Hegel's own discourses, there were links between Gans's points that Heine missed. Why exactly did the demise of earlier European social projects signal that the cause of freedom in the form of self-determination had momentum now?

Gans told Heine that he'd helped found the Society for the Culture and Science of the Jews to tackle precisely these sorts of issues. At first, all he and his associates thought to do was aid their fellow Jews howsoever they could in emergencies, and then deliberate the means whereby the malignancy of Jew hatred could be systematically uprooted. Some kind of collective response to the scourge had become necessary. They all agreed that the solution would have to spring from within their own community—in part because, for all the sorrow Christian prejudice caused their people, no Gentile could feel more dismay about the general state of Jewry than did the Society's own membership. By the summer of 1821, when the organization began publishing its bylaws, it had agreed on a twofold program for working to "harmonize the Jews, through self-reformation, with the present time and the states wherein they live." One track of the program was directed toward immediate problems, the other toward long-term amelioration. Top down, the Society would oversee "the dissemination of a clearer perception [of Jewish identity] through the establishment of schools, seminaries, academies, and through the encouragement of literary and all public activities of every description." From below, it would promote the "diversion of youth from petty trade to crafts, arts, agriculture and practical sciences, as well as a reform of accent and social circumstances, leading toward amalgamation with society at large."

Heine found much of this intriguing, but there was another disclosure Gans made that caught his interest as well. The Society had learned of a scheme concocted by an American sheriff and dramatist of Portuguese-Sephardic descent named Mordechai Noah to establish a Jewish colony on Grand Island in the Niagara River, partly as a refuge for persecuted European Jews. Gans had written Noah a plaintive letter in January in which he noted that the better part of Europe's Jews were "looking with the eager countenance of hope to the United States of North America, happy at once to exchange the miseries of their native soil for public freedom, granted there to every religion." Gans labored zealously on his project for raising fellow Jews up to European standards, and for making Gentiles conscious of this latest upgrade to their enlightenment. But if the glorious Hegelian synthesis of Jews and Christians stumbled, Gans also had a backup plan in motion for getting his people the hell out.

Chapter Twenty-two

GANS INVITED HEINE to join the Society, and he accepted on the spot. With his entire extended family pestering him to get his degree, convert, and set to work at lawyering, Heine now went all-in as a Hegelian Jew.

At the first meeting Heine attended, Gans delivered a windy speech about the organization's higher purpose. The Jewish community was itself a family within the Hegelian construct that implied the family's nesting-egg position inside the corporation and the state, he declared. Their movement was to be the bridge between Jewish domesticity and the Spartan halls of Prussian governance. The Fatherland was undergoing an enormous transition; and the Society was charged with changing the family of the Jews accordingly, so that Judaism could flow into European life like a stream into the ocean. But in order to achieve this noble end, members must relinquish personal aims—personality as such!

It didn't take long for Heine to start suspecting that Gans had not gone quite as far as he demanded of fellow members in sublimating his personality at the Society—let alone in overcoming his nature in other social settings. He savored the observation made by Rahel Levin Varnhagen, the peerless *salonnière:* even in the midst of his most impassioned disquisitions, when Gans reached his hand out absentmindedly for the sandwich platter at her evening teas, somehow he always managed to get hold of the ones filled with fresh salmon rather than those containing ordinary cheese.

Gans nominated Heine to be the Society's secretary, and enlisted him to teach seminars to boost poor Jewish students up the ladder of European civilization. Instructors should give whatever classes most interested them, Gans urged. He himself, for example, lectured on Roman law in relation to the Jews during Rome's imperial apogee, as well as on Mosaic and Talmudic laws of inheritance. (Some might suppose that such a course of study for an undereducated group of needy youth would prove a tad demanding. But Gans believed such reservations were undemocratically presumptive about the pupils' aptitude.) It was quickly settled that Heine would provide intensive French and German lessons, along with classes on the full sweep of German history, from its Roman tribulations through Napoleon, up until the present day.

Heine got along with young people and devoted himself to his teaching, even though the work was unpaid. He also attended all the organization's meetings. At these solemn gatherings, which rarely got a roll call of even ten participants, Gans invested the administrative process with the character of Hegel's idealized bureaucracy, manned by civil servants who embodied universal rationality.

But when Heine scrutinized his fellow members, listening to their recondite presentations, which strained to reconcile the latest theses of philosophy with age-old Judaic postulates, he couldn't help asking himself whether this was in fact the sacred cabal that would work such wonders among the Jews that Christian eyes would finally open wide. The Society's delegates were clearly gifted, but nonetheless the universal solidarity they aspired to was hard to picture in their presence, still redolent of dumplings and goose giblets. In later writings, he drew prose portraits of his compeers.

Ludwig Marcus was so slight he resembled a boy of eight, displaying the sort of wizened countenance that often accompanied a hunchback. How he loved just looking up things, Heine recalled. "I once made him happy by asking him to excerpt for me, from Arabic and Talmudic sources, everything that pertained to the Queen of Sheba."

Lazarus Bendavid was forever flogging his deistic line that God was an abstract intelligence who made the universe start ticking, then moved on to other business. He seemed permanently steeped in the sunlight of antique Greek serenity. Yet this noble old soul couldn't resist jigging along with the rest of the Society when it came to entertaining juvenile notions about the imminence of humanity's enlightenment.

Moses Moser, the scholar-businessman with his crisp, precise appearance, intelligent quick eyes, and lightly pursed fine lips, was diligence epitomized. He labored tirelessly in charitable work while maintaining an unassuming silence, fighting and bleeding incognito, never insisting upon his due. During their joint constitutionals, Moser would continually declaim in an elevated, Schillerian tone, even in the midst of pausing to relieve himself.

Leopold Zunz, with his auburn hair and gnomish features, was the prince of the bunch. There was no one Heine respected more—a man "who manifested unshakable steadfastness in a time of uncertainty and transition." Zunz rejected Bendavid's notion that if you believed in progress it was necessary to shed the whole of Jewish lore like an outgrown snake skin. "What prevents us from studying the totality of rabbinic literature, understanding it properly, explaining it felicitously, judging it correctly?" Zunz asked. There were untold treasures waiting to be wrested from the dross of superstition. Heine remarked that Zunz's wife took greater delight in her husband each day, even doting on his defects: "She maintains that his pockmarks are little spittoons of the amoretti," Heine noted.

In Heine's writing about the Society, we see him striving in detail after detail—and analogy upon metonymy upon synecdoche—to capture some aspect of these men's physical being that will pop them off the page, spin them round like singing tops, and make them spring to life. Because, for all of Gans's assurances that the organization was quintessentially of its time, Heine's nagging fear was that the project he'd committed to might prove worse than fanciful—might, in truth, be posthumous at birth. It was good to know his lineage could hold its own with any purely European provenance, but how much did it contribute to the messy struggles of the current age to create such fine-grained renderings of the existence Jews once enjoyed? Nor, for all its historical weightiness, was the philosophy these men espoused an emotionally persuasive substitute for the particulars of religious ritual they disavowed. Indeed, the more he learned about Jewish history, the more Orthodoxy's rigors impressed him—at least relative to recent efforts by reformers to make their faith more politic.

Gans had tackled Hegel directly on this score. It was not so easy to articulate exactly what gave the Jews abiding relevance once you had set aside the Bible. While Gans did eventually get Hegel to move beyond his conventional distaste for Judaism, and even to advocate for Jewish civil rights, the larger structure of Hegel's theory still compelled him to find something inimical to Reason in the notion of a person remaining actively Jewish in contemporary Europe, just as he would have to look askance at someone sacrificing to Pallas Athena along the Unter der Linden. God's relation to the Jews was basically a master/ slave dichotomy, Hegel pointed out, whereas there should have been a vibrant interplay that in time precipitated full unity. He'd never really discarded his early position that the fate of the Jews was that of Macbeth, "who stepped out of nature itself, clung to alien Beings, and so in their service had to trample and slay everything holy in human nature . . . and be dashed to pieces on his faith itself."

How could Heine help feeling sympathetic to the Society's efforts to make ideas change reality when ideas were being used to undermine their own legitimacy—and were, moreover, the only weapons the Prussian state would let them wield? Far deeper than any suspicions he harbored about Hegel's willingness to compromise with earthly powers were Heine's fears that in refining the old God of Christians and Jews beyond recognition, Hegel would create a void yawning to be filled with something else—even something more archaic and brutal. He was caught in an insoluble bind: the biblical God was a deadly drag on the joyous potentialities of humankind, and Heine wanted to be free of all strains of spiritual invalidism. But what came afterward? "The world is a great stable," he observed, "which cannot be cleaned as easily as that of Augeas because while one sweeps it the oxen remain inside and continually pile up more dung."

When Heine wrote so vividly on traits such as Zunz's pockmarks, he was trying to prevent these individuals from dissolving altogether in the ether of their own intellects: he strove to make a contrapuntal music between the fleshly and the notional. But the trap he set in doing so was that he also thereby advertised the fact that he couldn't take them altogether seriously. The embodied characters of these figures—rife with funny, tragic imperfections which were the means by which Heine made them real—made it harder for the larger world to believe in the reality of their ideas.

The contrast between the men's carnal selves and theories wasn't the only issue that provoked Heine's itch to ridicule. There was also the more basic gap between the Society's celestial ambitions and its prospects for achieving anything. The members' self-importance became a byword in the Berlin circles they frequented. One young historian described Gans's project as a product of "the stupidest arrogance of a few young people who imagine themselves sufficiently grandiose to change an entire nation that is unknown to them." Yet outside the synagogue there was no other group Heine could attach himself to in resisting the stigma against Jews. He yearned to believe that something in their gnarled, integral being still *mattered* to the larger world after so many centuries off time's main artery, tumbling down a kind of storm gutter edging the royal road of history.

When adversaries within the Jewish community identified the Society with Germany's budding reform movement, claiming it sought only to smooth away the Jews' idiosyncrasies so that they could seamlessly assimilate, Heine responded bitterly. He himself deplored those quacks who sought to cure Judaism of its skin troubles by bloodletting and had, as a result of their "clumsiness and their spidery bandages of reason," nearly bled Israel to death. Things had reached such a pass that "we no longer have the strength to wear a beard, to fast, to hate, and out of hatred to suffer; that is the motive of our Reformation," he railed in a letter. And yet, he acknowledged, he himself was equally deficient. "I haven't even the strength to eat *Matzot* properly," he wrote. He broke his teeth on those Jewish crackers, and could only solace himself with the thought that, after all, this was what it meant to be in exile.

Heine was sick of religion and philosophy, of the Society and the university, but Berlin harbored other social refuges where the company was often more sympathetic. These were mostly female and more concerned with poetry than with spiritual bureaucracy. On top of which they also offered lots of sandwiches, some with salmon filling, if you got there before Gans did.

Chapter Twenty-three

Rahel Levin Varnhagen had enchanting dreams, and she liked to share them. Her most striking visions came during Napoleon's occupation of Germany, when her social world was ruined. The collapse of her position was all the harder since she never took against the French. How could she when, as she announced to visitors around the time Heine showed up, this people had the republic in their bones.

The lights of the richly heterogeneous salon she had begun to convene in an attic-room when she was young and unmarried, still living with her oblivious mother and choleric father, had all but deserted her by 1812. Some because of the nationalistic disapproval of Jews that had been catching on in Prussia since its subjugation. Others—who knew why? She'd never been so alone, or so definitively bored, she told correspondents. Her German friends might as well have died, given how long they had kept away. The Schlegels had turned ultra-Catholic and kept their distance—sanitary, sanctimonious. The Humboldts were now such personages they'd gotten cautious about mingling with her. In a steel engraving from this period, her mouth gives an odd, half-tickled, half-jaded twist, while her dark eyes are judgmental, resigned, helplessly amused and curious.

In this mood, she began to catalogue her dreams: she found herself in a splendid palace with opulent gardens. All the rooms were dazzlingly lit, filled with scurrying servants. At the end of a long succession of chambers waited the true assembly of "the most distinguished persons," Varnhagen recalled. It was somehow impossible for her to cross the distance, though all the doors between them were open. She attempted to approach. When there yet remained many more rooms to pass through, an animal appeared beside her with a pinkish snout and paws. Part sheep, part goat, the animal adored her "*tremendously*," she reported: it gazed at her with more love than she recalled ever having received. Then it took her by the hand, and began leading her forward through the rooms, step by step, although at last it gently prevented her from joining the congregated elite for some reason she knew to be significant. The touch of the nameless beast aroused her senses, but her attachment was defined as well by "an overflowing of the heart in sympathy," and an understanding that "I alone knew that the animal could love and speak and had a human soul." No one but her could see the animal, which "seemed to be concealing a profound, highly significant secret." Only occasionally would she be jolted by the thought: "How can you give such caresses to an animal; after all, it is an animal!" This dream recurred with variations. Once, the animal was sleeping on its belly, very black with bristly hair. "My animal! My animal is back!" she shouted to the servants. Then by herself she went up to the creature and poked it with her toes. It rolled over, fell apart, and lay flat, a mere skin. "So it was dead!" she exclaimed.

Varnhagen quite possibly considered the idea, seized on by

her intellectual offspring, that the dream represented an allegory for both the history of German-Jewish relations and the chimerical mystery of Jewish identity. The architectural rendering of what it means to dwell among a population with respect to whom, despite the absence of visible barriers, one can have no access, poetically compresses the Jewish circumscription in German society. The sensual, primordial, secret-blessed companionship of her animal evokes some lasting truth of the Jew's relationship to Judaism—as does the sudden, fearful discovery that this strangely loving beast has expired.

By the time Heine appeared in her salon, Rahel was fifty, and had passed through the crisis of confrontation with her birth inheritance. After a torrid love affair, she had become engaged to Karl August Varnhagen, a decent, devoted man of liberal letters, fourteen years her junior. She converted briskly to make their marriage possible and—save for readings in febrile mystic testimonies—never much bothered about her Christianity after that.

It wasn't just her incandescent grappling with the experience of being Jewish in Germany that made it likely she and Heine would discover affinities; it was the way she could articulate her feelings about anything. Not only was she a scintillating conversationalist, Heine acknowledged Rahel to be a true writer, for all that her métier was personal correspondence, a form not accorded status within the reigning canon of classicist aesthetics. "I write letters in which blossoms and fruit lie together with the roots, and the earth on them from being pulled out of the ground. And worms," she told one correspondent.

Heine began finding his way into Berlin's principal salons from the moment he arrived. His poetic reputation carried him that far anyway. A large array of families were connected like linking rings in a magic trick, each circle revolving more or less intact from one gathering to the next depending on whose day it was. Beyond their clans, the presiding women were able to attract men from every part of society: trade, the arts, diplomacy, the military—even royals. Lady friends of the youngbloods trickled in behind them. Frau Elise von Hohenhausen, Byron's translator and the host of one such coterie, was infatuated with Heine, telling everyone he *was* the German Byron. At von Hohenhausen's salon he was often tempted into reading aloud. Once, when he recited a verse that ended "And loudly weeping I fling myself at her sweet feet," the room exploded with laughter. Heine was mortified, witnesses reported. He became more sparing in his performances after this—quicker, too, at firing off caustic observations about the poses struck by others. Heine also attended the Sunday musicales of Fanny Hensel, née Mendelssohn, at her home on Leipziger Strasse, slipping into the crowd at her neoclassical garden bower for large performances or, on more exclusive occasions, stepping into Fanny's high-ceilinged, celadon music room, where honey-tone floorboards matched the varnish on her pianoforte. On one occasion Fanny's artist husband, Wilhelm, drew Heine in pencil at his wife's salon: arms crossed, wincing mildly, stylishly waiflike, the floppy collar of his frock coat rising just below his shock of hair: Puck on the dole.

Henriette Herz, a senior figure among the *salonnières*, noted the rare opportunity for unconstrained intellectual camaraderie houses such as hers offered. Anti-Jewish prejudices were muted there because the climate was feminine. (It helped, she added, that the salons attracted some pretty women.) Of the women's characters, Herz said that their outlook derived entirely from figures like Voltaire. But the writings of such bold luminaries "had fallen on absolutely virgin soil." Members of her milieu had lost all traces of that education which transmits a heritage from generation to generation, together with the biases that accompany such schooling. This was why, Herz said, the salons conveyed an air of exuberance mixed with arrogance, a piquant relish for originality and utter disregard for the codes of polite discourse. Her friend Rahel Levin represented the supreme expression of this atmosphere, she concluded.

Rahel herself, as was her wont, saw things more jaggedly and dark: there was nothing on earth to which she was indifferent so long as she knew of it, she told a friend. But she was breathtakingly ignorant. "My education, which was non-existent, is no doubt to blame," she wrote. "I was taught *nothing*; I grew up as it were in a forest of people, whereupon Heaven took me under its wing." While it was true that few lies had reached her there, she had been kept in darkness so long that she was no longer capable of learning anything—not even faith. "I am just waiting for it from above, by which I mean either a name for the religion I now profess or the revelation of a new one." More than elation or arrogance, Rahel communicated to her visitors a mood of insatiable expectancy.

At the time Heine moved to Berlin, the Varnhagens were just settling back into town themselves. For seven years after her marriage, Rahel had traipsed around with Karl as he migrated between ministerial posts, before being forced into early retirement on account of his liberal opinions. She didn't like the itinerant lifestyle. "I'm too old, too clever, too lazy, too ugly, too poor and so on to find any pleasure in settling down in a strange place," she objected. Her health was never good and worsened over the course of their diplomatic tour—gout, migraines, palpitations. But she hadn't exactly been pining for her native city either. "Is it possible for a regular person to accept the pavements of Berlin as the world?" she asked a friend. And that was before war came, when the conviviality that gave life meaning "went under like a ship containing the loveliest goods of life, the loveliest pleasures." Sociability was the presiding genius of morality, she had vowed—"Actually that which is most human among human beings!" Absent faith that to another person someone's image "is the same as to us, that *he is* what *we are*"— there would be no basis for ethics, law, or thought.

She'd grasped Heine's character immediately—seen through him without deprecating what she found. He didn't startle her. After all, she considered herself a truth that still needed "to find room in which to assert itself, that presses violently into the world." The pair found some poignant mutuality: Rahel told friends that, because Heine was "sensitive and queer," she "frequently understood him, and he me, where others could make nothing of him." He needed a patroness—so far as she could tell he'd never received guidance in basic social conduct, let alone the writing business. (The Varnhagens brokered Heine's introduction to Gubitz, the publisher.) And Rahel offered sympathy, not only with respect to the limitations of that relationship, but also over the trouble that ensued after his printed work sparked controversy. She reassured him about the value of his best writing, while not hesitating to suggest improvements. And most of all Rahel talked with Heine endlessly—about literature, Jewishness, genius, Germany, dreams, love, and dancing.

When it came to art, Goethe was always her exemplar. The many-sided female characters he created seemed torn from her own soul, even as he eloquently promoted the causes of enlightenment and tolerance. "Goethe and life are still one for me; I immerse myself in both," she told a correspondent. Indeed, in the period of her first salon, before Goethe acquired Olympian prestige, Rahel had been among the most fervent proponents of his work, helping to consecrate his stature. Nietzsche later made Rahel's role in Goethe's success definitive: "We know the fate of Goethe in a Germany sour with morals and spinster like," he wrote. Goethe "had true admirers only among Jewesses." In fact, he wrote elsewhere, there was an element of the author which "achieved its perfection only in Rahel!"

She made clear to Heine that he'd have to reckon more intensively with the sage of Weimar, regardless of any self-doubt and ambivalence Goethe might provoke. It may have been at the Varnhagens' urging that Heine sent Goethe his first volume of published poetry, with a rapturous inscription: "I kiss the hallowed hand which has pointed me and the whole of the German people [toward] the road to the kingdom of heaven." Goethe didn't respond, which didn't alter Rahel's conviction that Heine could use some lessons in Goethean self-governance. Notwithstanding her attachment, Rahel did find Heine simply *too much* in his natural state. Sometimes after he'd been round she told her husband to hurry up and throw open the windows. She had to get some air.

Karl agreed with Rahel that while Heine had wonderful aptitudes, Nature, in her haste, had left out some vital points of character; in consequence "his brilliantly illuminated defects are now there for all to see."

Rahel told Karl that Heine had to learn how to become real, even if that meant he needed a thrashing. "Man, be real!" she'd plead.

One of the real dangers, Rahel opined, was his lack of judgment in choosing friends. She'd had own her missteps in love affairs, God knew. But at least her disastrous entanglements had been intended to enact the sublime theory of love developed by Enlightenment thinkers, based on true symbiosis between romantic partners. Heine's temptation lay elsewhere: in philosophically useless companions, particularly unbridled wastrels. He was too impressionable. That was why he needed to cultivate only the finest minds—like Goethe! In the company of such eminences he would learn to tamp down his pride so as not to squander what little social capital he'd thus far accumulated. Karl told Rahel about the night he and Heine dined at the palace of the Electoral Princess. Schlegel was in a cowardly, hypocritical temper, trying to safeguard his own standing in noble society by disavowing Heine's old tributes. Heine announced his intention to completely break with Schlegel, "but I wouldn't allow it," Karl said staunchly. (Heine waited about ten years, then flayed Schlegel for posterity in his history of the Romantic school.) Rahel approved of Karl reining in Heine's impetuosity. She was constantly telling him that he had to stop defiling himself—quashing his delight in playing "the dirty harlequin or hangman" just to aggravate people. Husband and wife sometimes seem to be bonding over their interrogations of Heine's naughtiness. They had no children of their own to fret about.

Uncharacteristically, Heine almost never chafed against their criticisms. He quickly became dependent on the home they had opened to him, calling it his "true country," and thanking them for having refreshed him "with macaroni and spiritual food."

Rahel understood Heine's outrage from the inside. Even when she'd passed the age of forty, she was still yearning to feel understood in Berlin society. Walking down the Unter der Linden, she had begun having hallucinations, never quite sure whether she was waking or dreaming: everything "strange, entirely strange and shabby." The terrifying unrelatedness of people overwhelmed her. "I among them, *still* more unrelated, with a full empty heart, thwarted in attaining everything desirable, separated from the ultimate."

"May no one have to return to his place of origin where he hasn't been for a long time!" Rahel cried at one point. Heine had long been preoccupied with fears about the way an inherited identity could surge up to subsume one's contemporary existence. But Rahel had gone deeper in her reflections on this matter. The guidance she offered Heine to Berlin's nightmare dimensions bled into her savagely analyzed experience of being a woman there—or anywhere for that matter. Another dream allegorized the situation: she was lying on a bed with two women near the world's edge. The three of them were no longer alive, but their eternal business was to ask one another what they had suffered. "Do you know enduring wrong, injustice?" "Yes, that I know!" they'd wail after each question. At last, Rahel asked the other women whether they knew *disgrace*; whereupon the women shrank away. "In a state bordering on madness I scream: 'I have not *done* anything. It's nothing I have *done*. I have not *done* anything. I am innocent!'" Rahel could tell the women believed her, but also that they could no longer understand her. "*This* burden I must keep; I know *that*. Forever! *Merciful* God! Woe!" Well, disgrace was Jewishness.

The source of her misery was an immovable *mountain*, Rahel once declared—as if "a supernatural being had thrust these words with a dagger into my heart: '*Yes*, have emotions, see the world as few see it, be great and noble, nor can I prevent you from constantly thinking; but *one* thing has been forgotten: be a Jewess!'" Her whole life was a process of bleeding to death, which she could prolong only by remaining absolutely still.

And this was the point where Rahel met Heine. The question of how she, he, and all their people, could surmount that congenital paralysis consumed her: they were like cripples, she declared. Each step they longed to take but couldn't reminded them of the larger ills of humanity that they yearned to struggle against and were prevented from addressing—which ended by making them feel more strongly their particular misfortune, "doubly and tenfold, and the one keeps heightening the other."

So Heine found in Rahel his muse of furiously humiliated alienation. At one point Heine told a friend he'd learned from her the phrase that captured his feelings more exactly than any other: *Meinem beleidigten Herzen*—"my offended heart." Indeed, Heine told her husband he was willing to wear a collar around his throat inscribed with the words, *J'appartiens à Mme Varnhagen*.

Heine's readiness to serve as Rahel's animal recalls her first recorded dream, particularly in light of an observation Heine made years later in a condolence letter to her husband after

Rahel's death. New generations would never grasp what the two of them had most wanted to do, or what they suffered, Heine wrote, because those goals were never openly expressed. "We never spoke our innermost secret, and we shall descend into our graves with our lips still sealed."

Chapter Twenty-four

BUT THEY ALSO just delighted in each other's way with language.

One of Rahel's friends said her self-expression was so fresh it seemed she'd invented each word that left her lips for her own distinctive purposes: she spoke of loving "green things," meaning experiences free of social rigmarole. Rahel meanwhile loved Heine's incomparable bons mots, as when he quipped of one well-connected author, "He'll be immortal as long as he lives." If Rahel joked about Eduard Gans's unflagging attention to his own best interest, Heine liked to narrate anecdotes that contrasted his own romantic temperament with Gans's coarser appetites. Once, when he and Gans had walked together from the Tiergarten to a party, Heine announced that they were unable to present the bouquets they'd bought, since he himself had sadly plucked the petals off his flowers and cast them into

the water, while Gans—here Heine gave a world-weary sigh—
"Gans has *eaten* his." Everyone broke into laughter.

On the one hand, Rahel wanted to tone Heine down; on
the other, his jests were elixirs for ennui. Heine knew he was
wrong to pull Gans's leg so relentlessly. But he maintained
to friends that really he was doing Gans a service: *because* he
truly respected Gans's intelligence, it pained him to witness his
friend's insights compromised by his public manner. "All the
world sees of this comet is his trailing tail," he once remarked.
Heine's sophistry hides some genuine anxiety about the pre-
sentability of the Jews at large, himself included. However, his
urge to make fun of others was also a tic he couldn't still even
when his jibes were only partly on the mark, and completely
undermined his interests. He's more persuasive explaining why
he could never relinquish his affection for Gans despite their
uncomfortable relations: it wasn't on account of the giant books
Gans wrote, or his noble deeds, Heine told his friend Moser,
but "because of the funny way in which he used to pull me
about when he was telling me something," and because of the
good-natured, childlike look that came over Gans in the face
of real adversity.

Heine's moral vision was always graphically embodied, but
how was this instinct to find literary fruition? Rahel embraced
her role as midwife-muse helping to resolve the question. His
triumph would be a battle won for both of them against their
common fate.

She had carefully considered viewpoints about what con-
stituted good writing. Commenting on the work of Ludwig
Börne, another influential Jewish writer devoted to the cause
of freedom whom Heine grew acquainted with, she noted that
his fiery spirit appeared more vivid in letters to a beloved than
in his published work. Börne can't write any more than I can,
she asserted. According to Heine, Rahel understood writing to

be "a calm arrangement, so to speak the editing of thoughts, the logical composition of rhetorical parts," that she enthusiastically praised in Goethe. It was a subject about which the two of them held "the most fruitful debates almost daily," Heine recalled, adding that the prose of the current age "was not created without much experimentation, consolation, contradiction, and effort." At first, he hadn't entirely appreciated Goethe's strictly regulated style, but Rahel brought him around. Not so their comrade Börne, who could never comprehend the Goethean manner. Börne, Heine said, resembled a child who, without grasping the dynamic significance of Greek statuary, "only touches the marble forms and complains of coldness."

What made her championing of classical forms especially laudable, Heine continued, was that she herself, like Börne, was one of the "bacchantes of thought who stagger after the god with sacred inebriation." Nevertheless, she revered "those circumspect shapers of words who know how to manage and, so to speak, sculpt all their thinking, feeling, and observation like familiar material disjoined from the engendering soul." Goethe and her husband were two ideals for her in this regard.

Everything Heine wrote about their exchange may be accurate, yet it still omits deeper strata of their dialogue. For while Heine prided himself on his mastery of metrical forms, the power of his writing also depended on his ability to drop refinement and crash the reader against reality's own discord when he saw fit to do so. Moreover, not long before he took Börne to task for his immature obtuseness with respect to Goethe's verbal sculptures, Heine himself had compared Goethe's masterpieces to beautiful garden statuary, noting, "They are only statues, after all. One may fall in love with them, but they are barren." Rahel may have helped Heine realize how formal issues can overlap with issues of identity. Did writerly conventions possess the same significance for a people scrawled raggedly into the margins of the Fatherland as they did for the firmly inscribed majority?

Rahel once told a Gentile male friend that everything *he* composed was deployed across the page like beautifully uniformed soldiers on a drill, while her words resembled "an unruly mob of rebels with sticks." To another correspondent she said of her anarchic punctuation marks, "sometimes, I know myself, that they are not correct, but I leave them, as they are, to insert a certain expression, and to give them a physiognomy, the one which I would like them to have." The German language wasn't at her disposal, she declared elsewhere. For language is our collective "lived life," and she'd been constrained to shape her own incongruous existence. Rahel was straining to put her living self, whole, throbbing, and incompatible with petty circumstances, on the page. "If only I could disclose myself to people the way one opens up a cupboard," she cried. The ambition was virtually identical to that which early critics spotted in Heine's work. Sometimes this quality was praised. Schleiermacher, the biblical scholar and philosopher, for instance, applauded the poet's courage. Then there were those like Thomas Carlyle, who exploded at the mere mention of the "blackguard" Heine, railing against "that slimy and greasy Jew— fit only to eat sausages made of toads."

The debates Rahel and Heine conducted couldn't have consisted merely in her telling him he needed to be more formally correct. They both saw a value in communicating the confused yearnings of flesh and spirit not just in terms of what was said, but also with regard to *how* that longing got expressed. Modern songs "refuse to pretend to a Catholic harmony of feeling but rather dissect all feelings in the cause of truth," Heine argued. He praised Rahel's allegiance to cohesive structure, but she may have been more influential in validating the effervescent restlessness of his voice—the will to switch direction at a snap, opening a new door where there had seemed to be a solid wall of precedent.

Given Rahel's defense of certain irregularities in her language as reflective of the disordered inner life she'd been condemned to by society's prejudices, one thing she may have talked about with Heine was how to mold their passions into something more politically significant. Rather than permitting himself to be simply groomed as a rejuvenated Goethe, Heine began to wonder what a Goethe who addressed the great liberal struggles of the age might sound like. In comparing Goethe's work to antique statues, Heine said they appeared to be awaiting the word that would "liberate them from their cold, motionless rigidity and bring them back to life." Such musings could have pushed both him and Rahel to contemplate the structural reconciliations a Jewish Goethe might accomplish. Increasingly, Heine saw his role in bridging sociocultural positions: German and French, Jew and Greek, Romantic subjectivity and enlightened Reason.

Heine read Rahel's letters twice, then "three, four, thirty, forty times," he informed her husband. Her words cheered his spirits, and his own mind became lucid in consequence. "When I read her letters, it is as though I had risen in my sleep, in the midst of a dream, had positioned myself before a mirror and had there held converse with myself, occasionally boasting a little," Heine wrote. At times he writes as if he were possessed by her the way he'd been by Red Sefchen in boyhood. Even his handwriting was becoming increasingly similar to hers, and this, he noted, was inevitable. "Our thoughts, after all, are as alike as one star is to the other—I mean, especially, stars that are many millions of miles away from the earth."

Concern kept resurfacing in Heine's writing that their real meeting place might be the starry canopy, or the next world. Once before a trip he wrote her begging that she not forget him, reminding her that their spirits had entered into a contract with time. If they met again after several centuries, when she had transformed into a glorious flower in a beautiful valley, he wished that she would greet him graciously as an old acquaintance, though he would probably be some prickly holly bush. Despite the humor of the pathos, the recurrence of this theme conveys real apprehension that the earthly prospects for their venture were unpromising. The "rebel mob with sticks" of her language was ranged against another, rougher gang wielding more deadly weapons.

In the wake of the Hep-Hep riots in 1819, Rahel gave a provocative diagnosis of what lay behind the antisemitism. "*I know my country! Unfortunately,*" she railed, calling herself "a cursed Cassandra." For years she had been saying the Jews were bound to be attacked. The Christians wanted to keep them around, only in order to mock and abuse them as Jewish lowlife—to reduce them all to little, needy peddlers, good for kicking. That would be the form of the brave German rebellion! And why? Because what this "most proper, good-natured, peace-loving, slavish people . . . ought to demand, it *does not know*." So they wallowed in darkness, then turned their rancorous befuddlement against the Jews, "whom one was, thanks to religious excesses, permitted to hate."

It wasn't only the economic order that exposed Jews to lethal jealousy, Rahel concluded, but the larger population's sense of exclusion from a way of thinking: Jews knew how to ask for things—they were eloquent in the language of misery and petition.

One way to view the articulation of psychic process in Heine's writing is pedagogical: an effort to take readers behind the scenes in the voicing of desperation and desire. The tearing down of customary forms of self-expression provides a kind of object lesson in cultivating a revolutionary imagination.

The problem of political responsibility in poetry had only just begun to prey on him in the early 1820s, however. Rahel wouldn't have tolerated him writing against Goethe then, even had he wanted to. Moreover, she detected Goethean melodies in Heine's verses, together with a comparable purity of subject matter. Heine's main chance for German valorization lay in fulfilling the promise of that resemblance, she felt.

The poems Heine composed under pressure from her to engage creatively with Goethe eventually repaid their efforts by bringing Heine fame. Still it's doubtful that what he wrote was quite what she'd expected. And the discrepancy could only have redoubled her conviction of his significance. For he had etched the lineaments of their predicament inside the frame of an archetypal German nightmare.

Chapter Twenty-five

ONE CONSEQUENCE of feeling that his relationship to Germany was unraveling was to make Heine rediscover everything he loved about the place. The "melancholy violets" in a maiden's eyes. The forester's hut with its stag antlers. "Bad tobacco and good fellows, grandmother's churchyard stories, faithful night-watchmen, friendship, first love, and all such sweet fads and fancies."

In the country's old, anonymously authored ballads one came upon the beating of the German popular heart, displayed in all its "somber merriment," Heine wrote. Here one found German wrath pounding the drum, and German love vouchsafing its special kisses. "Such naivete in German constancy! Such honesty even in inconstancy!" There was no other language in which Nature divulged its deepest, most secret work. He knew it wouldn't be so easy to divest himself of German character as he sometimes pretended. "German is to me what water is to a fish," he confessed to one friend. Were he to ever leap from his native German springs, he would "soon turn into a dry cod-fish. . . . At bottom I really love Germany more than anything else in the world."

Water. The Fatherland. Strange aquatic homecomings and terrestrial disorientation—German folk poetry rippled with such themes, and Heine was still bewitched by the timeworn genre. His recourse to its customary rhythms, in the form of four-line stanzas with several primary stresses and shifting counts of unstressed syllables, was so well known that the pattern came to be called Heinestrophe.

In early verses Heine had tried to resurrect the old popular style intact. But he came to feel that poets who strove just to replicate those productions were like producers of artificial mineral waters: they might imitate the chemical structure perfectly, and still the most vital element, the "indecomposable, sympathetic forces of nature," would elude them. Even Goethe didn't completely avoid this trap: time was so limpid in his eyes that he couldn't distinguish between himself and the ancient bards. He was immortal—*an* immortal, Rahel liked to say. But lacking real awareness of what separated him from the heroic age—from any original truth—Goethe was unable to persuasively question himself.

In Goethe's eyes, the source of ill fortune was the daemonic— a mysterious, destructive, but not exactly evil force, which he defined as a power that couldn't be analyzed by understanding and reason. "It does not lie within my nature but I am subject to it," he wrote. Part of his heroic old heathen charm was monumental unselfconsciousness. "If God had wanted me otherwise, he would have created me otherwise," Goethe once declared. The Jewish equivalent might involve a little foreshortening: "*Had* God wanted me, he would have created me otherwise."

If the original German folk poetry had been "artless" in the sense of being ideally naïve, and current practitioners of the form suffered either from the affect of a manufactured in-nocence, or (as was the case with Goethe) from ignoring con-temporary society, Heine would make self-awareness and its futility his real theme. He would foreground the chasm be-tween himself and the deep *Volkish* sensibility without denying its appeal.

During Heine's youth, numerous variants of a classic Ger-man legend involving female allure—liquid, not quite human, monstrous, divine—intoxicated male longing, and the threat of drowning, were circulating. Goethe's poem "Der Fischer" in-troduces a fisherman watching his line drift amid the mesmer-izing tides when suddenly a woman rises up, dripping from the waves. She sings to him, asking why he draws the fish "to the deadly blaze of day." If he only knew how freely fish thrived down below, in the same element where the sun and moon took their rise-and-fall refreshment, and where his own "mirrored form" naturally beguiled him, he would descend to be with them. The fisherman's yearning begins to grow: "Half drawn by her, he glided in / And was not seen again."

The poem is a meditation on primordial forces, both en-dogenous and exterior to the human subject. Goethe's water spirit is aligned with Nature, but this enveloping presence de-sires to come into relation with the fisherman, just as he is half willfully entering her. Their interaction is not a binary play between good and evil but something more suggestively con-trapuntal, directed at an unknown coalescence. The poem ap-peared in an anthology entitled *Voices of the People*, with a note by Herder stating that if German poetry *could* return to the original spring of the folk song, "Der Fischer" would be a tem-plate for that renewal.

An entire subgenre of the literary nexus between women, water, ambivalent male desire, and death emerged at the begin-ning of the nineteenth century around the Lorelei, a striking rock formation on the Lower Rhine that had older mythological associations. ("Lore" means a squinting elf; "lei" means rock.) Most influential upon Heine was the work of Clemens Brentano, the stern-eyed Romantic writer who was an occasional visitor at Rahel's salon. Devoutly Catholic and casually antisemitic, Brentano yet appreciated Rahel's intellect: he told a friend he would have spent more time at her home if conversation there hadn't been so "slovenly." Rahel registered his talent, but at heart she considered him a danger—all the more so because he himself was oblivious to the risks he represented. On the level of pure artistry, she also found his verses overblown: "Don't be a Brentano, I can't stand it," Rahel warned Heine. Yet the problem ran deeper than aesthetics.

After the last eruption of antisemitic riots, she had warned her brother, the playwright Ludwig Robert, another friend of Heine's, that the resurrected strains of archaic German faith, which members of the cultured elite were playing with, helped fuel the violence: "The new hypocritical love for the Christian religion (may God forgive my sin!), for the Middle Ages, with their art, literature, and terror, incite the people to the *only* terror they *can* be provoked into, because they remember having been permitted it as of old!" She singled out Brentano as one of those "highly positioned persons" whose contempt authorized bloodshed on the street. Anticipating Freud, Rahel suggested that people don't ever outgrow their cruelest instincts; these just get loosely sifted under conventional proprieties. When the ground shifts, people go back to what they know.

Brentano's version of the Lorelei developed from legends that attributed an echo heard in caves of the famous outcrop to a group of nymphs. But he was the first to transpose the rock's name onto a solitary temptress and elaborate a plotline. His tale tells of a beautiful sorceress from the nearby town of Bacharach who enchants many hearts, and causes much sorrow. Summoned to the lord bishop's residence for a reckoning, she declares that she longs to lose her occult gifts and die because she's been forsaken by her true beloved. The bishop assures her that she will be pardoned for her errors, but must withdraw into a convent. En route, escorted by three knights, Lorelei asks to climb the rock so that she can glimpse her lover's castle one last time. The ascent is harrowing. From on high Lorelei sees a boat sailing away down the Rhine; she decides her lover is on board. "He must, he must be mine," she cries, hurling herself off the crag. The knights are stuck up there; they die without receiving absolution.

It's an ornate neogothic tragedy with a heavy dose of Christian proselytizing: Brentano himself had recently retreated into a monastery, where he served as secretary to a visionary nun.

Heine had praised some of Brentano's earlier, less pious works, which filled the soul with "weird delight, with passion mixed with terror." In these writings Brentano had caught the sound of ancient sagas, "the deep roar of the dark Bohemian forests," with their "fierce Slav gods." Heine knew Rahel was right about the seductive menace of such scenes, but he too savored their macabre extravagance. Once you took that from the German people, they became either bourgeois dullards or cross-hugging zealots, he believed, identifying more clearly than Rahel had the dearth of good, safe choices in their homeland. As he himself took up the theme of the Lorelei, Heine focused on the mystery of German "passion mixed with terror," exploring as he did so the implications of cultural rapprochement about which he and Rahel daydreamed.

Even while writing his own version of the legend, Heine was envisioning medieval Bacharach from a perspective antipodal to its position as the seat of Christian forgiveness and authority. In the same year that he wrote his "Lorelei," he started a historical novel, *The Rabbi of Bacharach*, which was meant to do for Jews what *Ivanhoe* had done for the Scots. He never finished the book, but it remains Heine's most substantial effort at engaging with the trauma of Jewish history.

At the novel's outset, Abraham, the saintly rabbi of Bacharach, and his wife, Sarah, are hosting a Passover Seder open to the whole community. Humility and glad reverence abound until two tall, pale strangers arrive saying that they are Jews and wish to join the feast. The men are welcomed, and the festival continues until Sarah notices her husband overcome with anguish. Then suddenly he bursts into crazy hilarity—spattering the ladies near him with the drops of wine that symbolize Egyptian plagues. When it comes time for the ritual hand-washing, Sarah brings out the precious silver ewer. Abraham signals to her, and they surreptitiously slip away. He leads her down along the Rhine until they reach the base of a high rock looming over the riverbank, a dramatic bluff that in Heine's description sounds very like the Lorelei. Abraham begins guiding Sarah up the mount. On the summit, she's trembling with anxiety, while Abraham's face appears spectral—consumed with "pain, terror, piety and rage." All at once, he seizes the silver vessel from her hands and hurls it off the cliff into the Rhine.

Sarah falls at his feet, begging him to explain what has happened. Abraham recounts that, while they were reciting the Haggadah, he happened to glance beneath the table and saw a child's mangled corpse. The two strangers, so far from being coreligionists, had come to destroy them with the blood libel—that pogrom-inciting lie that claims Jews are guilty of secretly sacrificing Christian babies on Passover night.

Abraham promises Sarah that now they will be able to flee to safety. Casting the ritual vessel off the towering rock serves to initiate Abraham and Sarah's flight from their homeland into exile. In place of the fatal leap by Brentano's Lorelei into the river—an act sealing her Christian damnation—the Jew hurls the telltale attribute of identity into the Rhine in order to free himself and live.

But the choice enacted by the Lorelei in Brentano's poem was also in Heine's mind at the time. "I really do not know

what course to take in this bad situation," Heine wrote to
Moser at the end of 1823. "I'll turn Catholic yet for spite, and
hang myself." So he'll do the Lorelei one better: he'll both
adopt the alien faith *and* plunge into the void.

Overlapping motifs, together with Heine's flights of rheto-
ric about being a fish in the water of Germany who knows that
extraction from this medium will be fatal, suggest that Goethe's
"Der Fischer" was also present to Heine when he wrote his
Lorelei. Heine was doubly imperiled, however. Although the
Rhine is his native element, he's doomed to drown if he in-
dulges his love for his place of origin. His position flickers
between fish and fisherman, while the water swirls with contrary associations of its own. A Jew is "a water poet," Heine
told Moser. But one must be careful to employ the expression
correctly, to mean "A Jew who is not yet baptized, a water-
proof Jew."

In this mental state, Heine composed his own interpretation of the fable.

"Ich weiß nicht, was soll es bedeuten . . ."

> I do not know what it means
> That I should feel so sad;
> There is a tale from olden times
> I cannot get out of my mind.

In the poem's opening stanza, Heine shifts the emphasis from
the traditional legend into his own consciousness. As with so
many of his narrators, the singer here announces that he's
haunted by an ancient story; age and familiarity don't diminish
its heartbreaking force. But why this particular tale should
exert such a hold on him becomes its own melancholy conundrum, which remains unsolved in the poem.

The story is simple: In the cool of evening, the Rhine is
flowing peacefully and a rocky peak glitters in the setting sun.
On top of the rock, reclines a wondrously beautiful woman.

Her golden jewels are sparkling.
She combs her golden hair.

She combs it with a golden comb
and sings a song the while.

The song is as spellbinding as the female figure.

It seizes the boatman in his skiff
With wildly aching pain;
He does not see the rocky reefs,
He only looks up to the heights.

The last of the poem's six four-line stanzas returns to the poet's perspective,

I think at last the waves swallow
The boatman and the boat;
And that, with her singing,
The Lorelei has done.

The verses are at once so plain and eerie that it's unsurprising some early critics labeled it a cheap street tune. But considered in the context of Heine's other writings and struggles at the time, the blond-haired Lorelei with her golden jewels—twinned with the harsh crag she lies on—evokes the tantalizing, treacherous grail of Germanness as such, while the disoriented fisherman's relationship to the Lorelei echoes Heine's vision of the Jews' relation to that identity. Goethe's water spirit destroyed the fisherman by actively coaxing him into the water. Brentano's magical female willfully destroyed herself when she couldn't consummate her love. Heine's fisherman perishes not through any positive action of his own, but through a kind of overwrought, entranced passivity before the supine Lorelei: that self-absorbed, flaxen-haired beauty, the *schönste Jungfrau* with her *goldenes Haar*, proves deadly by making *him* fatally indifferent to the natural hazards he's navigating. The poet's character adds another layer to this entanglement: He's transfixed by the "passion mixed with terror" of the story, just as the fisherman is bedazzled by the Lorelei. There's a mise en abyme quality to the fateful conjunction.

Heine had experienced unrequited love with Amalie; but here he shapes a deeper, politically resonant meditation on this theme. At the same time, he shows that the singer's lofty awareness of the situation does not prevent the impending engulfment. Heine might have liked to think of himself, relative to Goethe, as embodying "the party of action," yet in these lines he presents himself as helplessly still—distracted from all possibility of motion by a cerebral interrogation of his own fascination with the tale. The fisherman will not be saved, nor will the poet be spared the sorrow of impotently witnessing the man's oblivious foundering on the high rock of the real.

But there's a further twist. If Heine is at once fish, fisherman, and mournful, impotent observer, he is also the elusive singer—the Lorelei herself, making a wondrous song. Once more, he ventriloquizes an enchanting female voice anchored in the depths of German lore. Perhaps part of the singer's sadness derives from the beauty of the music he himself creates, which is removed from harsh contemporary realities—just as Heine would indict Goethe's all-consuming aesthetics for hindering the cause of German freedom. Hegel had taught students that art ultimately needed to pass into higher forms of consciousness. "For us art counts no longer as the highest mode in which truth fashions an existence for itself," he had said. Even if Heine wouldn't yet go that far, he denounced its self-enclosure. "What matters," he wrote in 1823, "is to grasp the spirit of popular poetic forms, and with this knowledge to create new forms adapted to our needs."

In a final, compounding irony, the song of Heine's Lorelei, which ripples with the nascent threnody of Jewish-German history, proved irresistibly enchanting to the general populace. It was set to music by the country's composers more often than any other poem, and came to be considered so definitively German that even the Nazis could not safely expunge it from their songbooks, instead erasing Heine's name and attributing it to Anonymous.

Heine published "Lorelei" as one of a group of linked poems in which unrequited loves intersplice like waves, cresting, hissing, then bursting back to darkness. Numerous doppelgängers also make appearances; another way of reading that recurrent figure in Heine's work is as the unrealized, wholly German version of his own self. Singers pass in and out of antique reveries, slashed with modern spite and bitterness. In one verse, the poet asks how a former lover can sleep knowing that he yet lives and wakes. Fury at the thought of her repose dissolves his paralysis.

> Do you know how the old song has it?
> The dead lad rose up brave,
> Embraced his love at midnight
> And drew her into his grave.
>
> Believe me, child of beauty,
> Dear girl with golden head:
> I live, and have more strength than
> The strength of all the dead!

In another poem the singer regrets the loss of pleasant "olden days," replaced by the helter-skelter present with elbows shoving everywhere. "Pressure and stress on every side! / Dead is the good Lord God above us, / And down below the devil's died." One poem in the cycle consists only of four mordant lines that merge the personal and national morasses:

> Seldom have you understood me,
> Seldom have I you, in turn;
> Only when in filth we wallowed,
> We understood each other well.

Heine titled the section of his book in which these poems appear *The Homecoming*, and dedicated it to Rahel. To Gans he explained that he'd taken her name which was so dear to him and "nailed it to the doorpost of his book, and this has made it more homely and safe for me. Books too must have their *mezuzah*," he observed. But the notion of "homecoming" in these verses is a travesty—except insofar as the dedication mantles them with a suggestion that the only shelter for such wandering souls will be the relations they forge between themselves. By the time he wrote those words he, Rahel, and Gans had all received their Christian baptism.

Chapter Twenty-six

In the spring of 1824, Heine learned in quick succession that Byron had died ("He defied wretched mankind and its still more wretched gods—like Prometheus"), that Gans's plans for resettlement of the Jews in America had collapsed, and that the Society for the Culture and Science of the Jews had formally disbanded. Gans was stunned by the group's failure to win any material support, declaring, "Of all the wealthy brethren of our creed, there was no one who, however complete was his approval of our aims, however great was his enthusiasm for our performances, had given a single voluntary offering to the society or its institutions." Heine felt less surprise: though the Society's members had enormous gifts of mind and spirit, along with generous hearts, they had been trying to salvage a cause that was lost long ago. All the group managed to do was turn up the bones of older generations of warriors who'd perished in the same struggle on battlefields of the past, he wrote.

He returned to Göttingen, the "*Accursed Nest*," determined finally to complete his degree, but nothing conduced to that end. He thought too much about the Venus de Medici and the maid of one local councilor, he told a friend. He also took part in duels, pranks, and several ill-advised and unsuccessful lawsuits. He kept plugging away at jurisprudence but never seemed to make any progress, constantly interrupting his studies to read Jewish history. By the summer of 1824, he suffered from headaches seven days a week. A doctor recommended a break in the countryside. He felt too unwell to get to Greece, as Byron had done, or to Italy, like Goethe. Perhaps it was the Varnhagens who encouraged Heine to think about a trip to the Harz in September. Those low mountains might not have been heroic, but they were steeped in German folklore, especially their highest peak, the Brocken, which carried age-old supernatural associations. Goethe had set the Walpurgis Night dream Bacchanalia from the first part of his *Faust* there. Heine had been thinking about writing his own *Faust* for some time. Why not do a walking trip in Germany's bucolic literary backyard?

Moreover, he could tack on an excursion to Weimar to finally meet Goethe: that would certainly please the Varnhagens, who might have mentioned to Heine that when Goethe himself was twenty-eight—just a few months older than Heine was that fall of 1824—he'd made his own ascent of the Brocken. Goethe even wrote a Pindaric ode about the transformative experience, in which he called for his verses to mount the clouds of daybreak like a bird of prey, and contemplated the path of the fortunate man who runs swiftly and joyously along his prefixed way. Was he himself one of the blessed? he asked.

When Goethe first climbed the Brocken, he had been torn between the prospect of a comfortable existence at the court of his patron, Karl August, Grand Duke of Saxe-Weimar-Eisenach, and the lure of some vast unknown. His purpose in traveling to the Harz was to tour old silver mines, which the prince planned to reopen and employ Goethe to oversee. The decision to scale the mountain had been spontaneous. In winter, when the Brocken's winds and snow were notorious, the climb carried genuine risks. Goethe saw it as a kind of mythic test of his character.

Questions of what shape his life should take and whether he was one of destiny's favorites stormed about him as he struggled with the mountain's "impassable tracks," but the sublime majesty of the setting broke through his uncertainties. "Hide the solitary man/In your sheer gold cloud!" Goethe exalted. Let the

> winter streams plunge from the crag
> Into his songs,
> And his altar of sweetest thanks
> Is the snow-hung brow
> Of the terrible peak.

He reached the top—higher than the "marveling world"—and gazed down upon the "kingdoms and magnificence" of creation. He *was* one of the fortunate! He would stay at Weimar and flourish. Everything spread infinitely beneath him.

On the Brocken, Goethe had turned from the romantic interiority exemplified by his novel *The Sorrows of Young Werther* toward nature and science. He descended the shafts of local silverworks, observing miners and the process of smelting. On subsequent trips, he collected geological specimens. After descending the Harz on his second expedition there, Goethe traveled to Göttingen, where a professor gave him a presentation involving bubbles and bladders pumped full of gas to demonstrate the work of the Montgolfier brothers, who were just months away from enabling the first human flight in a hot-air balloon.

Goethe came to conceive of his vocation in terms correlative with that inspiring ascent. Literature was intended to "free

us by inward serenity and outward grace from the earthly bur-
dens which oppress us. Like a balloon, it bears us with the bal-
last which hangs upon us into higher regions, where the earth's
mazes lie clear before us." The most festive and serious creations had the same objective: to achieve, through a satisfyingly
correct intellectual representation, a moderation of "both joy
and pain."

Not quite the tone of Heine's experiences thus far, let alone
of his emerging aesthetics; but perhaps he would have his own
revelation in the Harz. Regardless, despite his apprehensions,
Heine knew it was time to encounter the great man of German letters. He was still young enough to believe he might find
some illumination with the genius, and of course he hoped that
Goethe would hand off the torch to him. Or at least toss down
a light.

He left Göttingen in the middle of September, traveling
north past donkey drivers, holidaymaking students jammed into
carriages, and other students emerging disheveled from myrtle
bushes alongside prostitutes. He walked from Nörten to Nord-
heim, on through the forested hills of Thuringia, from Oster-
ode to Klausthal, visiting silver mines en route. On September
20 he climbed the Brocken, hiking by ranks of majestic firs while
birds sang and brooks splashed. Past fallen giants, freckled with
lichen, their torn-up roots making dream sculptures, their nee-
dles turned amber, on through tufted grasses until the path became rockier and the temperature plummeted—ascending into
the mists, gasping for breath, until at the brink of exhaustion he
reached the summit where he came upon the incongruous sight
of the Brocken House, a low, thick-walled inn full of boisterous
guests.

Heine had surely contemplated the journey's literary potential before he embarked, but not the shape his narrative would
take—that derived from the experience. To the extent that he
had mentally mapped the project, his ascent of the Brocken and

appearance in Weimar were probably plotted as the tour's pinnacle events. The Brocken's character, Heine wrote, was "entirely German": calm, sensible, and bald, with a cap of white cloud that gave it a "somewhat philistine air"—together with a penchant for occasional mad, romantic debauchery. Conquering the mountain would carry obvious resonance. Goethe, meanwhile, *was* German literature, or at least German literature's past. Their encounter would join the eighteenth and nineteenth centuries.

Two epigraphs introduce his account of the tour. One is a citation from Ludwig Börne. "Nothing is permanent but change; nothing is constant but death," it begins. "Life would be a perpetual process of bleeding to death, were it not for poetry. It grants us what Nature denies us." The second is a poem by Heine himself that repudiates society's artifices in favor of pastoral liberty. He tallies up the attributes of Berlin's drawing rooms: stylish black coats and silk stockings, polished manners, suave embraces. "Oh, if only they had hearts!" he exclaims. "To the hills I shall ascend, / Where the breast expands in freedom." But the verses close with a signature jab. "To the hills I shall ascend, / And I'll laugh as I look down."

The first real stop on Heine's walk, however, was the mine district: like Dante, he descended into the underworld before starting his climb. If Goethe went into the silverworks to survey their operations in preparation for taking over their management, Heine wants readers to understand what it's like to be a miner. He describes entering chimneylike openings into a labyrinth of cramped tunnels dead-ending in a solitary miner struggling to crack ore from the wall, while surrounded by deafening machines. From his descriptions of the miners' prisoner-like outfits to the account of contortions he himself underwent while clambering down slimy, filthy ladders, dodging beams and rope, Heine conveys the work's oppressive tenor. When he remarks that he did not get down to the lowest level, where some

said you could hear people in America cheering for Lafayette—
the French hero of the Revolutionary War was then touring
the United States—the implication that an emancipatory spirit
would be welcome in this subterranean hive is clear.

Aboveground, Heine went on to the modest homes of
miners who shared old legends about the mountains, visits that
inspired him to speculate on the origins of German fairy tales.
The appearance of stasis in these people's lives belies the fact
that theirs is "a genuine, living life," Heine wrote. Indeed, the
unchanging nature of their habitations was precisely what enabled their thoughts and feelings to grow interwoven with the
furnishings. "The stove and cupboard are alive," Heine noted;
"a human soul has entered them." Such people acquired an
"imaginative whimsy and pure humanity" that allowed them to
narrate the most fantastical events in a matter-of-fact way: a
needle and pin depart from a tailor's shop and get lost in the
night. A shovel and broom propped on a staircase begin to fight.
In this charmed domain, even blood drops can speak, convey-
ing fearful messages. The circumscription of this people put
them into relationship with all creation.

Perhaps some of Rahel's ruminations on the enforced dor-
mancy of Jews and women—the socially dictated inertia that
fed her own unsettling imagination—contributed to Heine's
thoughts on the magical sympathies of those who dwelled in
the Harz. He tried more than once to link the fate of the rooted
but impoverished lower classes with that of the disenfranchised
Jews, whose roots run deep in ancient texts rather than the
earth. The Bible was the Jews' "portable fatherland," Heine
once wrote; there Jews asserted "an inalienable right of citizenship." But immersed in that book, they absorbed little that took
place around them: "States blossomed and expired, revolutions
stormed over the earth, but they, the Jews, lay bent over their
book and noticed nothing of the Wild Hunt of time that passed
over their heads!"

Instead of participating in the great contemporary struggles, Jews had visions, like the miners' families gathered around the stove, or the fisherman before the Lorelei. Dreams acquire an exceptional status among the confined and the isolated.

The enchanted perspective Heine discovered among the miners also evoked the state of childhood—not one of gullible innocence, but rather of radical, democratic attention to the world. In childhood, our lives are replete with meaning, he observed: we hear and see everything. Growing older, we exchange "the pure gold of contemplation" for the paper currency of "book-definitions." The trade-off entails a loss of depth. We— "the grand, grown-up people"—are continually changing houses. Our servants clean up after us, and we have no connection to our household objects, which may be someone else's tomorrow. "Even our clothes are alien to us."

The sense of disassociation induced by modern property links to what Heine has to say about the inhuman amorality of money. He never saw any silver in the mines, he wrote; for that he had to travel to the mint. There, the sight of all those "new-born shining dollars" prompted him to meditate on the migratory cycle of hard currency. "Young dollar, what a destiny awaits you! What good and evil you will cause! How you will protect vice and patch up virtue! How you will be beloved and accursed! How you will aid in debauchery, pandering, lying, and murdering! How you will roll restlessly along through clean and dirty hands for centuries, until finally, laden with trespasses and weary with sin, you will be gathered again to your own kin in the bosom of Abraham."

The economy of the imagination calls for its own revolutionary influx, which in turn can ripple through the political economy. In delineating the empathetic relation of miners to their domestic environments, Heine is cultivating empathy among his readers—enveloped in their own stillness by way of absorption in the book—an animating compassion for the remote lives of miners who draw society's silver from the earth, but have almost nothing of their own.

The conceit of household objects with souls fits on a spectrum with Goethe's pantheistic pronouncements. But the notion that the contemplative life of the working classes might have lessons for artists, let alone that art should play a revolutionary role in nurturing solidarity among disempowered peoples, is hard to locate in Goethe's oeuvre. Nor does it conform to Goethe's neoclassical model that Heine's experiences become more phantasmagoric, absurd—and occasionally infernal—when he *emerges* from Pluto's subterranean realm and begins to climb the mountain. Indeed, from a moral-spiritual standpoint, the underworld is closer to paradise than the top of the Brocken, which in Heine's narrative is filled with carousing, asinine students.

But perhaps the whole tour began to reorient in Heine's mind after his visit to Weimar. The account of his meeting with Goethe in *The Harz Journey* speaks volumes.

Chapter Twenty-seven

THERE IS NONE.

Before turning up at Goethe's gate, Heine had sent him a long, sententious note, providing credentials and reminding Goethe that he'd previously mailed him a book of poems and a packet of plays. "I beg your Excellency to grant me the good fortune to appear before you for a few moments," he writes. "I shall not trouble you. I shall merely kiss your hand, and go." Heine adds that it is for health's sake that he's in the Harz. "On the Brocken I was seized by an urge to make a pilgrimage to Weimar and pay homage to Goethe. I have come here truly as a pilgrim, that is, on foot, in weather-stained garments, and I await your answer to my prayers."

The letter shows the reverse side of Heine's bravado: an overweening longing for acknowledgment from German culture's *genius loci.* Molding Weimar into a center for the arts and learning, Goethe had turned the court theater into a stage of national renown, brought luminaries of European culture to sojourn there, and shaped its park landscapes to express classical ideals. Whatever ambiguities shaded his success, the imprint of Goethe's imagination was all over town. Years before Heine showed up, Goethe's celebrity was such that his barber, upon being asked for a lock of the poet's hair, was alleged to have said that every strand had been catalogued and presold.

In Goethe's presence, Heine would be at one remove from his platonic ideal of the Great Man, Napoleon. When the general invaded Germany, he had requested an interview with Goethe; they spent nearly an hour discussing literature and aesthetics. Napoleon made several adroit remarks favoring naturalism over artifice. He voiced his displeasure at "destiny plays," declaring, "There is no destiny, only politics." It was obvious from his incisive comments that Napoleon had read *Werther* carefully. *Vous êtes un homme*, Napoleon told Goethe, presenting him with the cross of the Légion d' Honneur. Such endorsement would have been Heine's dream!

Goethe admired Napoleon as the man who had brought productive structure to the tumultuous forces of the French Revolution; to Heine, Goethe's own life must have appeared a marvel of fruitful order. Approaching his house in dirty clothes through Weimar's dignified, complacent streets, after weeks traipsing the wooded hills, took pluck. No matter how often he told himself, "He's the past, I'm the future." Heine's heart must have been pounding.

Just to pass into the cobbled courtyard of Goethe's mansion, with all those windows glaring down from on high, might compromise one's sense of self-possession. Then up the broad stairs to the suite of rooms adorned with classical heads and torsos: huge, noble faces staring, beautiful and resentful, as if Goethe had somehow squeezed the gods themselves inside his townhouse, then ruthlessly dismembered them for some home-grown scientific experiment.

Every detail of Goethe's rooms had been orchestrated to illustrate the man's comprehensive life-art philosophy. Even the wide-ranging hues he had painted his spaces were expressions of a comprehensive theory of colors. "The eye needs color as it needs light," Goethe explained, noting that the optical organ felt happiness when something consonant with its nature appeared. So Goethe had to have a yellow room, because yellow was the color nearest to light and conveyed the quality of brightness—happy, vivacious, mildly exciting. And he needed to have a red-yellow room, since that shade conveyed an even stronger feeling of warmth and joy, representing flame-glow and the softer gleams of sunset. Then he *would* have a blue room because blue has its own distinct energy, although it also carried negative aspects. Cold and shadowlike, blue appeals to us "not because it attacks us but because it draws us along."

Who could even *think* of so much stuff—let alone acquire and arrange the sundry objects? All those minerals, busts, fine glasses, and engravings; the little statues, large drawings, and plaster casts of prize antiquities. How had Goethe constructed a domestic cosmos in which every strange thing serenely constellated? The decoration of Heine's rooms in Göttingen rarely went beyond a few measly family portraits. As a rule, he didn't give such matters a thought, but inside Goethe's house one realized what life *could* bring you. It was one thing to read about Goethe—to discuss Goethe, to hear Goethe endlessly praised—and another matter to be inside his materialized brain.

He might have met Goethe in the green chamber—ideally balanced between blue and yellow—where the writer routinely dictated to a handsome young scribe. Wearing a long cream coat, hands clasped behind him, Goethe stood erect, even though he was seventy-five and his hair had receded from his great forehead to form a wreath at the rear of his egg-shaped skull. He planted himself firmly, uttering words for the ages—while being ever ready to glance up inquisitively at each knock on the door.

Goethe's moods changed sharply day to day. Sometimes, unable to control his "negating propensity and skeptical neutrality," he was sophistical, sardonic, and contradictory, even though this state of mind displeased him. Other times, visitors found Goethe in "thoroughly good humor, restrained, communicative, informative, not in the least malicious or ironic or passionate or brusque."

Some afternoons, after lunching at court, he would sit around in his shirtsleeves drinking wine with close friends; if someone less intimate dropped by, he would have his servant shoo the intruder off: "Not when I have friends here who make me feel profound or sublime," he'd declare, glancing around at his cronies with relish. In these moods, even inside his yellow room, he was capable of asking, "What is more precious than gold?" Then answering, "Light." Then asking, "What is more refreshing than light?" And answering, "Conversation."

During one of these unbuttoned, slightly sloshy afternoon symposia, Goethe took up the question of the comic sensibility. "Only a man with no conscience or sense of responsibility can be a humorist," he announced. His pal Friedrich von Müller responded that the humorist's own emotional state meant infinitely more to him than the object of his satire. Goethe approved the comment. "How dare a man have a sense of humor when he considers his immense burden of responsibilities toward himself and others?" Goethe demanded. Then he shrugged it off, in a manner that allowed him to indulge in more extreme heresy: "I have no wish to pass censure on the humorists," he said. "After all, does one have to have a conscience? Who says so?" Intimates got the reference to Goethe's long-standing conviction that extraordinary men, like Napoleon—or himself—always placed themselves outside morality. Morality was a species of subordination, while the great behaved like fire and water.

Goethe excused the jesters to convey his larger point, but made it plain that he disdained them. He was reading Byron's

Conversations that fall. "How oversensitive he is about every foolish journalistic criticism," Goethe complained; "what a dissolute life he led with his dogs and apes and peacocks and horses; no logic or system in it at all." His own pleasure came from poetic meditations and creations, he noted, but there were "too many external and internal claims on my activity." If he had been able to live a more solitary life, he would have been happier and done more as a writer, he groused to his votary Eckermann. So even though he counted himself one of fortune's favorites, all his years felt Sisyphean, like "continually rolling a stone and having to heave it up again and again."

That was his mood when Heine showed up, unkempt and starry-eyed, bursting with unconnected thoughts—strewn with reminders of rough sleeping in the Harz.

Eleven years later, after Goethe's death, Heine finally wrote about their encounter, paying Goethe homage as a deity, while caricaturing his own cowed naïveté. Beforehand, he'd pondered all the profound remarks he would make to Goethe, Heine recalled. In the moment, realizing he was actually facing Jupiter, presence of mind flew out the window. He began expatiating on the excellent plums found alongside the road between Jena and Weimar. All the while, he stole glances at this man who projected perfect harmony between genius and appearance: when Goethe stretched his hand out, "it seemed as though he could prescribe to the stars the paths they should traverse," Heine wrote. He realized he ought to be addressing Goethe in ancient Greek, but instead helplessly babbled away in the vernacular about the tasty fruits of Saxony. In response, Heine wrote, Goethe *smiled* at him. "He smiled with the same lips with which he had once kissed the beautiful Leda, Europa, Danae, Semele, and many another princess or ordinary nymph."

Maybe. One student who saw Heine immediately post-Weimar got a different impression of how the encounter went.

He said Heine was *livid*—railing that Goethe had treated him with unforgivable frigidity—not bothering to read a single line of his poetry!

Goethe's own diary note of the encounter is succinctness itself: "Heine from Göttingen."

But it's also true that not long after Heine paid his call, Goethe began complaining about impromptu guests: "These visits always start one on new trains of thought which are not one's own, one has to think oneself into the situations of these people," he grumbled. "I don't want anyone else's thoughts, my own are quite enough, more than enough for me to deal with."

Whatever happened between them didn't take long: Goethe clearly found nothing in Heine worth encouraging. Yet he may ultimately have given Heine something more precious than compliments. Perhaps Goethe's icy reception helped propel him to pursue greatness on his own terms, catalyzing the decision to radicalize his treatment of the material he'd been gathering in the Harz. On returning to Göttingen, Heine began reimagining the odyssey he had just completed in ways that eventually made it the most celebrated walk in German literary history.

The Harz Journey combines sociological reportage with fiction, philosophy, and poetry. Instead of beginning the narrative at the start of the ramble, Heine opens with a comic evisceration of Göttingen—a beautiful town that "looks its best when you turn your back on it." The ensuing narrative is partially cribbed from travel manuals, as well as old histories of the region and legends—and old legends reconfigured as revolutionary manifestoes. A sense of social conscience flares up repeatedly—most vividly in the mines, but also aboveground in fantastical set pieces, such as dinner in the Brockenhaus, where the narrator reinterprets dance steps performed by the Berlin ballet as gestural hieroglyphics of the Prussian and European political scene. When a dancer "spins round a hundred times on one foot, without moving from the spot, he means the Federal Diet," Heine writes; "when he sways to and fro like a drunkard, he is signifying the European balance of power."

The one mention of Jews in the published version of *The Harz Journey* occurs on top of the Brocken, and chimes with Heine and Rahel's ruminations on the need to puncture their people's sociopolitical bewitchment. Heine's roommate at the Brockenhaus is a young merchant from Frankfurt who begins griping that Jews have no sense of beauty or nobility, and are guilty also of undermining business by selling English goods below cost. Heine decides to give a scare to the fellow. Having placed his pistols conspicuously beside his bed, he announces that he's a somnambulist and must apologize in advance should he disturb the man's sleep. The next morning, the man cries that he couldn't sleep a wink for fear of the damage Heine might do him while unconscious. *Beware the armed sleepwalker!* Heine suggests.

Throughout the piece, Heine challenges Goethe's contention that the purpose of art is to moderate joy or pain. Instead, Heine's art seems directed at heightening the passions and harrowing the soul—piercing every species of self-satisfaction without abandoning the role of humorist. If Goethe opined that humorists were defective in being more concerned with their own mental states than in the targets of their parody, Heine demonstrates that, to the contrary, the true humorist's psyche necessarily becomes a conduit for the consciousness of others. Whereas Goethe once announced that he'd outgrown romantic interiority, Heine in *The Harz Journey* fiercely reembraces subjectivity, but in a politically inspired voice that rejects the premise of an opposition between intense self-awareness and attentiveness to the external world. Goethe collected a dizzying sampler of earthly goods to adorn his private villa in Weimar. Heine celebrates the democratic commons of a bountiful imagination. At the same time, he reshuffles the traditional romantic hierarchy, demoting natural landscapes in order to highlight the perilous topography of culture. Most of Heine's walk, in the telling, comprises social interludes, realist, farcical, erotic, and supernatural. He cuts short contemplation of a spectacular sunrise to go drink a cup of coffee.

Heine's rearrangement of the grounds of German literary history is more extreme. The most significant poem in *The Harz Journey* begins as a spooky rustic idyll, then turns into a chivalric reverie. But so far from representing a nostalgic revival of the old, conservatively Christian romantic sagas, Heine's knight describes the stages of an evolving political theology. In his first youth, the poet recounts, God was his Father, the preserver and creator. When he came of age, he believed in the Son, identifying with benedictions of love. But now that he's older, the poet's faith rests on the Holy Spirit, who performed the greatest wonders of the past but has yet greater marvels in store.

> He who wrought the greatest wonders
> . . . .
> Smashed the citadels of despots
> And the yoke of slavery—
>
> Healed the mortal wounds of ages,
> Put the rights of old in place:
> All men are created equal
> In a single noble race.

He himself is a knight of this Holy Spirit, Heine announces as the poem progresses, thereby aligning himself with the fourteenth-century Italian revolutionary Cola di Rienzo, who took this title, along with that of People's Tribune, styling himself a scourge of the nobility and defender of the lower classes. Heine is thus a knight who comes to destroy the feudal hierarchy and Christian myth—a knightly knight-slayer. Goethe compared the role of poetry to a balloon that carries us far above the earth's confusions. Heine surrenders that Olympian viewpoint to cast his lot among the suffering individuals down below.

The true peak of Heine's tour occurs not on the Brocken but in his subsequent ascent of the Ilse Rock. At its summit, Heine drifts off into ruminations on German emperors, knights, and fair maidens, becoming so distracted that he loses his balance. He now sees the world literally upside down—the mountains on their heads, the red slate roofs of Ilsenberg dancing—until all goes green and blue before his eyes. Giddiness would have made him topple into the abyss had he not clutched in his dismay to the iron cross planted at the crag's highest point. "I am sure no one will think the worse of me for doing this in such an awkward position," he concludes.

The tour thus ends with Heine clinging to a cross—a symbolic gesture that would be more heavy-handed were his ambivalences about Christian identity not also so pronounced. There's a coda to his tale, however. "The Harz Journey is and remains a fragment," Heine writes, "and the colorful threads so prettily woven into it to form a harmonious whole are suddenly cut off as though by the shears of an inexorable Fate." Perhaps someday he'll continue the piece. Perhaps other things he writes will become sequels to the narrative. Rejecting the self-containment of any creative work, Heine declares, "In the long run it does not matter when and where something is uttered, so long as it is uttered."

The ultimate irrelevance of authorship isn't cause for melancholy, he adds. It's the first of May. Spring floods the world like an ocean of life. Flowers are in bloom everywhere and beautiful girls are carrying bunches of violets. Heine sees the beggar on the bridge looking as if he'd just won a lottery. The sun is shining with its most tolerant rays even on the shady broker who, not yet hanged, is charging ahead with his insidious, manufactured countenance.

Whatever emotion one might be filled with, if the gaze

keeps traveling, it will find the deprived and the depraved—the former poor, disowned and oppressed, the latter some variant on the selfish rich person. There's no rising above that cruel dialectic. Yet his narrative ends on a note of irrepressible joy. In the absence of transcendence, the panorama below keeps revolving. The writer is alive to creation, and the world, for all its sorrows, overflows with possibilities for love. Heine tells an imaginary female interlocutor not to feel alarmed if she hears a shot. It won't be the sound of him committing suicide, but of "my love, bursting its bud, and shooting up in radiant songs."

Chapter Twenty-eight

Back in Göttingen Heine plunged into writing his travel memoir, finishing a first draft before the end of November. Rahel's brother-in-law, Gottlieb Braun, agreed to publish it in a literary almanac he edited. After extensive revisions, Heine sent it to him in May in the exuberant mood that suffuses the last part of his narrative. Then he turned to his studies—while also resuming work on *The Rabbi of Bacharach*.

Although with *The Harz Journey* he'd written a work that would dramatically expand his audience, there was still the bleak lag between composition and publication to endure. In this case the delay was especially protracted since plans for the literary almanac were abandoned. Gubitz, the next publisher to take on the project, dithered as well. It wasn't until early 1826 that the work began appearing, in installments—fragments of the fragment which, Heine discovered, Gubitz was quietly expurgating. All his political references were vitiated. Gubitz blamed the censors, but Heine ended their collaboration, whereupon Gubitz began publishing nasty squibs against him.

Heine's first of May euphoria didn't last, though two days later he finally managed to squeeze through his preliminary exams for the bar. The end of his degree was in sight. But this achievement only heralded more profound trials. That same month, Heine paid a visit to a Lutheran clergyman in the town of Heiligenstadt who began giving him the instruction necessary to convert. On June 28 in the pastor's low, plain study, Heine was given the official examination for church membership. Years afterward, one examiner, Superintendent Grimm, wrote about the encounter. He said that Heine's answers revealed him to be well versed in Christian theology and to have thought deeply about the religion. This was not a candidate who simply memorized and spat back the mandatory teachings, Grimm said, but rather someone whose change of faith seemed driven by an urgent hunger from within.

Grimm would say that; but there are other indications that having decided at last to submit, Heine couldn't make his conversion entirely pro forma. After the encounter with Goethe, Heine undertook another pilgrimage that didn't get recorded in *The Harz Journey:* to Wartburg to see the spot where Martin Luther lived while translating the Bible into German. If the German people had lost some of its poetry in consequence of Luther's creed, they'd gained much by way of morality, Heine reflected. And what liberation had come with Protestantism! All the sanctimonious perversity of the monks had disappeared. Under "Brother Martin's" leadership, "thinking became a right," which then gave birth to freedom of the spirit.

It was as if with the visit he were working himself up to turn Protestant, touching the walls of the cell inside which Luther conducted his monumental labor in order to find a way into the spirit of his teachings. It was rare to encounter someone like Luther who was "at the same time a dreamy mystic and a practical man of deeds," Heine exclaimed. "His thoughts not only had wings, but also hands."

Heine had to persuade himself that with his conversion he was fulfilling some higher conviction—or at least acting in concert with a universal cause. He'd never thought of himself as a nonbeliever, Heine kept reiterating, ultimately composing his own doxology: "I do not belong to the materialists, who make the spirit body; rather I give the bodies back their spirits," he wrote. "I do not belong to the atheists who deny. I affirm."

On the other hand, he also reflected that his conversion was entirely the fault of Napoleon. If Napoleon hadn't been cavalier about the Russian winter, and so forfeited the Empire, Heine would still be French, and a licensed freethinker. Whatever admiration he might muster for Luther, Heine was also a self-conscious victim of clashing historical tides.

Heine insisted that it wasn't necessary for him to give his conversion a second thought, since he didn't believe in *any* religious institution. How could you change faiths when you didn't have one to begin with? On the other hand, however, since he didn't believe in any religious institution, how could he bring himself to pretend that he'd discovered the truth of the cross?

This was the society he lived in, Heine kept reminding himself and others. It demanded a certain type of pledge to a certain pattern of virtue as a prerequisite for just getting along. Rahel herself had accepted the need for this imposture, failing which one might end by discovering one had become no one at all. What was objectionable about repeating a few venal phrases, which once uttered were dispensed with, as if they'd never been pronounced, except for the fact that one was now free to marry who one pleased or make a living how one would?

The language in which the Bible had been written was dead now anyway—except for its subterranean persistence among the "murdered people," the "ghost of a people," the old Jews in dark ghettos to whom "German savants secretly descended in order to raise the treasure," Heine wrote. Luther had preserved the Jews' supreme work for the world by rendering Scriptures into the vernacular and in so doing had restored "the true religion." Luther created the Word for *us*, Heine avowed, and in this way he'd produced a new form of literature, *German* literature in the true sense of the word!

And even if there were something objectionable in the profession of new faith, hadn't he a responsibility to make an independent living? Besides which, his family wouldn't support him forever even if he'd let them.

All he wanted was to have as much freedom as he could in this world, here and now. To fight the battles that matter one must consign lost causes to the far side of time's Rubicon. If someone tells you "just say 'A' to gain B, C, D, and E—all the rest of the alphabet is yours," of course you say "A." "A" is simply the letter at the head of an alphabet that you want to make use of; in itself "A" is nothing.

It was only that somehow this particular "A" didn't sound quite right on the lips. It struck the wrong note, at a false clip. As children, he and Max held a metrical competition. Max prided himself on his proficiency at the exercise. Looking over Heine's shoulder while the poet wrote down his verses, he cried out, "Harry, this hexameter has only five feet." Heine ripped up the poem in a fit. But next day at dawn he showed up at Max's bedside saying he'd had a dreadful night. He'd fallen asleep very late and then was oppressed by a nightmare: that unhappy hexameter came limping up to his bed with its five feet, wailing terrifyingly, demanding its sixth foot. "Yes, Shylock could not insist more rigorously on his pound of flesh than this impertinent hexameter for his lacking foot," Heine said.

So that was the problem: Heine heard things in a certain way and the hexameter of his being had felt complete without that sixth foot of Christianity, even if it were the correct ending to his present lifeline. He knew the baptismal certificate was his "ticket of admission to European culture"; but why exactly did he need an entry document to something he was already physically, intellectually, and emotionally inside of?

He got a new name: Christian Johann Heinrich. At lunch after the ceremony, Grimm promptly flubbed it by introducing him to another guest as Heinrich Heine. At the meal, this guest noted, Heine kept silent but appeared extremely agitated. The clergymen kept glancing over at him with mild, grateful looks. Finally, Heine just thanked the men and left. There's no indication that they ever saw him again.

At first, he told no one that he'd done it. It was weeks before Heine wrote his sister that she should let her husband know he was now "not only Dr. Juris but something else too. It rained yesterday, as it did six weeks ago." In his first postbaptism letter to Moser he recommended that his old friend read Vasily Golovnin's memoir about his visit to Japan. There he would discover that the Japanese were the most civilized and urbane people on earth—"I may say a Christian people, if I had not read to my astonishment that the people holds nothing in such hatred and horror as Christianity. I will be a Japanese. They hate nothing so much as the Cross. I will be a Japanese."

Gans converted at almost exactly the same time, and Heine poured out his self-loathing on his old comrade's head in a poem excoriating the loss of youth's "sacred courage." "You have humbled yourself before the cross / the very cross that you despised," he wrote. The man who just yesterday was a hero had proven to be a cowardly knave. Heine never published the verses but kept the poem safe with the rest of his papers.

In December, Heine wrote Moser that "if the laws had allowed the stealing of silver spoons, then I would never have been baptized." He'd gone to synagogue and had the pleasure of hearing Dr. Solomon attack the baptized Jews, especially those who for a mere hope of getting *a position* were untrue to the faith of their fathers. It was an excellent sermon, he told Moser, adding that a mutual acquaintance named Cohen had been treating him magnanimously, inviting him to holy day meals: "He heaps glowing *kugel* on my head, and I crunch this sacred national dish." Kugel had done more for the preservation of Judaism than all three editions of the Society's periodical combined—and there was greater demand for it.

A year after his conversion he was still getting up in the middle of the night, standing in front of a mirror, cursing himself.

Chapter Twenty-nine

IT DIDN'T WORK OUT.

Not on any level at any stage in his life. It didn't enable him to buy the silver spoons he couldn't steal. It didn't make him feel aligned with the religion of progress. It didn't serve as his passport to European culture. Once Heine's baptism was done and unretractable he saw that it would accomplish nothing whatever—except bring him more enemies. Jews saw him as a traitor, while Christians viewed him as corrupting their faith from within. The whole venture had made him unlucky, Heine reported to Moser in January. Ten years later, its aftershocks were still causing him grief. In 1835, when Heine published his stirring paean to Martin Luther—his nearest thing to a "How I Could Bring Myself to Become Christian" statement—one Protestant leader was so outraged by the connection Heine drew between Luther's ideas and freethinking that he helped persuade the German Diet to ban all of Heine's writing.

Initially, Heine thought he might parlay his membership in the state church into a professorship at the University of Berlin. Wasn't the reason he'd ruled out an academic career the blanket proscription on Jews introduced because Gans got so pushy before his repentance? Well now Heine had foresworn his own absence of a foreskin, and he wanted to teach history. If he couldn't write all the time, he would give lectures on German history to young people, a bit like he'd been doing at the Society, only now with a steady salary, and not just to Jews. But his application in Berlin never went anywhere, so Heine turned his ambitions to the university in Munich. Its faculty was formidably reactionary, however, and without an inside track he couldn't get far there either, so Heine resolved to go back to Hamburg. In Hamburg he could surely take advantage of his uncle's connections and find work as a lawyer. He informed the family there of his plan, but job offers didn't exactly start springing out at him. Plus, Hamburg held only spoiled memories.

At one point he had thought of finding work in diplomacy: this wasn't such a bad line of work for a man of letters, so long as you stayed on the authorities' right side. But he'd had no grooming for the occupation, and no one familiar with his behavior was likely to promote him as a natural diplomat. It was a whim born of chronic frustration. Strip away literature and Heine's entire youth can be read as the story of a person looking fruitlessly, haphazardly for work in an increasingly aggressive economy that has no place for skeptics, regardless of their brains or education.

Obviously, he didn't have it in him to be a team player in either Germany's dynamic new financial industries or the burgeoning, consumer-oriented sector. Nepotistic opportunity was still his best shot, even if initial signs from Hamburg hadn't been encouraging. But before testing his credibility further, after the hard work of the past year, Heine felt he'd earned a little holiday (paid for again by Uncle Salomon). Off he went to the picturesque sand bluffs of another North Sea island. There he wrote some poems about nature's indifference, frolicked with young ladies of the local nobility, and stared morosely out to sea. The best of his new verses had a political edge that made their publication improbable. In one entitled "Seasickness," Heine gazes back longingly, nauseously, at the shoreline from a tossing ship, brooding over his fate—"age-old, ashen-grey reflections" known already to Father Lot when his drunken cheer began to turn "a little rocky." Heine considered to himself how Christian pilgrims on stormy sea voyages once kissed images of the blessed Virgin, while he himself just sat around chewing old strips of herring, wishing he were back on terra firma. It didn't matter that the soil of his dear German fatherland was covered with

> lunacy, hussars, bad poetry
> And vapid little pamphlets;
> . . . .
> What if your assembly of snails
> Thinks it will never die
> Since it crawls along so slowly,
> . . . .
> So what if folly and injustice
> Cover you completely, O Germany!
> Still do I long for you:
> For at least you are solid land.

Not your standard beach-resort doggerel.

Norderney was only partly transformed from an impoverished fishing village into a fancy holiday spot then, and Heine was alert to the discrepant fortunes and variant moral compasses of its two populations. The wealthy might do well to cover themselves up a bit, Heine advised. Should the local inhabitants, "poor as crows," peer into the brightly lit windows where the leisured classes gathered at night and see the feasting, gambling, and voluptuous dilly-dallying there, the consequences were bound to be drastic—most of all for the poor. All the money pouring into the bathing establishment would never compensate for the consuming new wants being awoken in them. And the church, which purported to offer the islanders spiritual defense by portraying all the world's splendors as gross bait set by Satan, was guilty in another way, Heine added. That "virtuous mob" wished to launch a crusade against the naked images of the gods just so that these could be replaced by their own set of costumed dumb devils: "the naked and divine is fatal to them." Only the other day he'd been thinking to himself that as a good Christian he really ought to go to church, but as he passed the sacred edifice, lines from Mephistopheles in Goethe's *Faust* ran through his head: "I know right well it shows a wretched taste, / But *crosses* never ranked among my fancies." Heine links "Wolfgang-Apollo" (as he now designated Goethe) with the destitute islanders who stood helplessly at the margin of a new age—pure hearts whose "unity of soul" had been disturbed by economic transformation. Goethe's writing revealed a kindred, archaic wholeness, Heine wrote. There was more morality in the "entire nudity" of a person like Goethe than in the hypocritical smiles of all society's camouflaged satyrs.

Self-consciousness was a disease, and the present age debased; but Heine couldn't help being burdened with the former and doing his best to capitalize on the latter's mongrel spirit. When one lady at Norderney engaged in a shallow aesthetic debate with other visitors asked Heine what *he* thought of Goethe, Heine, in an inspired conflation of values, cultures, and faiths, crossed his arms over his breast, bowed his head and declared, *La ilaha illa Allah, wa-Muhammed rasul Allah.*

As a freshly baptized Christian, Heine immediately began critiquing the church and genuflecting to Allah in the persona of irreligious Goethe; and as a newly minted doctor of laws he went on holiday and critiqued the vacationers, especially the seductive gamblers—while also gambling himself, unsuccessfully, with Uncle Salomon's money, and having a fling with a local fishergirl. With his family on tenterhooks waiting for him to start lawyering, Heine turned his attentions to the humble laborers whose exertions would never earn them the pleasures of their social superiors. He remembered his own yearning, as a boy, for lovely, fragrant tarts that he could sniff but never taste, and recalled the fashionably *un*dressed women who had promenaded by just out of reach when he was older. Then he rechanneled these personal recollections into a revolutionary sympathy with the local workers, whom he also confessed he found unbearable at close proximity because they stank of fish. The instinctive recoil from the odor of poverty was a recurrent issue for Heine—but he noted also that once the lower classes had money and opportunity to keep themselves clean, he knew the problem would cease. He doesn't, in other words, gloss over the squeamishness induced by unsanitary circumstances, but sees the taint as contingent, and remediable by a just distribution of resources.

After Norderney, Heine went to visit his parents at Lüneburg, where he found his reputation had grown to such an extent that he was invited to all the best houses. Then he got to Hamburg, and immediately felt suffocated. "Rain, snow, and too much food," he wrote friends on arriving at the house of his sister and her husband, Moritz.

Moritz continually sniped at him. It was true that Heine had promised Charlotte he wouldn't come to Hamburg if he didn't have a source of income lined up. But Moritz took his difficulty in finding a job as a kind of moral scandal. It incensed this stiff nullity to find that instead of devoting himself around the clock to securing steady work, Heine sought out a little palatable company. Yes, he'd befriended a handful of musical composers—along with an author-physician who was a relation of Varnhagen's, an obscure local poet, an older literary scholar, a cultured young merchant named Merckel, and a bon vivant joker named Prätzel. Did that make him wicked?

In the midst of his brother-in-law's attacks, Heine told Moser that civil war had broken out inside him as well. What was he even doing trying to live by the terms of a city concerned only with shopping and business? He'd now become a true Christian, he continued, "toadying up to rich Jews." He was in revolt against the whole world and himself most of all. As a Christmas present, he was sending Moser something really special, Heine announced: the promise that he wouldn't casually shoot himself.

Anything socially untoward he might actually have done came from his being openhearted and childishly attached to his friends—and to friends of friends, Heine acknowledged conscientiously. In any case, he obviously couldn't continue living in his sister's house. Not to mention which, he was getting no support to speak of from Uncle Salomon. It was as if the man were just waiting to be fed poisonous rumors about him, Heine told his brother. "Every creeping thing, which could ruin my good name" received a royal reception in Salomon's house. Long after he'd left Hamburg, Heine told another writer that the whole city revealed "a timber-deep thick-headedness. . . . This hypocritical citizen morality, combined with a libertinism devoid of all grace of fancy—how horrible was all that! Berlin was very wearisome—very dry and very unreal—but Hamburg!!"

Still, his stay there wasn't a complete write-off. One winter day in 1826 he walked into a bookshop asking for a copy of his own tragedies—speaking of the volume derisively, perhaps defensively—only to be gratifyingly rebuffed by the store owner, Julius Campe. On the spot, Campe became Heine's publisher and remained so for the rest of Heine's life.

Portly, large-featured, quick-eyed and relentless, Campe could be generously jolly or shrewdly calculating as occasion required. He also had a streak of sloppy, warmhearted theatricality that, together with staunchly liberal politics, made him Heine's kind of *confrère*. All through his career, Campe took pleasure in outfoxing the censors. Only volumes shorter than 320 pages had to be submitted to the authorities for scrutiny, since the assumption was that longer books would never find enough of an audience to become meaningfully incendiary. Campe bumped up page counts with standard tricks like manipulating margins, enlarging fonts, and stretching out the spacing. He also devised new tactics for evading officialdom: packing the work of controversial authors inside bales of dry goods; sending a book's title page to readers in one post, then mailing off the actual content in a second parcel under a name indicating it to be a treatise on grammar or religion. In *Ideas: The Book of Le Grand*, published the year Heine started working with him, Campe even took the risk of printing Heine's bold satire of the censors themselves. It made Heine crazy that they simply substituted blank dashes for words deemed suspicious, as though what was left out made no difference to the narrative, so he decided finally to turn their own technique against them.

Chapter 12 of *Ideas* begins with the words, *Die Deutschen Zensoren*—the German censors—followed by line upon line of slashes interrupted only once by the word *Dummköpfe*, blockheads, followed by more slashes—until the chapter breaks off. In Heine's work there is *literally* no content being masked by the marks. He leaves it to the reader to link *Zensoren* with *Dummköpfe*.

For all his wiles, Campe kept getting into trouble—at one point stirring the full German Diet to lodge a protest with the Hamburg town council about his behavior. But though his press intermittently got shuttered and he himself was once thrown into prison, Campe kept his publishing house in business, insisting that the future "belonged to the young, and he was sure of remaining true to progress while he kept on enrolling them in his ranks." He told Heine that since he wasn't trying just to feed himself but to fulfill a vocation, he was compensated for the torments of his business. Campe's true ambitions were directed toward something higher than lucre—though still at times he cut deals that appear retrospectively to have taken advantage of Heine. Certainly Heine swore as much, though he also maintained outlandish expectations. While a small number of his works sold well, most did just modestly. Campe never abandoned Heine even when few readers bothered with him.

Heine was part of the first generation of writers in Germany for whom it was even conceivable to make a living from book sales. Until then, authors either found a patron, had a separate career, or lived off inherited wealth. Bookselling was still a germinal business, and readers couldn't afford to pay much for books, though production was expensive. Neither writers nor publishers yet had a firm grasp of the economic implications of their collaboration. Copyright was virtually nonexistent. Writers were not paid a percentage of sales. Instead, they received a lump sum at contract. A run of thirty-five hundred copies was considered substantial and brought a meager advance. The bestseller mark was roughly ten thousand copies, and Heine hit that milestone only once near the end of his life.

At the same time, however, the coming transformation of publishing into a mass-market enterprise was visible on the horizon—not actualized but tantalizingly within sight. A period of intense technological and sociological change in the industry began just as Heine's career took off, without quite crystallizing in his lifetime.

The first great reading revolution is often dated to the latter half of the eighteenth century. It has been difficult for scholars to get a firm handle on why exactly that initial expansion happened: less God and more science, plus revolution, a bit more leisure time, and greater financial investment in the business help explain the phenomenon. Yet something remains elusive.

The second surge was dramatic and somewhat easier to chart. Book production tripled between 1821 and 1845. Through those years and the decades to follow, industrialization of the book trade coincided with a rapid rise in literacy, which fueled the market for more miscellaneous reading choices—newspapers, periodicals, novels, and histories—as well as for more variety within each genre. Writers who survived on their work were almost always dizzyingly prolific—and also took editorial positions at journals. Except for a brief six-month stint with a publisher in Munich in 1827—the only time in his life that he held a steady job—Heine did neither. But one way to think about the intensely heterogeneous nature of his work, its radical, multigenre confabulation of voices, would be to view it as an intuitive channeling of the expanding hunger for content that characterized the age. His eclectic, democratic imagination complemented the curiosity of a new reading public.

In *Ideas*, Heine links the kaleidoscopic character of consciousness directly to the disjunctive array of available reading matter. At night, his inner life got fast and wild, Heine wrote: "A congress is held in my head by the nations of the present and the past, the Assyrians, Egyptians, Medes, Persians, Hebrews, Philistines, Frankfurters, Babylonians, Carthaginians, Berliners, Romans, Spartans, Arabs, Street-Arabs—" but it would take too much time to describe, he breaks off. "Just read Herodotus, Livy, the *Haude and Spener Gazette* [a major Berlin daily newspaper], Curtius, Cornelius Nepos, the *Companion* [a literary periodical]—Meanwhile I will have breakfast."

Campe acknowledged Heine's brilliance. On at least one occasion he even discouraged him from publishing something that ended up selling briskly because he felt it had been written in a slapdash fashion that detracted from his genius. But there was not a direct correlation between Campe's respect for Heine's writing and the rate of remuneration. Heine complained that Campe's payments were so low they were killing him. In any case, he had a tendency to spend everything he got no matter the sum, and for a time he was in fact among the best-paid German authors. Campe kept trying to make Heine accept that his audience was limited. "You treat love and your Self, and again Your Self, and people see that as stinking egotism," Campe said. This approach was simply not going to prosper at a moment when, Campe explained, books were evaluated on the basis of their suitability as gifts for ladies.

Both men at different points likened their thirty-year association to a conjugal relationship. Campe rhapsodized over their ability to speak about everything that mattered, "like man and wife." He referred to Heine's books as "their children." The two fought badly at different moments: "There is pouting in marriage when one of the couple oversteps the natural boundaries," Campe observed. But that didn't mean they need ever part ways. From their first conversations, Heine knew he could count on Campe to put his work into circulation. Furthermore, and of crucial importance to Heine's sense of his vocation, he trusted Campe not to censor a word of his manuscripts without first having done everything possible to slip it past the censors. Even more than honorariums, the confidence that he would be able to see the current of his imagination rendered in print as it had flowed from his pen gave a crucial boost to Heine's self-respect.

Eighteen years after they met, in his epic masterpiece, *Germany: A Winter's Tale*, Heine made room to salute Campe by name. For all the glories of Venice and Florence, the republic of Hamburg had better oysters, Heine wrote, and the best of the best were at Café Lorenz, where he went one fine evening with Campe for a dinner meeting washed down with Rhenish wine. As he "gobbled and guzzled freely" Heine mused,

> I thank the Lord who made the grape
> And the vines that cling and kiss earth,

And gave me Julius Campe as
My publisher on this earth!

I thank the Lord whose mighty Word
Tells nature to replenish
The oysters growing in the sea
And, on the land, the Rhenish!

—Who made the lemons grow, to squirt
The oysters as He blessed them.
Tonight, Lord, grant that I shall have
The stomach to digest them!

It may be the poem's lightest scene, but the teasing affection and joie de vivre are contagious.

At such moments Heine forgave Campe for having at first shown little interest in the *Buch der Lieder:* It was Heine's prose that seemed to him to have a future. Campe finally agreed to publish the poems in 1827, paying a pittance for the collection that established Heine as one of Germany's foremost poets and went through thirteen editions in his lifetime. Campe's coup has been compared to the windfall reaped by the printer who gave Milton five pounds for *Paradise Lost.* But it did give Heine the opportunity for a witticism. He liked in later years to say that he did have at least one awesome monument erected to him in Germany: Julius Campe's new mansion, built from the proceeds of the *Buch der Lieder.*

Chapter Thirty

TRUTH BE TOLD, Heine hadn't seen success coming from his songs either.

Since visiting Goethe, he'd deepened his commitment to the principle that the age of lyric verse was finished—superseded by new material realities and coinciding struggles for progress. "The hubbub of a common European brotherhood of peoples," with its "sharply mingled pain and jubilation," made its own kind of music, Heine declared. Although many of the poems from the *Buch der Lieder* were more politically inflected than lyric poetry customarily allowed for, Heine wanted to signal an ideologically driven break with the genre as such.

Indeed, the age of art, which Goethe had emblematized, was now in retreat, Heine proclaimed in 1828. "A new era, a new principle" was emerging that required aesthetics to be fully engaged with "the movement of the time." Each period had its problem and mission, Heine wrote, and the great problem of their own time was emancipation: "Not simply the emancipation of the Irish, Greeks, Frankfurt Jews, West Indian blacks, and other oppressed races, but the emancipation of the whole world."

The pursuit of freedom for all humanity wrapped together Heine's passion for Napoleon and the French Revolution with the best of Hegel, the Society's most noble goals, Rahel's wildly transcendent voice, a hint of Jewish Messianism, and his own iconoclastic creative spirit. "It will be some time, I know, until emancipation is achieved," Heine allowed, "but it is bound to come, this blessed time." Then, in unity, people would battle against the other great evils of the earth—"perhaps at last against death itself," he decided, though death's "stern system of equality" was neither so oppressive nor so ludicrous as "the theory of inequality held by aristocracy."

It may not be chance that Heine's clarity about the greater cause occurred as he sloughed off all pretense to pursuing legal work, while in the glow of a fancy-free ramble through Italy. Heine later saw this period as the most delightful of his life. "It was a time when I ran exulting from one peak of the Apennines to the other," he wrote Rahel's sister-in-law, the celebrated beauty Friederike Robert. "The ichor of youth and amorous bliss filled my veins, and I dreamt great wild dreams in which my fame spread the whole world over to the farthest islands, and old sea-salts would tell of my deeds." The fact that Heine delivered his manifesto to freedom as part of a travel narrative—one of several rambunctious Italian sketches he wrote in these years—indicated that liberation would extend to a new formal amplitude. Heine advised readers to skip half a dozen pages every so often: "There is nothing so stupid on the face of the earth as to read a book of travels in Italy—unless it be to write one—and the only way in which its author can make it in any degree tolerable is to say as little in it as possible of Italy," he stated.

But as previous aesthetic programs began to be supplanted by the flowering of what Heine now labeled "the so-called art of political poetry," he watched with dismay as "the Muses were given strict orders . . . to enter into national service, possibly as *vivandières* of liberty or as washerwomen of Christian-German nationalism." German poets were particularly afflicted, he wrote, "by that vague and sterile pathos, that useless fever of enthusiasm which with absolute disregard for death, plunges itself into an ocean of generalities." Both his predecessors' failure to reckon with sociopolitical realities, and the current instrumentalization of art—even for progressive agendas—seemed misconceived. Suddenly people found a new, mortal weapon against genius: "the antithesis between Talent and Character." The masses valorized the latter in the shape of persons who "proclaim their life program in the marketplace once and for all in popular language." But "it takes more than an opinion to build a Gothic cathedral," Heine quipped to a friend.

At one point Heine even told Karl Varnhagen that it appeared poetry was at an end; he could only hope to live the longer in prose. But this renunciation was never a position he could really sustain, or embrace as politically necessary. The point was not to kill poetry but to change it, so that it would both *matter* in the struggle for emancipation and remain true to the divinely unaccountable imagination. His chief business, he declared in later years, was "to defend the inalienable rights of the spirit" by overthrowing pieties and the form's status quo, while denouncing humanity's oppressors. Heine's description of his self-appointed mission increasingly resembled that of a biblical prophet.

Ultimately, he contended, poetry was simply truer to people's experience of mundane reality than was a dutifully prosaic documentation of events. In their histories, people wanted to see the facts "dissolved again in the original poetry from which they sprung." Poets knew this, Heine said, and took mischievous delight in remolding the collective memory, perhaps to heap scorn on those historians who flaunt their aridity as a badge of gravitas.

Still smarting from his dismissal by the faculty in Berlin, Heine aimed his venom at the state archivists who were, he noted, as desiccated as the parchment they wrote on. But there was a deeper layer to his argument. The problem with conventional works of history was that when the public opened their pages what they found simply bore no relation to the world they actually lived in. Heine argued that people from all classes experience reality filtered through the lens of imagination into far richer tableaux than official chroniclers acknowledge. These hybrid perspectives, spirited and porous to the fantastical, inspire our actions—or at least our understanding of events as we live through them, before their inscription in the pedantic annals. When a fussy companion on his Italian trip quibbled that Heine seemed to be advocating "falsified history," he countered that poets "give the *sense*, in all its truthfulness, though it be clothed in inverted form and circumstance." For this reason, "it is with poets as with dreamers."

The naked facts of Heine's life over the latter half of the 1820s were undistinguished. He carried on brief, jaunty love affairs and fulsome quarrels. He wrote, published, and postured. He scrabbled to get by, meandering from place to place, in Germany but also in England and Italy. However, if the externals of Heine's existence made for a series of choppy vignettes, his inner life was an inexhaustible font of ideas and imagery. In addition to cross-genre travel diaries and poetry, Heine wrote *Ideas: The Book of Le Grand*, his most radical experiment in autobiographical fiction.

The book is strewn with details of Heine's childhood in Düsseldorf, his early manhood in Hamburg, and his evolving intellectual outlook. In earlier works he had shown the way our private dramas reinhabit the contours of a timeless sequence of love, indifference, and disillusionment: the "old story" keeps repeating. But while this temporal slippage universalized private experience, in *Ideas* the narrator's persona shifts and diffracts through distinct characters as well, destabilizing the whole conceit of individual being. There's neither a discrete self nor a universal. A tale that seems to trace the development of a single personality unfolds in a series of monologues by disparate selves that present the same core dilemmas from multiple, converging angles: unrequited love, the temptations of abstract thought, the intersection of personal and world history. The speaker is first a tourist in hell, then the "Count of Ganges" at a restaurant in Venice, then an exuberant pantheist, a lovelorn poet in contemporary Germany, a Venetian knight, a wide-eyed child in Düsseldorf during the era of Napoleon's conquest—and a melancholic in the years of German decline post-Waterloo. Yet all these personae share a voice and experiential trajectory. As self-portrait it's psychological cubism.

Nor is it only the narrator's own persona that's dramatically mutable. His female addressee shifts as well, between a "She" and a Signora Laura (who may be based on Amalie), a "Madame" (who is often assumed to be Rahel's sister-in-law), and a figure denoted as "Little Veronika." Geographical locations fluctuate, too, from central Europe to the Himalayas. If the task of the age was to be "emancipation of the whole world," Heine here conducts a vibrant prelude to that liberation— loosening the fixed attributes of place, love object, and self to communicate the feel of delirious freedom. For years, Heine had struggled against the notion of being constrained by any fixed identity. Here, he unfastens himself from all society's assigned roles by hoisting the anchor on Creation.

One visitor to Heine's home during this time described the place as feeling as if it were occupied by someone who had arrived the night before and planned to leave the next day. "An open portmanteau, linen scattered about, two or three volumes of a circulating library, some nice walking-sticks still in a state of packing, and before all the man himself," with his air of restless nomadism. But Heine developed a political defense of this lightness of existence also, linking it to the imperative of creative autonomy. He was aggravated with himself, he noted, for having purchased a tea set, discovering that china impeded his writing by making him cautious: "I shouldn't be surprised if the china salesman was an Austrian police agent and Metternich lumbered me with the china in order to tame me." He was still strong enough to break his porcelain shackles, he warned. If his anger got roused, the domesticating articles would fly straight out the window—watch out below!

Sometimes Heine marveled at the persistence of the myth of the Wandering Jew. A favorite of Christian mothers looking to frighten their children into remaining close to the hearth, it wasn't even a Jewish story, yet it kept playing out in the Jews' actual experience. "We are the heroes of the tale and do not know it," Heine told Moser. The day was coming when he would have to leave his German fatherland, he announced. "It is less desire to travel than the torment of my personal situation (for example, the never to be effaced Jew) which drives me hence." No barber could "shave the white beard, the ends of which time is forever blackening with new youth."

In one of Heine's most startling anthropomorphisms, Time itself became the reactionary artist, perpetually renewing the stereotypical features of hounded, homeless, postexilic Jewish identity.

Chapter Thirty-one

A NOTE FOUND among Heine's papers from this period cat-alogued his vision of bliss: "A humble cottage with a thatched roof, but a good bed, good food, the freshest milk and butter, flowers before my window, and a few fine trees before my door; and if God wants to make my happiness complete, he will grant me the joy of seeing six or seven of my enemies hanging from those trees. Before their death, I shall, moved in my heart, for-give them all the wrong they did me in their lifetime. One must, it is true, forgive one's enemies—but not before they have been hanged."

Christian virtue had its benefits, at least for connoisseurs of vengeance.

The numbers of Heine's enemies—or anyway those he dis-cerned to be such—grew in tandem with his audience. He was becoming a public figure, but the elevated stature heightened a sense of vulnerability. It's true that he was regularly attacked in print, and more than once in the flesh, yet Heine saw conspiratorial adversaries everywhere. In Hamburg, in 1826, he claimed to Moser that one stinking Jew had begun telling lies right and left about having beaten him up: the "pig-dog" *had* assaulted him in the streets, but he'd barely even managed to grip his coattails—and then denied everything to the police when Heine reported him. It was all filth not worth writing about, he concluded, before proceeding to spread the story to others. Eventually, he began picturing an unknown man lurking in the shadows, waiting to stick a knife into him.

Life swung between triumph and affliction. In 1827 he told Campe that wherever he went he found his travel writings in vogue: "Everywhere enthusiasm, complaint and admiration." But what he wanted was to *live*—to feel himself free and unthreatened by the dreadful climate prevailing in the cities where he could make a name. Watching a performance of *The Merchant of Venice* in Drury Lane the same year brought him to speculate that while Shakespeare might originally have wanted to please the mob with a comic portrayal of "a hated fabulous being who yearns for blood" then is stripped of everything, the world-spirit inspiring Shakespeare was too powerful for such trite formulae. Instead, the playwright ended up depicting an unfortunate sect, burdened by Providence from inscrutable motives with the hatred of both the lower and the higher classes. Shakespeare showed "neither Jews nor Christians, but oppressors and oppressed"—and the madly anguished exultation of the latter when they can pay back their injuries with interest.

His own brutal caricatures were by then notorious. During his trip to England, one relative in London refused to let Heine even mention her pianist-husband in his travel notes, convinced that Heine, ill-equipped to understand the man's music, would settle for making a fool of him. Old acquaintances shied away in fear of what he came to call "the sword and flame" of his lyre. He told one friend he had found that by just making someone appear ludicrous, you'd "stoned them to death." For those who had reason to be anxious about Heine's opinion, he took on the air of a nimble gorgon in cap and bells. Dodging his gaze was hard, but vital if you wanted to avoid being petrified.

In the spring of 1828, Heine unenthusiastically took a job in Munich, coediting the *Neue Allgemeine Politische Annalen*, a journal of ideas published by debt-juggling magnate Baron Johann Friedrich von Cotta. Varnhagen had lobbied hard for Heine with Cotta, whose firm had an unimpeachable pedigree as Schiller and Goethe's publisher. But the money wasn't great, and the clerical perfume of Munich's cultural life made him cringe. As happened repeatedly, Varnhagen had tried to address Heine's distress in a straightforward way—Heine had been complaining of his unreliable finances, Varnhagen would find him work—and so missed the deeper ambivalences of his plight. No sooner was Heine hired than he began fantasizing again about a teaching position at the University of Munich. In one particularly misconceived ploy he tried to get Cotta himself to take three of his books directly to King Ludwig with hints that his double-edged pen could be contracted for attacks or puff jobs at the royals' behest. Nothing came of the scheme but fresh opportunities to spot traducers sabotaging his progress.

Even in the midst of his Italian travels, when that country's beauty was restoring his sense of the world's original promise, Heine felt shadowed by dark intimations. Suddenly, he turned around and began traveling north again. Somewhere near Venice word reached him that his father's health was deteriorating. By mid-December, he had reached Munich. When he finally headed for Hamburg, where his parents had moved the past summer, he learned en route that his father had been dead for several weeks.

Though Samson had been fading for years and Heine's visits home were rare, the news struck him a body blow. Decades later he told a friend that he simply couldn't absorb the loss. He moved in for a time with Betty, and his own health declined. He retreated far away, first to Berlin and then to the imperial hamlet of Potsdam. In that monumentally overwrought and peculiarly desolate suburb he lived, he told friends, like Robinson Crusoe. In the spring of 1829, he remarked on how tame he'd become since his father's death. Once he had dreamt of all the wonderful deeds of derring-do he'd perform. Now all he wanted was to be an old tabby curled before the hearth listening to others spin yarns of their exploits, he wrote Friederike Robert.

To his lawyer friend Rudolf Christiani, Heine's cry was more naked. "Yes, yes, they talk about seeing him again in transfigured form," he wrote, of his late father. "What use is that to me? I know him in his old brown frock-coat, and that's how I want to see him again. That's how he sat at the table, salt-cellar and pepper-pot in front of him, one on the right and the other on the left, and if the pepper-pot happened to be on the right and the salt-cellar on the left, he turned them round again. I know him in his brown frock-coat, and that's how I want to see him again." The blunt home truth of his lament negates the grandeur of the church's promised resurrection.

As the months wore on, the pace of his writing slowed and he brooded on his ill fortune. The question of who was blocking his university appointment obsessed him. No doubt, the Munich clergy had intervened against his interests, but Heine was convinced they hadn't acted alone. In August he withdrew to a red sandstone plateau in the North Sea archipelago of Helgoland. Campe pestered him to finish the next installment of his Italian sketches—it had been two years since he'd published anything. Time to feed his audience! Heine agreed, but the spark was missing.

Then he read a new verse drama, *Romantic Oedipus*, by one Count August von Platen, and abruptly began writing at a furious clip. He completed the final pages of his manuscript so rapidly that he boasted the volume had come off the press before it was written.

Much of *The Baths of Lucca* is bracingly funny and formally inventive. The book is a kind of picaresque *Bildungsroman* interspersed with philosophical digressions on literature, religion, and politics. Its chief protagonists rank among Heine's most imaginative character sketches: the banker Marchese Christophero di Gumpelino, a pompous, baptized Jew, and his valet, Hyacinth, formerly a lottery-ticket salesman, and still a Jew, though he notes that Judaism is not a faith but a misfortune. It's Heine's most vibrant fictional exegesis of Jewish experience on the cusp of modernity—one foot caught in the shame and glory of a historical identity, the other straining and stamping in space, trying to get purchase on the new era of capital. Assimilation is the leitmotif, a grail and conundrum. A character remarks of Gumpelino that despite his nose, the man possesses superb qualities. "For instance, a great deal of money, common sense, and the desire to embody in himself all the follies of the age." Explaining his dedication to self-improvement, Gumpelino announces, "Money is round and rolls away, but culture remains." He demonstrates his refinement by gestures like naming his mutt Apollo.

Along with the comedy, there's poignancy. Hyacinth's account of the nascent Reform movement, centered around the new Israelite Temple with its "orthographic German hymns," allows Heine to probe the loss attendant on the embrace of a "good clean religion" which accommodates the profit-taking priorities of contemporary life. That is contrasted with the faith of "Lumpy," an old Orthodox peddler who spends the week bent under his wares but on Friday evening, after lighting the candles, takes his seat before a fish baked in "nice white garlic sauce," beside his "crooked wife and crookeder daughter," sings the psalms of King David, and is replete. Hyacinth remarks, "The man is happy, he does not have to worry about culture, he sits wrapped contentedly in his religion and his green dressing-gown like Diogenes in his tub."

Yet even Heine's depiction of the poor man's majestic state of Sabbath wholeness hints at something more than purely beatific delight. Hyacinth observes that the peddler is glad also "that all the bad people who did anything bad to them died at last," while he lives to eat with his family. His pacific bliss is contingent on the extinction of his persecutors, and the comparison to Diogenes—the savagely candid and critical founder of Cynicism—raises its own questions about the Jew's chosen role in society.

After his rhapsody on Lumpy, Heine introduces the real-life character of Count August von Platen, whereupon the entire narrative swerves into a garish vivisection of that writer. The onslaught seems to burst in out of nowhere, but its roots date back to 1826.

Before publishing his second volume of travel writings, Heine had an idea: why not have other writers contribute flourishes of their own—turning certain pages into a kind of graffiti board for his friends? Heine didn't solicit just any passage from his pals, however; he asked them to deride people who might be expected to oppose their generally dissident mind-set. Almost everyone was repelled by the scheme and declined to participate. The sole exception was Karl August Immerman, who had written one of the earliest positive reviews of Heine's work and remained loyal. He sent thirty-six satiric epigrams to Heine, which Heine duly incorporated into his book as the work of an "esteemed co-worker." The last of Immerman's epigrams reads: "These poor poets eat too freely of the fruit they steal from the garden groves of Shiraz, and then they vomit *Ghaselen*."

The reference was to poems composed by Platen on a Persian model that Goethe had been first among the Germans to adopt (a rhymed couplet at the opening is repeated every other stanza). Immerman's words don't read today as wildly scathing, but Platen took the publication as an intolerable affront—perhaps the cause he'd been waiting for his whole life. The ensuing melee between him and Heine resembled a game of blindman's buff played in explosive suits. Many thousands of words have gone into examining the carnage without ever clearing the smoke. What's certain is that those watching the conflict were horrified, and almost everyone, excepting Varnhagen, viewed Heine as the malefactor.

Platen came from an old, noble family. He was given a rigorous scholarly education, and by the late 1820s had made a name for himself as a serious poet disdaining Romanticism for the Attic ideal. Highly skilled technically, Platen thought of himself as superior to other, more celebrated writers by every measure, though the wistful, peevish content of his verses made little impression on the broader public. The only living author Platen would defer to was Goethe: he saw himself as Goethe's sole heir. Just as he looked down on his fellow writers for being less metrically accomplished, he held the general reader in contempt for failing to appreciate his purity of language.

But instead of being dismissed as obnoxious, Platen exuded a tragic vulnerability that his literary peers sympathized with. The family wealth hadn't extended to his branch. He had few close friends. He was known to be homosexual—in an elevated classical manner. Between his ignoble resentments and his lofty sense of purpose, everything was a struggle for Platen, and this tension seemed to find expression in the strained, pathetic quality of his verses. Italy was Platen's ideal, and he spent increasing amounts of time in the country. But his eyes always turned back toward Germany, where he couldn't win the unlimited acclaim he alone knew he merited.

The moment Heine's volume with Immerman's epigrams was published, Platen was determined to retaliate. Writing his friend Count Fugger, Platen fulminated that the "Jew Heine" had crossed an inviolable line. Platen's antisemitism was perfunctory, but these circumstances excited it. Immerman's lines were in themselves forgivable, he wrote Fugger. But the fact that Heine had given the epigrams the platform of his own publication, and therefore caricatured him through a third party, was "unpardonable and incidentally, a typically Jewish maneuver." Platen began concocting a riposte in the form of a full-length verse drama—*Romantic Oedipus*—which would dazzle the world and teach what it meant to impugn a literary Olympian.

The satire, which was published while Heine was traveling north from Italy, found a well-disposed audience in certain minor aristocratic circles. It characterized Heine as a foolish romantic and the "Pindar of the little tribe of Benjamin." It featured spritely challenges—"Pride of the synagogue, who do you think you are?"—and would-be withering insults. The character Nimmerman remarks, "I am his friend, but I don't want to be his darling; his kisses stink of garlic." Other poetic sallies Platen composed over the course of their feud give a fuller sense of his wit.

> Let your daily prayers offer thanks, o little Hebraic jokester,
> That you live with Germans and not among the Greeks:
> Were you to appear naked in the manly sport of the Palestra,
> Tell me, how would you conceal that mutilated part of yours?

To Fugger, Platen wrote, "The fact that he is or was a Jew is no moral failing, though it is a comic ingredient in the whole situation. Discriminating critics will be able to judge whether I haven't used this ingredient with Aristophanic subtlety."

As Heine read the *Romantic Oedipus* in Helgoland, stirred by contemplation of the sublime ocean, he had a kind of revelation, he later wrote. Suddenly, he saw this "high-born writer" with his "blooming decay" exactly as he was, "a writer forced without force, piqued without being piquant, a dry, watery soul." This "dismal debauchee" had the nerve to think he could imitate Aristophanes, the most powerful poet of the Grecian world! Nowhere in Platen's work was there a trace of the foundation of every Aristophanic comedy—Heine invented a word for it: *Weltvernichtungsidee*, a profound, world-annihilating idea. Out of Weltvernichtungsidee grew the "fantastic, ironic magic tree" of all Aristophanes' work, Heine wrote, "bearing in its branches singing nightingales and capering apes." Such a notion with its "death merriment and the fireworks of destruction" couldn't, of course, be expected from the poor count. But Heine knew from Weltvernichtungsidee, and Platen would allow him to demonstrate it. From his aristocratic lineage and antisemitism to his aesthetic preciousness, Platen appeared the perfect adversary for a life-loving, warm-blooded Jewish poet.

While reading *Romantic Oedipus*, Heine realized that the fury which had been building in him for years over all the ways his German identity had been undermined—the withholding of work, money, acceptance, and *freedom*; the injustice of being crucified by Christians for his Jewish birthright; the urge to revenge himself on himself for the self-betrayal of his own conversion—could be channeled into an effluvial deluge of comedy that would blot out the work's author, while displaying once and for all his own indomitable potency.

The irony that Heine's assault was wreaked on the composer of an Oedipus play—and a proxy for the Fatherland—in the wake of Samson's death may not have been lost on him. In theory the whole project, casting himself as a kind of Shylock, and then recasting Shylock as a vengeful Superman, had interest. (If you prick me, do I not obliterate you?) In practice, however, Heine had caught the wrong man.

Platen *was* an aristocrat; but he had neither ideological investment in his genealogy nor reactionary political impulses. In fact, he supported much the same democratically minded reform program Heine championed. His Christian devotion was minimal and certainly meant less to him than his lyric Greek paganism. The elevated status he sought to assign the poet was not so different from that which Heine believed in. Platen was at core a humanist, and their battles against German censorship were kindred. Moreover, Platen was also embroiled in a bitter, philosophical struggle with German identity, which ultimately drove him into exile. Even Platen's antisemitism comes off as lightweight, more careless than venomous, and contravened by a number of his writings.

Not only was Platen a problematic focus for Heine's wrath, Heine's vehicle for assailing him was indefensible: a lurid exposé of Platen's homosexuality. There have been latter-day efforts at extenuating Heine's attacks as structural in purpose, aimed beyond Platen himself at societal biases and literary conventions with which the poet was intrinsically aligned. Nonetheless, on the face of it, Heine was publishing crude verbal cartoons of Platen's self-abasing pursuit of anal intercourse. And after making fun of Platen's sexuality, Heine went on to mock his poverty—which he then viciously linked with the insinuations of pederasty.

The Platen satire consumes the final forty-plus pages of *The Baths*. There are interesting moments, which make its ugliness still more dispiriting. Heine suggests that the crimp in Platen's personality is a result not of his preference for men but of a society that outlaws this preference, so that Platen "meanly and soberly and anxiously sneaks among the paths of friendship." In antiquity, Heine writes, such desire could show itself "with heroic openness." In this sense, his erotic situation was not so dissimilar from Heine's Jewish dilemma. There might have been other ways to be actively Jewish, just as there are other ways to be homosexual, but these dignified models weren't available to either Heine or Platen.

Not only are the sparkling first parts of *The Baths* lost in the cruelty of Heine's portrait of Platen, the one truly remarkable passage in the satire itself gets muddied. When Heine introduces himself overtly into that portion of the narrative, he notes that in *Romantic Oedipus* the reader will discover how he's "a real Jew; how I, after writing love-songs for a few hours, immediately sit down to clip ducats. . . . How I on Easter night slay a Christian." The list of stereotypical Jewish offenses builds to an exaggerated crescendo, whereupon Heine abruptly reveals that actually none of these scenes appear in *Oedipus*. The play is riddled with missed opportunities to execrate his people: Platen is so feeble, he can't even hate properly. Heine has to teach *him* how to hold a Jew up for ridicule.

The notion that Heine might redeem Jewish character by showing that a Jew is better even at despising himself than are his oppressors *is* radical. He's developing a metaphysics of hatred that calls the entire model of Christian forgiveness into question—linking this with the larger, tradition of theologically and politically dictated resignation to historical destiny.

That Heine himself was apprehensive about the implications of his argument is borne out by the fact that he cut his most daring theological speculation from the manuscript before its publication. Remarking on the irreducible strangeness of the fact that a Jew invented Christianity, Heine observed, "Murdered Judaea was as cunning as the dying Nessus, and its poisoned robe—poisoned with its own blood—consumed the strength of the Roman Hercules so effectively that his mighty limbs grew weary, armor and helmet fell away from his withered body, and his voice, once so mighty in battle, dwindled to a prayerful whine. Miserably, in a death-agony that dragged on through a thousand years and more, Rome dies by the Judaic poison."

The portrayal of Jesus as the Jews' revenge on Rome for the Temple's destruction—a kind of Trojan Horse savior who reveals that if you can't overthrow the Empire by military force, you might yet vanquish it from within by an enfeebling pathogen—is inspired. But Heine knew his satire already represented a dangerous provocation. Near the end of December 1829 he mailed off one of the first copies of *The Baths of Lucca* to Immerman, writing, "Poor Platen! *C'est la guerre!* This is no playful game, but a war of annihilation." Yet he added that he had written the book in "bad circumstances," under pressure to publish, which adversely affected its tone.

By early January, German literary society was waking up—in shock—to what Heine had done. "Now as always after an execution, there is compassion for him," Heine noted to Varnhagen. "I should not have handled him so severely. But I do not see how a man can be overthrown with gentleness." The combination of mild remorse and truculence placated no one. "It was a war of men against men," Heine continued, "and the reproach which is publicly made against me, that I, the humbly born, should have spared the noble estate, makes me laugh—for that was precisely my motive." A genuine satirist always trampled over class boundaries.

A month later, when the extent of the damage he'd inflicted on himself was clear, Heine swung out more wildly. Yes, he had offended the public and done himself immeasurable harm—but he'd had no choice. "The revolution enters literature," he declared, grandiosely and unpersuasively. When the Munich clerics first went after him, he had dismissed the whole business as silly, he insisted, but then he'd sniffed conspiracy—the priestly contingent was in league with Platen. "I saw through the intention of Platen's satire, when the booksellers told me that similar poisonous productions were crawling about in manuscript—then I girded up my loins and hit out as hard and fast as I could." Platen was responsible for mobilizing an aristocratic and clerical cabal to wreck his reputation. Platen was responsible for his being slighted by the university! It's unclear whether Heine himself ever really believed these meritless charges.

When his friend Gans was attacked, his fellow convert had suffered in proper Christian fashion, maintaining a prudent silence, Heine rattled on. But he was different, and that was good; he could "carry out ruthless and pitiless retribution for himself and others." In this light, the whole attack on Platen can be understood as an extraordinary attempt at *de*-converting— repudiating every vestige of Christian forbearance in the name of the ancient Hebrew God.

Platen himself never publicly responded to *The Baths*. Not long after its publication, he went into self-imposed exile in Italy. Five years later he was dead. The university at Munich now made it clear that Heine was never going to get a professorship—not because of intriguing by Platen but because of Heine's assault on the man. Readers and friends dropped him. Immerman went quiet. Rahel's brother Ludwig cut off their friendship. Close allies from the Society broke with him. Even Gans ended their long association. Moser himself stopped communicating. Heine seems to have been unable to absorb the full measure of rejection, carrying on with his letter-writing campaigns of self-vindication as though things must come right again. Notwithstanding the differing motivations of the people who censured Heine, there's something remarkable about the way a large swath of educated nineteenth-century German society acted to decisively repudiate an antihomosexual burlesque.

However, that wasn't quite the whole story. Outside the literary coteries familiar with Platen's circumstances, in places where *The Baths* could be read impersonally, Heine was gratified to learn of the book's being embraced as an indictment of Germany's repressive clerical-noble power alliance—exactly as he claimed it was intended.

In the summer of 1830, Heine was back in Helgoland, pondering fate. In an open letter to the public he wondered "that I of all people should have been destined to whip my poor fellow Germans out of their comfortable ease and hound them into movement. I, who like best to spend my time contemplating passing clouds, figuring out metrical word magic, listening for the secrets of the elemental spirits, and immersing myself in the wondrous world of old folk tales."

Now he was tired and wanted only rest, but peace was impossible in Germany. Where could he go? he asked. South? Ever since the Habsburg occupation of northern Italy, Austrian sentries roared out their terrible challenges from beneath every lemon tree. To "damned England"? "Never again to this vile land where machines behave like humans and humans like machines."

Should he sail to America, "that enormous freedom prison, where the invisible chains chafe even more painfully than the visible ones would at home, and where the most repugnant of all tyrants, the mob, exercises its crude sovereignty"? He'd once loved that "Godforsaken land"—before he knew its true nature, Heine wrote. Oh yes, German peasants, go to America, he urged. "Where there are neither princes nor nobility, all men are equal, that is equal boors, with the exception, of course, of a few million that have a black or brown skin and are treated like dogs!"

Most horrifying of all were the reports from German and French writers who'd traveled to the United States describing how even in provinces where slavery was abolished, free blacks and those of mixed race had to suffer the vilest insults, while white Americans crowed about their Christian piety. "Worldly advantage is their actual religion and money their god," Heine wrote. In New York, he added, there had recently been a case in which a Protestant minister gave his daughter permission to marry a Negro; a mob stormed his house, stripped her naked, smeared her all over with tar, rolled her in a slit-open feather bed, then dragged her through the city, taunting her the whole way.

Heine's outrage was exhilarating. But he was a pariah.

Goethe shook his head on learning of the quarrel with Platen. It was all so wasteful. The world was wide enough to live and let live—one's strength should be reserved for the fight with one's own talent! The thing about a certain modern German poet with negative tendencies akin to Byron's was that he had many brilliant qualities, but lacked love, Goethe told Eckermann another day. The man valued his readers and fellow poets as little as he valued himself; and without that, Goethe observed, "though he spoke with the tongue of men and angels, his voice was as sounding brass or a tinkling cymbal." The public leapt to the conclusion that Goethe meant Heine. Eckermann later said his target had been Platen. Either way, for all Heine's amorous posturing, readers sensed the blade of ice in his heart. Here he was, thirty-three years old, with no significant romantic interest, alienated from most of his family and almost all his friends, estranged from his faith and his homeland, all his writerly powers devoted to scoffing and scourging. Intentionally or no, Goethe had hit on a terrible secret: *Heine didn't know how to love.*

Chapter Thirty-two

Only it wasn't true.

Or was so, except for all the ways his writings and actions disprove the judgment—those myriad instances where Heine can be found loving passionately or cozily, faithfully, and play-fully. His friendships with Rahel Varnhagen and her husband Karl endured. Relations with Moser were partly mended. He kept trying to maintain a collegial bond with Gans, even when Gans warded him off. After leaving his sister's house in angry disgust, Heine patched things up with her; similarly with Uncle Salomon. His mother became more and more important to him as he grew older. He made new friends continually, some of whom became lifelong intimates. He gained a reputation for being delightful with children and they adored him.

He loved people who sacrificed themselves for the causes of freedom and justice—loved the people's aspiration to their own liberation—loved humanity's joy and those who released it. He loved the power of the imagination to see beyond this heartrending hour and conceive new, gaily plentiful existences. In art, he called himself "a supernaturalist."

At Helgoland in 1830, in what might have been his most isolated moment, he read Genesis voraciously. Each word was like a phenomenon of nature—tree, flower, ocean, stars, man, woman. As he read, "the holy prehistorical world roved like long caravans" through his mind. He cherished the vision of a time before positive religion and political legislation, when morality operated purely by "the rationality of the heart." Then he leapt to the New Testament and found himself enchanted by the Gospel of John, where it was written, "I have yet many things to say unto you, but ye cannot bear them now." So, Heine glossed, "the last word has not yet been said, and perhaps here is the ring to which the new revelation can be attached. It begins with deliverance from the Word, makes an end to martyrdom, and founds the kingdom of eternal joy." When he wasn't reading the Bible, he devoured revolutionary histories day and night—and when he wasn't reading anything he bathed in the sea trying to get healthy. Then he learned of the July Revolution in France, and it seemed a continuation of the glorious images already coursing through him.

Fishermen were saying the feudal lords had been cast down, and the poor were victorious. Thick bundles of newspapers arriving from the mainland resembled "rays of sunshine wrapped in printed paper." Heine rejoiced that the people had chosen a "citizen king," with a cream felt cap for a crown and an umbrella for a scepter, who wandered down the street, shaking hands with grocers and artisans. "I felt I could set the ocean alight right up to the North Pole with the flares of the enthusiasm and the wild joy that blazed within me," he wrote. The entire ocean smelled of cake! The Seine had spread the good news into its waters, where "beautiful nixies, who from time immemorial have been well disposed to all heroism, immediately put on a tea dance to celebrate the great event." He ran around his boarding house like a madman, kissing all the occupants.

At some point—though it occurred more slowly than Heine let on—he found his longing for island quiet had evaporated. "I now know again what I want, what I should do, what I must do," he wrote. "Flowers! Flowers! I will wreathe my head for the fight to the death. And the lyre, too, hand me the lyre, that I may sing the battle song." Declaring himself the "son of the Revolution," he caught a boat back to the mainland.

On arriving, he traveled first to Hamburg to visit his family. Bursts of activity inspired by the French insurrection had begun crackling across the country. But Germany being Germany, things went a bit crosswise. In Leipzig, the workers wrecked the printing press of the venerable liberal publisher Brockhaus. In Berlin, the people rose up against the taxation of dogs and the ban against smoking in the Tiergarten. Right after he got to Hamburg, the revolution broke out there—and took the form of anti-Jewish rioting.

Once again shouts of *Hep, Hep!* clattered off the city's stones. Men armed with cudgels smashed windows. Salomon's house was attacked—all his munificence now irrelevant. In his journal, Heine noted that it wasn't only the mob on a rampage but also respectable shopkeepers—the ones who liked to stand in their doorways in house slippers, conducting business in proper, comfortable fashion, unlike Jewish peddlers with their ungainly packs, who offended bourgeois etiquettes of moneymaking.

That was the other thing about Heine's refusal to turn the other cheek—his decision to unleash the whirlwind against the delegates of German small-mindedness that night-bloomed into prejudice—he was right that the phenomenon had to be called out unabashedly. Anti-Jewish sentiment, even in its milder, socially convenient forms, was entangled with populist strands that posed a threat to the Jews' physical survival. During the riots he jotted in a notebook: "One Jew says to another, 'I was too weak.' This saying commends itself as the motto for a history of Judaism."

Rahel, who had long prided herself on her ability to temper Heine's reactions with seasoned perspective, took a passionate line on events: the revolution in France was profound and beautiful, and dangerous—perhaps even destined to destroy its participants. She remarked that whether the Republic would benefit or injure them was impossible to say, but—like the struggle for a constitution in Germany—*There is no other path to the future.* She called the French "my vanguard people." Heine agreed with both halves of her assessment: the peril and the necessity of radical action.

But as great as Rahel's sense of the inevitable progress toward democracy was her revulsion at the latest round of violence against Jews. Of all the miseries that occupied her thoughts, she told Heine in the fall of 1830, this enduring blight topped her list. The project of assimilation that had shaped the atmosphere of her youth seemed ever more fantastical. After the events in Hamburg, she and Karl provided Heine with introductory letters to acquaintances in Parisian literary circles: he should get out while he could.

Departure would not mean abandoning their shared responsibility to fight for freedom from oppression, Rahel insisted. She hoped that in France Heine could attain the clarity necessary to mount an effective campaign against the demagogues orchestrating these grotesque scenes—one that would strike its real target. From France, he must tell the world, in a language people would listen to, just how dire things had actually become in Germany. Rid at last of the dreadful confusions and prejudices of their homeland, he would carry on the struggle for justice. For these latest riots had been totally predictable, she told Heine. "No 'bridal wreath,' no elephant crossing stage bridges, no charity list, no hurrah, no condescension, no mixed society, no new hymnal, no award of a bourgeois decoration, nothing, nothing could ever appease me," she wrote. "The pocks themselves must be extirpated." Their dream of a Republic foundered on Judeophobia. Rahel tasked Heine with carrying on the battle for the Jews' deliverance in her name. "You will say all this in wonderful, elegiac, fantastic, incisive, always exceedingly witty, melodic, stimulating, often thrilling ways; say it soon," she implored. "The text from my old offended heart will always have to be your own." Heine's answer is lost, but his actions suggest he accepted this charge from his patroness and muse—a Jewish riff on the chivalric trope in which a noble lady assigns her paladin the quest to kill a fire-snorting dragon.

Heine had been complaining about the diseased character of life in Germany for years. Ever since the French were driven out, the country's pernicious elements had been slowly congealing. Now Prussia's selfish, petty, bellicose attitudes were openly in the ascendancy. Every day the country's atmosphere grew more unwholesome. Lately, he'd started having visions. Clouds gathered and made gruesome faces at him. Nights, he dreamt of a black vulture gnawing at his liver, while in daytime the sun resembled a Prussian cockade. An old lawyer friend who had spent time in the fortress at Spandau told him just how unpleasant it was to wear irons in winter, when the only fowls on offer were flies. Heine began worrying that such a fate might soon be his.

Then he met a traveling French merchant who talked of how merrily people were living in Paris, singing the Marseillaise from morning to night, with *Liberté, Égalité, Fraternité* painted on all the street corners. Suddenly the possibility that he might actually get out of Germany became real. Though he wasn't planning on emigrating, the prospect of a long respite from his birthplace in a country that treasured freedom became more and more preoccupying. Still he dithered for months, drifting around Germany, writing and getting into scrapes, until—

just as it seemed he'd need a kick to actually get moving—another inducement appeared, almost magically.

In the wake of the July Revolution, *Le Globe*, the chief publication disseminating Goethe's work in France, was taken over by disciples of a new movement dedicated to the political, religious, economic, and aesthetic regeneration of society. It was, in many people's eyes, a new religion, albeit a scientific faith, based on the rational organization of all parts of society and the universal brotherhood of man. When Heine got hold of the recast periodical he was enraptured. For the essays in *Le Globe* seemed to answer his own concern that while the old social order had to fall in the name of freedom and a more equable allocation of the world's blessings, if the existing forms of government merely yielded to popular rule, prejudice and mob justice would run rampant. Instead of enthroning the masses, this movement conferred sovereignty on the ranks of expert bureaucrats.

Its founder was the impoverished revolutionary Count Henri de Saint-Simon, a disciple of the polymath Jean-Baptiste le Rond d'Alembert who had fought heroically in the American War of Independence, supported the French Revolution, then devoted himself to encyclopedic research on how best to organize society for the new age. Saint-Simon had died in 1825, but his followers continued writing and lecturing prolifically on innovative measures to ameliorate the human condition. For Rahel and Heine, the key attractions of the philosophy were its elevation of merit over hereditary privilege and its overall commitment to discarding the shackles of precedent. Saint-Simon's exponents relocated the Golden Age from the past to the future, while declaring that the means to create an ideal society lay in embracing the dynamics of modernity, not looking backward for some original purity. Thrillingly, in their precepts, technological capacities were understood to be already sufficiently advanced that scarcity was artificial; the privileged classes just remained perversely suspicious of how dramatically increased agricultural production and industrialized manufacturing could benefit all levels of society. The influential economist Thomas Malthus hadn't calculated the potential of machines to redouble earth's resources, and many of the rich saw the large-scale reduction of poverty as predicated on the diminishment of their own status.

But to reap the benefits of the age's continual advances, society needed to be rationally systematized. Artificial trade barriers should be dropped. A new bureaucratic hierarchy would empower professional ingenuity in those sectors of the economy that were defining the times: finance, industry, large transportation projects. Saint-Simon's most radical insight was that economic relationships were the chief drivers in history. (Hence his importance to the young Karl Marx.) Maximizing industrial and mercantile efficiency required a social transformation: Saint-Simon's followers meant to open the floodgates of opportunity for all individuals regardless of sex, class, or religion. Relations between men and women would necessarily become freer. The domains of Caesar and Christ should never have been separated. By establishing a cooperative meritocracy in the workplace, and Christian love without Christian abstinence at home, the New Testament's promises could be realized on earth.

The compulsory inaction of both Jews and women that so tormented Rahel would also be done away with under the Saint-Simonian program. For outweighing the problem of which political system ought to be in power was the question of what enables people to *move* in the world—to act out their will and attain personal fruition. Those who met Rahel at this time spoke of her being openly "at war with the artificial life of our civilization." Real change couldn't be confined to systems of commerce and property ownership. Time and again she reverted to the domestic condition of women, "its falseness, its absurdity, and its benumbing influence." All social institutions needed to be revolutionized.

The goal of the "rehabilitation of the flesh," which for Saint-Simon's followers was bound up with the enfranchisement of women, elated Heine. He had long deplored the Judeo-Christian tradition of reviling the body. The Saint-Simonians believed in human perfectibility in a physical sense, as well as morally and intellectually. Indeed, many of the dichotomies that plagued Heine's consciousness were theoretically reconciled in these doctrines—spirit and senses, faith and reason, practicality and beauty. Irresistibly, poets were to be granted a quasi-sacerdotal role in the new social order. Saint-Simon had declared that "in the great enterprise of working directly for the establishment of the system of public good, the artists, the men of imagination, will lead the way." Heine saw himself elected to this artistic synod, dreaming up new paradises that scientists and industrialists would actualize.

Rahel told Heine that Saint-Simon's legacy had become her "nourishment, entertainment, occupation." The man's theory touched "the great old wound, men's history on the earth. It operates and sows." As Heine declared in one ebullient flourish: "We have measured the lands, weighed the forces of nature, reckoned the means of industry, and behold we have found that this earth . . . offers everyone sufficient space on which to build the cottage of his happiness." The poorer classes need not be consigned to the mercy of heaven.

It's a measure both of the pair's buoyant resilience and their rope's-end desperation that after so much grim disappointment they could be stirred by the vision of a materialistic utopia based on a program of overbearing prototechnocratic policies.

Yet people of their ilk were categorically different from the leaders of the French Revolution, Heine asserted. "We are not fighting for the human rights of the people, but for the divine rights of humanity." They had no wish to be sansculottists and frugal burghers, who demanded "simple modes of dress, austere morals, and unspiced pleasures." He and his allies meant instead to found "a democracy of terrestrial gods." They desired "nectar and ambrosia, purple mantles, costly perfumes, luxury and splendor, dances of laughing nymphs, music and comedies. . . . To your censorious reproaches we reply in the words of Shakespeare's character: 'Dost thou think because thou art virtuous, there shall be no more cakes and ale?'" In a letter to another friend, Heine put matters more plainly. People would better understand the Saint-Simonians if they were told that "they will eat beef instead of potatoes every day and work less and dance more." The revolutionary imagination challenged reality to become more attentive to humanity's festive dreams, not the opposite.

He'd been a drum-banging Napoleonist, a semi-demi-Schlegelian, and a selective Hegelian. Now Heine would charge forth a blazing Saint-Simonian. But to realize his new great-man passion, he had first to get to France, where the movement was centered and constantly galvanizing fresh droves of adherents. On the first of April 1831 he told Varnhagen that every night he dreamt he was packing his trunk and traveling to Paris, there to inhale fresh air, "to give myself up entirely to the sacred feeling of my new religion, and perhaps to receive the final consecration as a priest of it."

He crossed the Rhine on May 1. Two days later, Heine rolled through the triumphal arch of the Boulevard St. Denis.

Chapter Thirty-three

JUST TO HEAR French spoken everywhere, mingled with Parisian street sounds—the shout of the *coucou* driver, the bell of the *coco* seller—made Heine euphoric. Apologies rang in his ear like Rossini melodies, so he tried to get himself bumped into repeatedly. The city's "sweet pineapple perfume of politeness" refreshed his soul, which in Germany had been compelled to breathe tobacco fumes, sauerkraut, and vulgarity. He flirted with flower girls and visited the giraffe, the three-legged goat, and the kangaroo in the Jardin des Plantes. Roasted ducks flew straight into his gaping mouth—one after another. Heine wrote a friend back in Germany, "If anyone asks you how I am, tell him 'like a fish in water,' or rather, tell people that when one fish in the sea asks another how he is, he receives the reply: 'I am like Heine in Paris.'"

Perhaps he'd forgotten that some years earlier, he had used a nearly identical phrase to characterize his relationship to Germany: German was to him what water is to a fish, and without it he'd become dried cod. It may be salubrious not to recall former revelations too clearly. What he registered most powerfully was how France reincarnated his childhood enthusiasms. The ubiquity of Napoleonic imagery, for one thing, amazed him. During the years of the Restoration, when representations of the general were banned, coins and medals stamped with his countenance had been illegally circulated, while busts and statuettes were clandestinely marketed. When Heine arrived, after the proscription had been lifted by Louis Phillipe's government, the range of items bearing Napoleon's likeness burgeoned, ranging from clocks, biscuits, and tobacco pouches to fans, envelopes, wallpaper, and crockery.

It was difficult for anyone outside France to really fathom the public's idolization of Napoleon, Heine wrote. The name alone remained magical. Just as the Jews did not utter the name of God lightly, "Napoleon is here rarely designated by his name; he is always called 'the man' but his image is everywhere." Once, on an obscure side street, he came upon a small child lowering himself onto the ground before a tallow candle, "mumbling a song to the glory of the great Emperor."

Such sights were both rousing and disorienting: the dreams that had illuminated his youth were again vividly present, but here they took a decorative form, as if in the sacristy of a cult religion. Nonetheless, Napoleon's continued veneration meant that revolutionary ideals were alive. The emperor had set the pattern for a Saint-Simonian ruler, Heine declared, just as his meritocratic army had prefigured Saint-Simon's ideal social hierarchy.

Within a day of arriving in Paris, Heine attended his first Saint-Simonian meeting. Soon thereafter, he met the entrepreneur-reformer Prosper Enfantin, who, with his lush locks of hair and small, clear eyes, was considered one of the Pères Supreme of the movement. Initially, Heine found Enfantin's vaulting ambitions inspiring. Enfantin preached that "the translation of pantheism into political language equals the association of people with themselves and of humanity with the earth." This notion seemed to validate some of Heine's own cherished speculations. But within a few weeks, Heine's pristine view of the movement cracked and he found himself fighting back tears. Tears of laughter, for the most part.

Once again, he had sought contact with the embodied representatives of ideas that excited him and then, once he'd had these encounters, found he couldn't stop picking at the silly bits about them. The badge reading "Père" that Enfantin wore on his breast; his preference for being referred to as the "living law" by disciples; the apparel he developed to stress codependence— it could be buttoned only at the back, so required another person's assistance—all such elements carried low-hanging comedic potential. In his journal, Heine marveled at how much God had done to allay the world's sufferings: during the Mosaic age he'd performed miracle after miracle; as Christ, he had been flagellated and crucified. Now in the person of Enfantin, God had made "the ultimate sacrifice on the world's behalf: he made himself ridiculous."

Before long, the revolution lost its luster as well. From up close, Lafayette's silver hair, which Heine had pictured cascading majestically down his shoulders, proved to be a brown wig matted to a narrow skull. In July 1830 the people had bled not for themselves but for others. It was another "old story," like his unrequited love passions. They had fought this time for the bourgeoisie, who revealed themselves to be no more sympathetic than the nobility. The people had won nothing but remorse and greater poverty. Saint-Simon's enthusiasm for the energies of the middle classes had been institutionalized by the new regime, but without unleashing that expansive altruism which Saint-Simon thought was intrinsic to their character and would lead its representatives to share the spoils of their enterprises. The businesses kept growing—railways, canals, investment houses—and some of the Saint-Simonians grew extremely rich; yet so far from spreading their wealth, they only consolidated more exclusive monopolies.

As for Louis Phillipe, he wasn't strolling about so much these days, Heine observed. People were saying that when he'd gone out handshaking in public formerly, he used to wear a dirty rough glove put on expressly for this purpose, which he'd then switch for an immaculate kid leather pair when he went to visit "his banking-ministers, intriguers, and amaranthine lacqueys." Every day there was new evidence of history regressing. Just as the cobblestones that had been used as weapons were being pounded back into the streets until no trace of revolution remained, the people were being hammered back into place and trodden down.

Not three months after Heine got to Paris, his mood tumbled. It was a trip to the Pantheon that did it—reading the gold inscription there, *Aux grands hommes, la patrie reconnaissante*— To the great men, a grateful homeland. What a mockery! he wrote Varnhagen. Exactly the kind of thing petty men say about the heroes after they've died and can no longer be relieved of their miseries. As for himself, he had discovered that right in the middle of Paris he was surrounded by Prussian spies. "It would be easy to flee if one did not drag the Fatherland along on the soles of his shoes," Heine observed. All he had wanted was to leave the endless fighting to others and withdraw into poetry. But he was forced to wage war. "In my cradle lay my line of march marked out for my whole life," Heine wrote.

Still, when he thought back on the situation in Germany, he didn't know what else he could have done. Here anyway he was "in the vortex of events," the dayspring, the roaring revolution. "While I drown in a wild sea of men, I also burn by the combustion of my own nature," Heine reflected. He felt as if he were made entirely of phosphorus.

Another discovery Heine made in France was that aversion to Jews and anticosmopolitan impulses weren't the only troubling tics of the left. In Paris, he reconnected with the revolutionary writer Ludwig Börne, whom he'd last seen in Frankfurt four years earlier. When the two met up at the Hôtel de Castille, sparks glittered ominously in Börne's eyes. He perched before Heine in a multicolored dressing gown, craning his narrow little head suspiciously up from the fabric, like a turtle from its shell. "Welcome to Paris!" Börne cried in a trembling voice. "I am convinced that all the best-intentioned people will soon be here. Here is the assembly of the patriots of all Europe, and all peoples must reach their hands out to one another for the great work."

Heine hadn't reckoned on being lumped with his fellow countrymen as zealous ciphers in a common cause. Börne insisted that they had to unite in order to keep Europe's royalty from combining forces to suppress German freedom. "Revolutions are a terrible thing, but they are necessary, like amputations, when one limb or another has begun to petrify," he said. "Whoever out of pity or fright at the sight of blood stops the operation half way, acts more cruelly than the worst fiend." Marat had been correct to declare that the human race needed bleeding, Börne continued, and if he'd gotten his 300,000 heads, millions of better people wouldn't have died and the earth would have been healed of its ancient evil. On and on went his quavery tirade. What a way to begin a conversation! All vestiges of good humor were gone. Everything had turned arid and homicidal. The escalation of political insanity in just four years astonished Heine. He learned that Börne had recently gone up to Montmartre with six hundred journeymen tailors to sermonize from on high, "persuasively, popularly; naked, artless." Heine couldn't get over the image of this man who'd grown up swaddled in silk reborn as a fiery agitator. Was it despair over the sodden degradation of the Fatherland that had done it, Heine wondered—the realization that for all this man's intelligence and moderation, he had achieved literally *nothing* in his endless invocations of freedom? At last, "seized with the ghastly pain of a misspent life," Börne had drawn his cap down over his head, cut himself off from all sights and sounds, and "plunged into the howling abyss."

Heine thought back to his own mood on the North Sea strand. Young and histrionic, he'd made speeches to the waves, as they "roared and howled," while dreaming of becoming an orator, like Demosthenes. But in Paris, confronted by this pack of brawlers around Börne—some of the tens of thousands of German workers and artisans who had come to France after the July uprisings—Heine realized he could never play a prominent role in the battle. Maybe Börne was being rhetorical when he remarked that if a king were to shake his hand, he'd thrust it in a fire to purge the stain. But Heine was being literal when he said that if the people were to grab *his* hand, he'd scrub it afterward. Once more, he refused to romanticize the physiology of poverty. He didn't see why that should be taken as compromising his commitment to improving the peoples' circumstances—if anything, the opposite. It was necessary to have seen them for oneself, sniffed them with one's own nose, heard with one's own ears "what this sovereign rats' nest had to say" in order to grasp why Mirabeau said the revolution would be no lavender-scented romp.

When they walked out together, Börne's politicizing was interminable—every sight they encountered got tuned to the key of his righteousness. In the Tuileries, Börne remarked that the chestnuts were secretly singing the Marseillaise. It was holy ground! Heine should take off his shoes! Oh look, look up that way, toward the Rue de Rivoli. That was where the Jacobin Club used to meet, Börne cooed. And there at the Tuileries Palace had gathered the most radical faction of all—Titans, compared to whom Bonaparte was just little baby Jupiter. Börne raved away until the limb of one of those hallowed chestnuts suddenly came crashing down, nearly killing them both. In time, even venerable growths can turn rotten, Heine noted. Börne just hissed in irritation that this was a "bad omen."

The real problem now struck Heine: liberals like himself, attached to rational French ideals of freedom, were probably in the majority. But the regenerate Teutomaniacs fueled by a religious fanaticism would invariably spark greater enthusiasm. Börne's faction shouted out "Germany!" and "Faith of our Fathers!" and cast a spell that words such as "humanity," "reason," and "truth" simply couldn't elicit. At no time would he have hesitated to join Börne on the field of action, Heine added; they shared the same foes and dangers, after all. But he would never even be permitted to fight alongside them since, with their "turbid partiality," the German radicals refused to recognize his existence.

On the one hand, Heine had to contend with representatives of Metternich's "great hand" scraping the alleys of Paris for potential subversives. On the other, there were the compatriots Heine met over foul sausages in dens at the backs of remote courtyards. The latter deplored the oppressive, commerce-minded Germany just as much as he did. But in their graceless, murderous saintliness they were not "his people" any more than were the reactionaries.

Soon, the ultraliberals started to discern Heine's ambivalences and turned harshly against him. They registered the entrée Heine got through high-placed connections to some of Paris's select salons. Note was taken when he didn't sign their petitions and failed to show up for their protests. As Heine's political writing took on what seemed to them a cynically balanced tone, they countered with malevolence, accusing him of taking money from the Austrians—eventually branding him a political apostate.

Börne began writing a series of public letters, calling out

Heine's weird love for kings and inexorable aestheticism. One could make allowances for children's games and youthful passions, Börne wrote. "But when, on the day of the bloodiest battle, a boy chasing butterflies on the battlefield gets tangled with my feet, when, on a day of the greatest urgency . . . a young fop comes by seeing nothing in the church but the pretty girls and flirts and whispers with them—that can, notwithstanding our philosophy and humanity, well make us angry."

Heine was a poet, an artist, Börne wrote, and the one thing he lacked was the ability to accept that this was his entire identity. People knew he was able to accept something as true only when it came in a guise he found beautiful. But truth was *not* always beautiful: "Heine would worship German freedom if it were in full flower, but because it is covered with manure on account of the raw winter, he does not recognize it and holds it in contempt." It was impossible to believe anyone who believed nothing himself. The eyes of Marie Antoinette would have teased lovely verses from his pen! If he'd seen Mirabeau smoking a dirty pipe—well so much for Mirabeau and freedom! He who has frail nerves and shies back from danger, "let him serve art, absolute art, which deletes every rough thought before it becomes a deed and polishes every deed until it becomes too puny for misdeeds." Heine found his own accusations against Goethe turned back against him with a viciousness far beyond what he'd directed at the Sage of Weimar.

What was more, Börne continued, Heine fixated on the importance of individuals. But individuals were only heralds of the people at large. To satisfy the democrats, Heine claimed that the Jesuitical-aristocratic party in Germany abused him for defying absolutism. Then, to make the nobles happy, he sounded off about how bravely he resisted Jacobinism and had always been a royalist at heart. He turned from one to the other. Now *boldly defying* the Jacobins! Now *boldly defying* the absolutists. "If it were for the sake of a crown he could not suppress any smile, any mockery, any joke, and if, misapprehending himself, he nevertheless lies, nevertheless dissembles, appears serious where he should laugh, humble where he would like to mock, everyone sees it right away, and from such pretense he has the reproach but not the advantage."

Börne's judgment against Heine thundered on for pages: a stunning indictment of the poet's contradictory nature. But only Heine possessed the brilliance to go Börne one better by reproducing huge blocks of this screed verbatim in his own work. Heine channeled his adversary as a part of his memorial portrait of Börne himself—dancing dialectically with his Nazarene enemy—on his adversary's grave. By foregrounding the critique within Börne's obituary, he subverted it. One way of mastering an antagonist was to appropriate his voice, then recontextualize it.

Yet the politics behind Börne's attacks could not be so neatly dispensed with. In a private journal, Heine wrote of Parnassus being flattened and smeared over with tar to prepare for a highway or railroad. The revolution *was* coming. A savage, gloomy age was imminent, and a prophet who set out to write a new Apocalypse would need to invent beasts so terrifying that those accompanying Saint John's Revelations would seem like gentle doves and amoretti. "The future smells of Russian leather, blood, godlessness and many beatings. I advise our grandchildren to be born with extremely thick skin on their back."

Increasingly, Heine felt trapped in the bind of his own revolutionary logic: Since all men had an inalienable right to eat, and they were not being adequately fed under the current system, there was only one conclusion to draw: "The existing society has been judged and condemned!" he cried. "Let it suffer what it deserves! Let it be crushed, this old world, where innocence perished, where selfishness flourished so mightily, where man was as a prey and plunder to man! Let them be radically destroyed, these whited sepulchers, where falsehood and raging wrong were enthroned!" And blessed be the grocer who would turn the paper his poems were printed on into bags to hold coffee for poor old women who'd been deprived of such goods for too long. "Let justice be done and the world perish!"

So it must ever be Heine wrote. For, as he expressed matters in one work,

> There are two kinds of rat:
> One hungry, and one fat.
> The fat ones stay content at home,
> But hungry ones go out and roam.
>
> . . . .
> These wild and savage rats
> Fear neither hell nor cats;
> They have no property, or money too,
> So they want to divide the world anew.
>
> These roving rats, alas!
> Are near us now en masse.
> I hear their squeaks—straight on they press—
> Their multitude is numberless.
>
> . . . .
>
> No cannon, not the biggest guns,
> Can help you now, my pretty ones!

Part of Heine savored the prospect of this revenge of the rats. Part of him dreaded it. When he pictured the coming slaughter, the promise of a glorious new paradise receded far into the future. Yet when he turned his eyes from politics to his new home, Heine sometimes felt he'd found his Eden, kaleidoscopically substantiated here and now.

Chapter Thirty-four

OLD PARIS hadn't quite disappeared yet. Most of the city was still lit by oil lamps with metal reflectors—badly placed, people complained, with a reddish flame that hurt the eye up close and gave little light below. At night, after rainstorms, one walked the uneven, crooked stones at a precarious pitch, paying urchins to lay planks over the overflowing gutters. Small trades with long pedigrees thrived everywhere—cheap illustrators, vegetable steamers, rabbit peddlers, worm sellers, pipe seasoners, wine vendors, and parrot dealers. The wooden galleries of the Palais Royal were in their last mazy shudder—harboring "wild mirth and a babel of talk," Balzac wrote. There, amid hobnobbing capitalists and businessmen, were representatives of the burgeoning publishing houses: "poetry, politics, and prose, new books and classics, the glories of ancient and modern literature side by side with political intrigue and the tricks of the bookseller's trade." Under the colonnades were gambling places, tables for dice and *trente-et-quarante*, roulette wheels, girls for the victors, and punch flambé for the unrestrained, while highborn ladies monitored the scene through black velvet masks.

Each outing was a splendid adventure. Heine went to operas, balls, cathedrals, concerts, and art exhibitions. (Delacroix's painting of the July Revolution at the 1831 Salon taught people to stop grieving over ancient graves and believe happily in the resurrection of all races, Heine avowed.) Even the new bazaars of commerce resembled Venetian palaces, springing up from the ground as if at the flick of a fairy wand. Every time he went into the Bourse it vexed him. He couldn't help appreciating that marble edifice, built by Napoleon in the noblest Greek style, yet consecrated to the most contemptible business: swindling public funds. But he always relished his promenades up Boulevard Saint-Martin to the great romantic theaters. Théâtre de la Porte-Saint-Martin, built by Lenoir in forty days on the orders of Marie Antoinette, the Folies-Dramatiques and the Fantaisie, where Heine declared, theater attained its zenith before starting to degenerate toward the round-the-year carnival at Franconi's, with birds doing tricks, savant dogs counseling domino players, fleas tugging carts, and dwarves, giants, skeletonmen, and Mademoiselle Rose with her head on the boards and her feet twinkling high in the air.

Paris was a stage on which some of the world's most terrible tragedies had been played, Heine wrote. But he was continually reminded there of a night he'd spent at the theater watching a heartbreaking drama while seated behind a woman wearing a huge bonnet of pink gauze, and so casting the tragedy "in the most cheerful and most rosy light." The populace's thirst for passionate experience, as if death were about to call them away the next hour, was infectious. For here, Heine declared, could be found everything that defined civilization. The human spectacle gathered in the great Parisian salons and saloons brought to mind curiosity shops "where the relics of all ages rest higgledy-piggledy—a Greek Apollo near a Chinese pagoda, a Mexican Vizleputzli near a Gothic *Ecce Homo*, Egyptian idols with dogs' heads, holy little imps of wood, of ivory, of metal." Here were the old *mousquetaires* who'd once danced with Marie Antoinette, mild Republicans who'd been idolized in the Assemblée Nationale, pitiless, immaculate Montagnards, "faded mutilated deities of all ages." Paris materialized in one place Heine's vision of creation as the dream of a drunk god. He disagreed with most of what Madame de Staël had to say about Germany, but her pronouncement on Paris struck home: "Here one can dispense with good fortune."

In time, the city's *joie de vivre* even helped him clarify his vision of history. Those who believed in cyclical time, and who therefore claimed there was nothing new under the sun, shrugged off all political enthusiasms with indifference. Those who rejected that fatalism in expectation of an intervention by providence—which made the current hour a mere evolutionary phase—while more honorable than the conservatives yet failed to satisfy the vital emotions of human experience. "We take ourselves too seriously to consider ourselves only as a means to an end," Heine wrote. He championed a third way that valorized the present without dimming the promise of the future: "Life is neither end nor means; life is a right," he wrote. Each created thing had its own integral purpose. "Life wants to enforce that right against the cold hand of death, against the past, and this enforcement is revolution." Saint-Just's declaration *Le pain est le droit du peuple* was "the greatest declaration made in the French Revolution," Heine announced.

He met Franz Liszt, and gave the delirium inspired by the pianist-composer's concerts the enduring name of Lisztomania. Richard Wagner became acquainted with him—and snatched Heine's version of the Wandering Jew legend as the basis for his opera *The Flying Dutchman*. Théophile Gautier, Honoré de

Balzac, the Princess Belgiojoso, George Sand, Alexandre Dumas, Frédéric Chopin, and Gérard Nerval all grew to be friends with him. Heine disdained the reactionaries, and swerved from his fellow radical refugees into the glitter of Parisian artistic society. "What happy days!" Nerval remembered, shortly before sinking into madness. "We gave balls, suppers, costumed parties. . . . We were young, always gay, and often rich."

Gautier said Heine appeared like a god, mischievous as the devil, but good-natured withal. He would give away the clothes off his back, even when he himself was debt-plagued; yet "extravagantly as he expended his wealth and health, his expenditure of *esprit* was more lavish still." If Heine privately rolled his eyes at the oddities of the Saint-Simonians, he kept writing in the idiom of their most ecstatic beliefs—preferring their pink-lit giddiness to the politicians' stern grimaces. For, he wrote, a person could feel "a new form of art, a new religion, a new life is brought into being here, and the creators of a new world feel here active and full of joy."

Rahel was writing him regularly during his Parisian initiation, telling him how much she herself was taking from Saint-Simon. Wasn't the movement's real mission "to beautify the world: my old topic—freedom to all human development?" she asked. She'd felt increasingly unwell of late, she confessed, but her spirit was exhilarated. How she longed to speak with him about these ideas!

Only the religious conceits of the Saint-Simonians really interested him, he told the Varnhagens, but these needed merely to be spoken "to become embodied in life sooner or later." Long after he'd ceased idealizing the actual movement, he made its most utopian hopes into a lyric catechism: "Happier and more beautiful generations, conceived in freely chosen embraces, who grow up in a religion of joy, will smile sorrowfully at their poor ancestors, who gloomily abstained from all the pleasures of this fair earth." The dark present couldn't dim to-morrow's radiance. "I believe in progress," he wrote. "I believe that mankind is destined to be happy, and thus I think more highly of divinity than those pious people who think mankind was created only to suffer."

Cholera struck Paris less than a year after his arrival: at its height, eight hundred people were dying daily. Heine described the disease as a new, more horrifying reign of terror since its execution took place so swiftly and mysteriously. Initially the city's great balls were more crowded than ever. People tried to drown themselves in the roar of music, taking iced beverages as the fever intensified, until suddenly the merriest harlequin would feel his legs grow numb, and tear his mask off to expose a violet-blue face. Soon he too was carried off to the Central Hospital—followed by the retinue of carousers, who died and were buried in their fantastic fools' garments. Everywhere you looked there were funerals or, sadder still, hearses with no fol-lowers. One day Heine traveled to a neighborhood near Père Lachaise to visit a friend, only to find the man's corpse being loaded into a hearse; so he headed to the cemetery to pay the visit there. At the gates, his carriage was trapped in a line of hundreds of conveyances queuing before the narrow entrance.

Hygienic measures imposed by the authorities exacerbated the chaos. Heine wrote of the *chiffoniers*, or ragmen, who used to make their living picking through the city's filth, being de-prived of their employment by the new sanitary commission, which tried to get all the street refuse carted beyond the perim-eters of Paris. The chiffoniers began rioting, while other groups, seeking to sabotage the government, began spreading rumors that the hastily buried dead were victims not of disease but of a cabal who had discovered how to slip poison into market veg-etables, meat stalls, bakeries, and wine. The police—eager to appear responsible and informed—fanned the flames of popular fear by announcing that they were on the tracks of the murderers. The poor became terrified to eat or drink. There were outbreaks of mob violence against suspected poisoners.

One hundred twenty thousand passports were said to have been issued in April 1832 alone. The rich and famous were fleeing, taking with them their doctors and drugs. But Heine stayed, raising eyebrows when he appeared in salons, since everyone knew that no great business detained him. In fact, Heine was occupied caring for his cousin Carl when that young man became ill and the risks of contagion were greatest. Dismissing any imputation of bravery, however, he told Varnhagen that he'd remained simply because he was "too lazy" to leave. The Saint-Simonians vowed that none of their church could die; the Bonapartists were declaring that at the first symptoms of cholera one of their ranks had only to stare up at the column of Place Vendôme to be saved. Each man had his special faith, but for himself, Heine wrote, "I believe in flannel."

His devotion to Paris only deepened at the sight of the people's wretched helplessness. Next to a deathbed one could study how to await the end calmly; but to learn how to be buried in a grave of quicklime—that was beyond him. He walked up the cemetery's highest hill to a point overlooking the city, in all its glory. The sun was sinking. Twilight vapors draped Paris like a shroud and Heine began to weep bitterly, "over the unhappy city, the city of freedom, of inspiration and of martyrdom, the savior-city which has already suffered so much for the temporal deliverance of humanity." For all its venal tendencies, he never experienced the sense of spiritual incarceration in France that so oppressed him in Germany. He never stopped believing in the country's future, however long salvation might be deferred, likening the country to Penelope, daily weaving the same shroud to gain time until her true paramour arrives. The air of freedom—of love—of love as freedom, and freedom as love—still animated the metropolis.

It was true that Louis Phillipe turned out to care only for his own crown; but the constitutional monarchy he inaugurated was a mold ready to be filled one day by some truly great individual. Heine cherished his memories of the first Revolution and its heroes. He admired Robespierre and Saint-Just, yet acknowledged, "I would not like to live under the *régime* of such great souls, I could not endure being guillotined every day."

It wasn't contradictory that he loved the French Republic without wishing for a return of its original, bloodthirsty radicalism. Even less could he pine for the events that would ensue at the hour of a united Germany's awakening. The German revolution would not prove mild and pacific simply because it had been preceded by so much elevated philosophy. To the contrary, Heine prophesized, it would be descendants of the German idealist philosophers "who, with axe and sword, will mercilessly tear up the soil of our European life in order to destroy the past to its very roots." In time, some child of Germany's godless philosophies would "conjure up the demonic forces of Old Germanic pantheism . . . which does not battle to destroy, or to conquer, but solely for the sake of the battle itself." Christianity had partly tamed the "brutal Germanic lust for battle"—that was the religion's greatest merit. But whenever the restraining talisman of its cross broke for good, the old stone gods would "emerge from their forgotten ruins and rub the dust of millennia from their eyes," he wrote. "A play will be enacted in Germany which will make the French Revolution look like a harmless idyll."

Hegel died in 1831. *Les dieux s'en vont*, Heine wrote after Goethe's demise in 1832. Death had become an aristocrat, singling out the giants. Though, he added, more ambiguously, perhaps in truth death had decided to favor democracy by destroying earth's celebrities, freeing people's minds from their authority, and thus promoting intellectual equality. Two years earlier Heine had used the occasion of Goethe's eightieth birthday to denigrate the poverty of a German nation that would name as its greatest man this figure who'd subsided into prosperous, hieratic complacency. There was more relief than heartache for Heine in the loss. But it wasn't only the titans who were passing away. Before the end of 1832, cholera had killed Friederike Robert, then her husband, Ludwig. Uncle Simon van Geldern, whose attic had nurtured Heine's imagination, passed away in March 1833. And that same month, he learned that Rahel's long illness had finally taken her life at the age of sixty-one.

His letter of condolence to Karl was an incoherent outburst of grief. The earth seemed a battlefield. She had earned her laurels, he cried. Now he understood the saying "Life is war." Friends were falling all around him. Time, the cunning Saturn, healed every wound only to carve new ones deep into our hearts. He could not write for weeping. Alas, we must fight with tears in our eyes. He himself had been ill of late. But he would not yield his sword until his hand sank into the earth.

Moses Moser and Eduard Gans were dead before the end of the decade—both in their early forties. Heine discovered that Ludwig Marcus, the most devoted exponent of the Society for the Culture and Science of the Jews, was living near him in Paris; but this modest man, who had never sung a note in his life, now sat on the floor of a relative's home chanting obscenities at the top of his lungs, and throwing his manuscripts, ink jar, pens, and purse out of the window. Marcus was taken off to a sanatorium, where he died two weeks later in terrible agony. The picture filled Heine with angst. "One is tempted to say that insanity is the national malady of Germans in France," he observed.

He missed his family terribly. It wasn't some vain desire that had led him to leave everything precious behind; he'd thought his homeland didn't need him anymore. "For once, I'll live for myself and write lovely poems, comedies, stories, tender and gay word-comedies," he vowed. "I'll quietly slip back into the land of poesy, where I lived so happily as a boy." But when he chanced one day on another group of Germans who had felt compelled to flee their birthplace, he became overwhelmed with despair. These people weren't rebels—just common, provincial families. Heine asked them why they were leaving and they answered, "The land is good, and we would gladly have stayed, but we could stand it no longer." Speaking in a straightforward, stoic tone, they recounted a little of what they'd suffered at the hands of the nobility. Their last words cut the deepest: "What was there to do? Should we have started a revolution?" Heine swore by "all the gods in heaven and earth" that if one-tenth of what they had endured had been inflicted on the people of France, it would have provoked several dozen insurrections—in addition to costing several dozen kings their crowns and heads.

Patriotism was an odd thing, he decided. A person might love his country and never realize it, though he lived until he was eighty years old. "But then he has never left home. . . . Love of the German Fatherland begins at the German frontier." One morning he came upon some lines Rahel had written in a foreign land. She recounted having broken down sobbing "bitter tears of feeling and mortification." I never knew that I cared so ardently for my country until now, she exclaimed. "I'm like a person who does not know scientifically what blood is worth; yet if you take it away from him, he will collapse just the same."

"That is it," Heine cried. "Germany—is ourselves."

Then, the year after Rahel died, Heine fell in love.

Chapter Thirty-five

ONLY NOT EXACTLY ROMANTICALLY. Or not romantically in the manner he'd hitherto understood love to be: remote, lofty, cruel, otherworldly, Lorelei-Germania-Amalie-style love this was not. Crescence Eugénie Mirat was a nineteen-year-old peasant from Seine-et-Marne, apprenticed to her aunt at a boot shop in an arcade near the law courts. In a surviving photograph, she's chrysalised in a huge black silk dress. Her Italianate coiffure is mantled by a lengthy ripple of white lace. Her eyes are dark and low-browed, her full lips are spread. She looks very young, a little wry, unfocused, dauntless, and ready for fireworks.

Some people say the first time Heine saw her she was dancing. Others, that the first time Heine went out with her, in October 1834, he took both her and her Aunt Maurel to a dance-hall. Perhaps both are true. Either way, people agree that Mirat was eager to kick up her heels. For six months after they first met, Heine vanished from public view. When he finally contacted one friend, he rhapsodized: "Rosy waves are rushing around me with such powers, my brain is still so deafened with the furious scent of flowers, that I am not in a condition to converse reasonably with you." Have you read the Song of Solomon? Heine asked. "You'll find there everything that I would tell you."

He renamed her. First Nonotte, then poor dove, finally Mathilde. Crescence Eugénie was just too much name to get out of the mouth—it hurt his throat, Heine protested. His literary friends condescended to her ruthlessly, even when they acknowledged her good nature or were amused by her tempers. They called her an illiterate, a spendthrift, a child. She didn't clean. She couldn't cook. It was incredible that a German poet would submit to such circumstances!

She never even read a word of his poetry, people said. Some remarked that Heine wanted it that way, since then he felt she loved him for himself, not his fame; others claimed he'd simply purchased her outright for hard cash from her aunt. The only German she knew was the handful of phrases Heine taught her for fun: *Ich bin eine wilde Katze,* was one. Certain of his friends called her enchantingly pretty. Others said she was unpretentious and lively. Over time, most agreed, she grew homely, coarse, and plump. She was capable of fits of self-pity—wailing over everything Heine didn't give her, and she wanted a lot. Lace especially, but also champagne, and green frocks. Heine acquired one of the age's most celebrated books of animal illustrations. Mirat loved paging through the volume—but only because she was salivating for the fur coats, people smirked.

Alexander Weill, a waggish short-story writer, gossiped about scenes in which Mirat began beating herself with her fists, crying that she was the worst-treated creature on earth, biting her own clothes, her flesh, raging and weeping. The incredible thing was that she'd have these tantrums right in front of Heine's guests, and no one pitied her in the least, Weill reported. When her hysterics went nowhere, Mirat herself would suddenly burst into laughter, shaking so that she "showed off the graceful movements of her waist and divine hips," whereupon everyone felt fond of her. It was impossible for anyone to be angry with her for long, Weill added. Once, when he himself commented that the fish she was serving looked a bit shopsoiled, she picked up the platter and hurled it smack into his face, almost breaking his nose. And *he* still felt amused by her.

She and Heine fought all the time; everyone said so. Heine provoked the quarrels as often as she did. She spent all his money! She loved having birds about, and they made noise so that he couldn't work, but she just got more of them! Then, on top of her aviary, she got Minka, the poodle. Heine was wildly jealous—hated her dancing with anyone else, and she liked dancing with everyone. He attacked students who stared at her. He watched the clock when she was late coming home from anywhere. He panicked that she might have left him for good whenever she flew off after a squabble. He wrote her scores upon scores of letters. "You are the only joy of my life. Don't make me miserable." Most said something like that. In return, she wrote him ten brief notes over twenty years, and the awkwardness of each pen stroke drives home her ignorance. They jousted like kittens; onlookers chuckled. But the fights always ended with "Homeric laughter" on both their parts—followed by passionate embraces. Yes, one of those relationships. Except that Heine praised her to the heavens far more than he complained. She was "an honorable, good creature, without deceit or malice," he told his mother. They were extraordinarily happy living together, he informed one friend: "That is, I do not have a moment's peace day or night." Well, he owned, "I have always been an opponent of the theory of renunciation."

Only once, less than a year after they first shared a dance, did he decide he couldn't take their scrapping any more; he ran off to the estate of his worldly friend Princess Belgiojoso, near Saint-Germain. He couldn't work. He despaired at his own character. The princess persuaded him to lie down beneath the majestic trees and talk out his misery. He followed her prescription: sophisticated conversation, long strolls, refined concerts, until finally his spirit was hushed. Then he wrote a letter to his publisher Campe with two lines of verse up top: "Before the poet tries to sing, / The man must learn to live— poor thing!" He apologized that in his agitated state he hadn't written anything for months. Now, however, he reassured his publisher, everything was quiet and cheerful; he lived in a congenial circle—all of them "distinguished individuals and distinguished individualities." His soul had been cleansed of dross. "My piety will be purer, my books more harmonious."

But nights at the castle were dreary beyond words. His ultracultured fellow guests just sat about twitching like marionettes at loose ends. Enough with the chamber music! He took off abruptly for a hotel in Boulogne, where he befriended an eleven-year-old English girl. Twenty years later she still vividly recalled walks they'd taken by the sea together and the stories he told her of fish, mermaids, sirens, a violin—and a poodle. He couldn't stop missing Mathilde. "I am condemned to love only the most humble and foolish!" he cried to a friend.

He returned to Paris with a great bouquet of flowers and a pair of cute thrushes. They lived from then on as husband and wife—marrying six years later, when Heine wanted to secure her inheritance. The ceremony was a full church affair in the Catholic tradition. "For no consideration would I shake this dear being's belief in her inherited religion," he declared. Not to mention which, friends recounted, he hid his Jewish origins from her almost to the end—no real accomplishment, they said, given that Mathilde was so naïve that she refused to believe that the name of Heine's cousin Cohn just might indicate Semitic ancestry. Heine pledged that their offspring would be educated in their mother's religion. He knew child-rearing wasn't his specialty, much as he liked having kids around to make up pretty stories for and treat with fancy cakes. The couple remained childless, adopting a parrot instead, which they named Cocotte. He cursed it in exquisite German. Cocotte swore back at him in high, fluent French. Mathilde's affection for the bird tickled him—and the parrot swinging in its cage while deriding him was a promise that Mathilde hadn't completely abandoned him whenever she ran off. She'd come home for Cocotte, if not him.

Sometimes he moaned to friends that her hunger for new garments was ruining him. He wrote letters in which he jokingly tried to tabulate the exact number of poems he'd composed to get her an opera cape. But he loved indulging her, all the more as his health began to founder. He told his brother Max that his passion for her towered over his illness: in that emotion he was strong, even as his limbs degenerated. Two years into their marriage the fingers of his left hand were nearly paralyzed. His left arm was crippled to the elbow. One foot dragged so badly that children parodied him. Both eyes were enflamed and perpetually dilated. His headaches were so severe he couldn't work for days on end. Mathilde cared for him devotedly year after year. Heine never said otherwise—never once regretted having wedded her, he told his mother. Given all the rotten unions in France, their marriage should be preserved in spirits! he cried.

Perhaps even her immoderate purchases reflected Mathilde's understanding that Heine needed to feel he could make a queen of her: he loved seeing her dressed up, loved watching her grow more physically abundant over the years—calling her his "treasure," his material plenitude. During one trip without her, he wrote Mathilde how terribly he longed to see her "fat little behind jigging about at the family ball." He relished the flamboyant unpredictability of her character, telling friends she brightened life "with the consistent inconsistency of her whims."

The dramatist Heinrich Laube, one of Heine's closest friends in the last years, commented that Mathilde had a unique gift for drawing out from him the childlike charms and graces that readers discovered in his best poems. She provided a haven into which the elaborate tribulations of Jewishness, German politics, and publishing barely infiltrated. With her inimitable French cheerfulness, his wife did not permit him "to sink into melancholy dreams to which I am too much inclined," Heine told his brother.

There was just cause for his moods. Prussia's censors made every publication a trial. What began as a voluntary removal to France became a forced exile after an arrest warrant was issued in his name for affronts to royalty and "instigations to discontent." This writ was renewed annually, accompanied by posters featuring a sketch of an ugly, fat, elderly man with a large, predatory beak. *Heinrich Heine, litterateur,* reads the caption. The poster added tips on identifying him: he had a "pointed nose and chin; and markedly Jewish manner. He is a libertine, whose wasted body denotes dissipation."

But still Heine slipped back over the border twice; and at moments would write of his homeland with indissoluble allegiance, declaring that his tombstone should be engraved with the words "Here lies a German poet." His letters to his mother became more and more frequent, alternately reassuring, anxious, and bathetic. He addressed her as his "sweet old cat," and "dear, kind, precious tyrant." He constantly asked after his sister and her children. Hamburg suffered a catastrophic fire in the spring of 1842, and Heine raced about haphazardly for twenty-four hours awaiting news. When he learned that his mother's house had burned, and that Charlotte had rescued one of his manuscripts in the face of the flames, he cried out that next to her, Wellington was a coward!

For all his misgivings about Hamburg, when he saw the city on a visit home in the fall of 1843, after twelve years away from Germany, the devastation shocked him; it resembled a half-shaved poodle, he thought. Some of the buildings etched most deeply into his memory were gone: the home of the firm that printed the travel writings that brought him fame, the house where he got his first kiss, the oyster cellar where he slurped his first salty mollusks. His mother's health had drastically declined. She was folded over with anxiety and sorrow, Heine wrote Mathilde. Every bit of news worried her now. The worst change of all, however, was to her proud sociability. Since the conflagration, her living quarters had been reduced to two rooms, and she no longer felt able to accept invitations since she hadn't the wherewithal to reciprocate.

Things went surprisingly well with Salomon that trip, who appeared relieved that Heine hadn't come to beg money. (He'd ordered Hamburg's fire brigades to blow up his town house in order to stop the conflagration's spread: a costly, public-minded sacrifice that may have left him especially reluctant to indulge his nephew.) Heine also spent time with Campe, who affirmed Heine's stature by agreeing to publish his complete works.

When he returned to Germany in the summer of 1844, this time with Mathilde, the visit went less well. Charlotte's husband, Moritz, met them at the Havre steamboat. Picking up one box, he immediately dropped it again, yelping with pain. Cocotte was inside, and had managed to bite Moritz's fingers. Mathilde cried in anger at Moritz's rudeness to the parrot, particularly after he'd been so seasick on the journey. Her lack of German and informal manners irked the family. Mathilde herself was bored stiff by the family colloquies in Ottensen. After a fortnight she announced that her mother was sick and sailed back to Paris. Heine might have welcomed her departure, given the tensions she'd stoked. Once Mathilde left, he tried to wheedle some financing from his uncle—and ended by so aggravating Salomon that the old man clopped him with a stick. His discomfort went beyond domestic travails: Heine received a hint from a well-placed individual that he'd do well to flee.

Before leaving Hamburg, Heine wrote a statement addressing his reputation as a traitor. He could hear the "beery voices" of his detractors sputtering with indignation, Heine wrote. But he assured them that he loved Germany just as much as they did—indeed this love was precisely why he'd been in exile for the past thirteen years and might now make his exile permanent. It was true that he was a friend to the French, he acknowledged, just as he was a friend to all reasonable, good people. Despite the accusations, however, he didn't even reject outright Germany's claims on the lands won by Napoleon. If the Germans would finish what the French began—"if we save the god that dwells within people on earth from his own degradation; if we become the redeemers of God; if we restore to their proper dignity the poor people disinherited of happiness, genius scorned and beauty ravished"—then not just the disputed territories, but the whole of France, the whole of Europe, the whole world, would become German. "This is *my* patriotism," Heine vowed.

He left Hamburg on an oracular high. A few weeks later, Salomon died, and all the poet's expectations tumbled into the gutter. Salomon's will ordained magnificent bequests to his children, grandchildren, servants, and philanthropic interests. Heine got a mere 8,000 marks. (Approximately $120,000 in today's money out of a fortune estimated at over $120 million.) Moreover, the will specified that if he contested this legacy, he'd lose it altogether. Carl, the principal beneficiary, told Heine that to receive his bit he'd have to agree to never write another satire mentioning the family. He also announced that given Heine's reckless improvidence, he had decided to hold back the capital and pay him four percent interest on it, while also cutting back the allowance his uncle had paid him for years. "You have no claim on it," he informed the cousin who had nursed him back to life during the cholera epidemic.

Heine was flabbergasted. He wrote his brother Gustav that his toes were itching uncontrollably, and Lord have mercy on the rear end they first struck. He told Campe he would raise the ire of the popular press against his own family. A single fistful of mud would no doubt be sufficient, Heine assured a journalist friend, while cajoling him to place a series of articles in the Hamburg papers, letting the world know that his family was trying to blackmail him. "These people are not used to filth, while I can endure whole carts of it; like flower beds, they only facilitate my digestion," Heine wrote, adding that it would be a cinch to win public opinion over to the side of a poet against millionaires.

But matters weren't so simple. Salomon's charitable commitments were extensive and sincere. He might honestly have wondered how much help his now famous nephew truly required—certainly in comparison with the genuinely indigent. Carl behaved condescendingly and controllingly, but he was justifiably terrified of what Heine might do to the family for a laugh. Heine had a way of looking back lightly at the devastation he wrought, even when his victims were still buckling on their backs, coughing dust.

A long, ugly battle ensued. It was "a murderous assault," Heine told Karl Varnhagen: "Sneaking mediocrity, which, consumed with envy of genius, waited for twenty long years, had at length attained its hour of victory." For many years Heine's perspective on the feud dominated the narrative about Salomon's will, but more recently both Salomon's and Carl's decisions have been viewed with more nuance. And though Heine wrote of his shock at finding himself so meanly remembered, it's also the case that part of him had been waiting his whole adult life for the rich to do scandalously ill by him.

At the end of all the fighting, Heine still didn't get what he claimed Salomon intended to bequeath him at a minimum, yet he was offered more than the original sum—and he even partly reconciled with Carl. One day, he had confronted Carl directly with his anxiety about Mathilde's future. Carl's "affectionate readiness" to see that Mathilde was never in want moved Heine immeasurably. It was all he really cared about. When the young man gave Heine his hand as a pledge, Heine brought it to his lips.

Death had become an intimate temptation. In 1846 Heine wrote Varnhagen that his eyesight had so deteriorated he could barely see his own handwriting. His speech organs had become partially paralyzed. He had trouble swallowing food and had begun suffering fainting fits. Everything he ate tasted like earth. Reading even ten lines at a time was beyond him. "Had I not wife and parrot," he wrote Laube, "I would—God forgive me the sin—like a Roman put an end to my misery."

It has proven difficult to chart the progress of Heine's illness. Were the headaches that plagued him since youth the first symptoms? Certainly, Heine began having serious health troubles while still a student. The eruptions of his maladies came in waves, and over the years at diminishing intervals. By the mid-1840s, the problems had intensified to where his whole body continually tortured him. Syphilis was almost certainly at least part of the trouble. At the last of the many flats in Paris he rented, on the top floor of a building just off the Champs Élysées, Heine was sometimes carried out onto the small balcony and handed an opera glass to observe the street life below. One day, he watched a dog urinating against a tree, then lowered his gaze: ashamed to stare when he himself could no longer manage even so much as that.

The suffering made Heine renounce atheism and pantheism both. He was candid about the motivation for this final turn of his devotions back to the original font of greatness, stating that he needed a personal god to weep his heart out to in the late hours when no one else was around. He'd never been an atheist anyway, he reminded readers. Even in the 1830s, when he was writing on Spinoza, he took umbrage at the notion that the philosopher's disavowal of the providential God of Abraham who operated outside nature made him an unbeliever. Indeed, Heine argued, no one ever expressed himself more sublimely about the divine than had Spinoza: "Instead of saying that he denies God, one could say that he denies the human. For him, all finite things are only modes of the infinite substance."

The problem with pantheism was more complicated, Heine argued. The system threatened to let the world stagnate. For if God were equally present in everything at all times, why bother to change anything? Better to propose that God appeared "in different degrees in different things, and everything feels within it the stress of aspiration to a higher degree of divinity." That made for "the great law of progress in nature." Besides which, there was a problem with God himself in the pantheistic scheme: the monotonous pantheistic divinity "is interpenetrated into the world and grown into it, imprisoned in it as it were," Heine wrote. "To have a will one must have a personality, one must be a person, and, in order to manifest it, one must have one's elbows free. If one desires a god to help one . . . one must accept too his personality, his externality to the world and his holy attributes."

Heine told the younger poet Alfred Meissner that it was inevitable, being "sick, sick to death and broken down," he'd come back to a personal God; why should that be a crime? But there was something beyond bodily anguish bringing him back— a "sort of heavenly home-sickness." Suddenly, he found himself on the same platform as the American Uncle Tom, Heine wrote. That platform was the Bible, and he knelt there by the side of his dark-skinned brother, praying with equal fervor. "Poor Tom," indeed, seemed to have seen more in the holy book than he could because Tom grasped more deeply "those ceaseless blows of the whip" described in the Gospels and Acts. "A poor negro slave reads with his back, and understands better than we do," Heine commented.

Still, his new attitude as a supplicant never made him guilty of piety.

All through these years, he wrote one caustic, imaginatively profligate masterpiece after the next. Epic poems, such as *Atta Troll*, which Heine characterized as the "last free song of the Romantic," projects the political muddle of German liberals and reactionaries onto the saga of a boorish dancing bear. The poem marks Heine's most inspired testament to the pitfalls of politically relevant art—and to the conviction that nonetheless poetry is our most urgently relevant source of hope and insight. "Children, we possess the future!" roars Atta Troll, the bear.

> If all bears thought just as I do,
> And likewise all other creatures,
> With our forces thus united
> We'd make war against the tyrants.
>
> . . . .
> Unity! and we shall triumph!

Atta Troll proceeds to outline the laws of the new ideal state:

> Strict equality! Each ass will
> Have a right to highest office
>
> Yes, yes, even Jews will likewise
> Then enjoy full civic rights, and
> Legally be made the equals
> Of all mammals whatsoever.
>
> Only, dancing in the plazas
> By a Jew shall be forbidden;
> I make this amendment solely
> In the interests of my art.
>
> For this race is wholly lacking
> In a sense of style, of movement

With a strictly plastic spirit—
It would spoil the public's taste.

Another narrative poem, *Germany: A Winter's Tale*, written after Heine's last trip to his homeland, culminates with Germany's destiny being revealed to the poet by Hammonia, the goddess-protectress of Hamburg—in the interior of an enchanted chamber pot: "The things I saw there I can't reveal," the poet cries.

My oath makes it unlawful;
But I can tell you this much now:
My God, the smell was awful! – – –

It turns my stomach still to think
Of those odors blended together—
. . . .
As if the filth were being flushed
From thirty-six sewer trenches. – – –

. . . .
This scent of the German futurity
Was ever so much stronger
Than anything I ever smelled.

X-rays of the manuscript reveal the history of the poem's emendation. Heine knew the German censors were sharpening their quills for this work, and one can track Heine's process of anticipating their intervention. First he crosses out more and more parts of the poem that he knows will raise objections. Then he goes back in again—now reinstating section after section that he'd taken out, finally adding new, excoriating segments until the last version became even more aggressive toward the Prussian regime than the first had been.

Along with his epic compositions, Heine wrote shorter, gripping works, among them "The Slave Ship," considered Germany's first antiracist poem. In its stanzas, Heine channels

the consciousness of a Dutch ship captain transporting a load
of six hundred slaves, who are dying in the fetid air of the vessel's hold. The captain tries to calculate how many lives he can
afford to lose before his profit is gone. On a doctor's recommendation, he finally brings the chained men and women up
on deck, forcing them to dance. Their guard, "the master of
revels," whips the naked invalids into a frenzied glee. They kick
and stamp with "madly whirling feet," while the captain prays,

> Oh, spare their lives for Jesus' sake
> Who did not die in vain!
> For if I don't keep three hundred head
> My business is down the drain.

And finally, near the end, Heine wrote a series of anguished,
Job-like interrogations of God and his own character over age-
old questions of suffering, love, and history. "Drop those holy
parables/and Pietist hypotheses," one late poem begins.

> Why do just men stagger, bleeding,
> . . . .
> While the wicked ride the high horse,
> Happy victors blest by fate?

"Who's to blame?" the poet asks. Isn't God omnipotent?

> Or is evil His own doing?
> Ah, that would be vile indeed.

> Thus we ask and keep on asking,
> Till a handful of cold clay
> Stops our mouths at last securely—
> But pray tell, is that an answer?

In another poem, Heine begs God's forbearance as he confesses to being shocked at what's befallen him. With due respect, it seems the Lord has made a blunder. "You formed the
merriest poet and now/You rob him of his good humor." If the

pain continues, he warns, he'll turn Catholic and load God's ears with sobbing in proper Christian fashion.

Finally, in "Parting Word," the poet inventories the hatreds and desires that have departed from him since his health declined, until suddenly he cries, "Within me death alone lives on!"

The bloodshed of the 1848 revolution filled Heine with horror, for all his belief in the righteousness of the struggle. "The beautiful ideals of political morality, legality, civic virtue, freedom and equality" of which his generation had "heroically dreamed" seemed to have been trodden underfoot like fragments of a porcelain bowl, he wrote a friend.

He was leaving his apartment less and less frequently by this time. His legs felt like cotton, while his attachment to life resembled "a gentle nun in the old ruins of a cloister: it haunts the ruins of my *ego*." But one May day in the midst of the street fighting, despite his weakness, he dragged himself out with his stick to take a promenade on the boulevard. The tumult in the streets soon proved too much for him, and he limped haltingly into the sanctuary of the Louvre. The vast palace was almost deserted. Heine crept around the huge silent rooms until at last he reached the chamber of ancient gods and goddesses.

All at once he found himself standing before the Venus de Milo—the "ideal of Beauty, the miracle of an unknown master." He felt overcome by emotion. Here was the pinnacle of what humanity could produce to redeem reality. Heine fell to the stone floor, weeping uncontrollably. The lovely lips of Venus appeared to smile compassionately yet powerlessly down at him; radiating an empathy without solace.

"Don't you see," the goddess seemed to say. "I cannot embrace you. I cannot help you. For I myself have no arms." He staggered home down the streets, through the furious melee, and never again left his mattress grave.

Yet he spent seven years there, never stopped writing, and people visited him constantly.

Chapter Thirty-six

ELISE KRINITZ might have stepped out of one of Heine's dreams, and she savored her effect. In the summer of 1855, she appeared at his door on Avenue Matignon from—no one's quite sure. Exotic and lonely, she traded in the glamour of everything unknown about her. The past incidents she chose to reveal flashed like jewels when she gestured with her fine hands, which she did frequently. Heine wrote in one poem that Krinitz dreamt she was a lotus, "God bless her, / And really believes it, almost."

In her reminiscences, she said she'd come to Heine from Vienna bearing a few sheets of music that an admirer of Heine's asked her to deliver. After she handed them over to a servant, a sharp ring sounded from the next room. Krinitz was surprised by a rather imperious voice forbidding her departure. A door opened. She walked into a dark space, stumbling against a screen covered with colored paper meant to imitate lacquer. All around her, she caught a "certain indescribable aroma of former Bohemianism," which recalled, Krinitz wrote, "the laughter of *grisettes* and the exploits of pianists." She inhaled her imaginary vision of the poet's youth—that "unhealthy past," which artists of the day, so adept at assuming "the airs of respectability," kept their homes clean of, she commented, derisively, while herself breathing more deeply.

Behind the screen lay a man sick and half blind, stretched across a low divan. "Imagine if you can, the smile of Mephistopheles passing over the face of Christ"—that was how Heine struck her. He raised himself on his pillows and held out his hand, saying he would be gratified to speak with someone from "yonder." Before she left, he'd given her a book and asked her to come again. And so it began, Krinitz wrote.

Except that the original letter she sent Heine asking to visit makes no mention of any gift, or of her own role as envoy. And she signed that introductory note Margareth. Some years before, she'd been the lover of Heine's friend Meissner, though Heine didn't know this. She'd told Meissner her name was Margot. On public documents, meanwhile, she signed her name Camille Selden. It took decades to ascertain that her legal name was Elise Krinitz; but that was still not her birth name, which might, or might not, have been Müller.

She was born in Prague—probably—the illegitimate daughter of the debonair Count Nostitz. A German family adopted her and brought to Paris. When Heine met her, she was about twenty-seven, though she looked younger. She may have shown up at Heine's flat just because she'd been devoted to his poetry since childhood; her mother had given her exquisite editions of his works. Thanks to Heine, "Nature seemed to me transformed into a terrestrial Paradise," she stated.

No one who knew her described her as beautiful, exactly. Heine himself wrote his sister of a strangely talented young woman who had turned up and begun helping with proofs of his work. She succeeded in blending French *esprit* with German sentiment, Charlotte decided after meeting her, noting also that her hands and feet were small and neat, while all her motions were unusually graceful.

How had she worked up nerve to intrude on the famous poet's last struggle? Krinitz attributed her preparation for the encounter to a "somewhat cosmopolitan education and much travel." She'd been around, that's certain. When very young she was married off to an abusive Frenchman, who had burned through whatever money she inherited. Visiting England, he swept her off to the family of friends in a fine country house, where an old gentleman received her in a most pleasant manner. Once inside, her husband disappeared and she discovered she'd been dumped in a madhouse. She went into convulsions, and lost the power of speech for more than a month. When she finally persuaded the keepers to release her, it was on condition that she return immediately to Paris. From then on, she made her living giving German lessons. At least that's the version of her story she gave Charlotte, who liked her.

Krinitz was frank about the nature of her attraction to Heine. She didn't mind the rough sides of his character, she declared. While defending him, she felt she was defending herself—training for the day when she would have "to strive against the wickedness and folly of the world." Moreover, he was instructively free of commonplace affectations. Heine's fifth-floor flat resembled "third-rate furnished lodgings," with "no trace of good taste, no attempt even at comfort." The only art she noticed were two engravings from the early years of Louis Philippe's reign, *The Reapers* and *The Fishermen*, both ideological works by Léopold Robert embodying Saint-Simonian conceits: the sanctification of matter and daily labor as an act of reverence. There was no sign in the room of a woman's presence, she pointedly added. For that, you had to go into an adjoining chamber, where you'd find a "display of imitation lace lined with transparent muslin," cupboards coated with brown velvet, and a full-length portrait of Mathilde herself placed in good light, depicting her in "a low-necked black bodice, and bands of hair plastered down her cheeks—a style in the fashion of about 1840."

Heine, for his part, was instantly smitten with Krinitz. He invited her to return at any hour, early or late. "I want to imagine, superstitious as I am, that a good fairy is visiting me in a sad hour," he wrote. "Or are you a bad fairy? I must find out soon." He called her the last flower of his gloomy autumn. She approved Heine's judgment that she had shown up "opportunely, in fact, just when I was needed." And she was probably correct in her surmise that he'd detected a similarity between their spirits. Heine saw in her, she wrote, "the horror of routine, of ugliness, of vulgarity, the hatred of expediency, the contempt for bombast, as well as for empty sentiments and phrases, before, and above all, an exceeding love of imagination."

He added to that roster the observation that they were both rather flea-bitten and probably touched in the head.

Margot, Margarethe, Camille, Elise Krinitz Müller—whoever she was, she had a seal embellished with a fly, and Heine named her Mouche. He craved her presence fluttering around him, he told her repeatedly. When she left town and returned, he couldn't bear it if she didn't drop round at once. He longed to smell the musk of her gloves, to hear the sound of her voice, to make a living impression on her face, he said after one absence. He wrote her poems in which he pleaded that he could bear flaying or having his flesh torn with red hot pincers, but she must not make him wait and wait and wait! In other verses, he artfully lamented the impossibility of making their love physical.

Never was a poet more miserable than he in the midst of total happiness, he swore, for "imagination is all I can offer you." Though sometimes, also, there's a hint of relief that he couldn't consummate their relations—it took the pressure off, licensing him to express inexhaustible, dangerous machismo, strictly hypothetically. One letter expressed joy at the thought of seeing her soon again and of placing *une empreinte vivante* on her sweet features. "Ah! That sentence would bear a less platonic meaning if I were still a man! But I am only a spirit now, a fact which may suit *you*, but scarcely satisfies me!" After nights of particular anguish when he didn't feel well enough for her visit he wrote crushed notes of remorse, telling her he would have to delay until tomorrow, or the next day. "How vexatious! I am so ill! My brain is full of madness and my heart is full of sorrow!" he exclaimed.

She was devoted to him: reading aloud in a voice people described as richly resonant, chatting about anything, often quite knowledgeably, and serving as his amanuensis. Most of all, she just sat with him for several hours each day, as he drifted in and out of consciousness—at ease with his twilight dreamself. This state was attributable partly to his illness, partly to morphine. Heine was continually drugged by then. His physician kept open a series of incisions along his spine so that opioid powder could be inserted directly into the wounds.

Mathilde tolerated the relationship—just barely, refusing to let Krinitz dine at their table, almost ignoring her greetings, stalking out of the sick room whenever Krinitz walked in. Still, she never forbade her from coming. And why exactly should she have embraced this beguiling young woman, so enamored of her own vagabond unconventionality, who alone had the power to make Heine feel hungry for life again? Krinitz, for her part, described Mathilde as a "dark stout lady, with a high color and a jovial countenance, a person of whom you would say she required plenty of exercise in the open air." It would be absurd to idealize this woman when Heine himself never did, Krinitz wrote, adding that there was something appalling about the contrast between this robust woman and the gaunt, dying man.

There were always people around. In addition to the nurse Catherine, Krinitz noted a lame, slavish friend of Mathilde's named Pauline who did light maid's work, a secretary from Saxony, and an elderly half-paralyzed Jew who called himself Dr. Loeuvre. Heine kept him on retainer, having delegated him to manage "the small system of secret police which he fancied he was bound to maintain." The unpaid hangers-on didn't add to the place's charms—"relics of the past, waifs of politics or love," members of the "princely demi-monde," as Heine himself labeled them. Krinitz had no patience with the Princess Belgiojoso, whom Heine himself once called the "most accomplished of all beings." The lady complained incessantly, bewailing "her ruined digestion which obliged her to partake only of iced food at midnight," Krinitz wrote. A second princess in attendance was no more glamorous: "another wreck from Weimar," who reeked of tobacco and had her hands constantly full of little pamphlets "in praise of the god of her adoration who allowed her to have her own way." Krinitz shared, or developed under Heine's tutelage, an eye for the elegantly annihilating detail.

The apartment was dim and squalid, but she saw how it conduced to Heine's entranced remembrances. He lay there in his sunset state, conjuring his student years, "no great passions, but many petty love affairs . . . many hours wasted in drinking, in idle discussions," amid "broken glasses, hiccups, duels, brawls, and perhaps even sighs." So much for Heine's glory days. Yet part of him remained, in her estimate, ingenuously, sentimentally German. It came through in the way he could never get over the ill treatment he received at the hands of his countrymen. He forgot, Krinitz wrote, that people don't raise statues "to those who call them stupid and bourgeois."

Sometimes, in all honesty, he made her feel smothered with his longings. Her own health wasn't the best. The women in Heine's fantasies were too unearthly and subtle. And he could be so sardonic, overflowing with arrogance, surprising one "by the audacity of his imaginary desires. . . . With the true skill of a *raffiné* artist, he knew how to keep cool, while making you shudder." How many times, she wondered, would she be greeted with that needling refrain, *Here you are, at last.* Sometimes she felt death pursuing her in Heine's person, trying to drag her, living and young, down into the gulf. Then suddenly he would tell her how deeply he loved her. She had to realize that she was forever his "dear *'mouche'*" and that his miseries became "less distressing when I dwell on your sweetness." Heine signed this letter, Nebuchadnezzar II, "Formerly atheist to his Prussian Majesty, now worshipper of the Lotus-flower."

All the poems Heine wrote for the Mouche were love poems of a sort. The last one—perhaps the last he ever wrote—was profound.

It begins with the poet remarking that one summer night he dreamt that he found himself amid the ruins of both renaissance buildings and classical columns under a moonlit sky. Amid the building fragments lay shattered statues: centaurs and sphinxes, satyrs, chimeras—all the mythical creatures in which man and beast are compounded. And there were also stone female figures, covered with grass, embraced by the weeds. Time, the "worst kind of syphilis," had stolen part of a nymph's face.

In this vast field there stood one undamaged open marble casket, inside which lay a dead man with a face of gentle suffering. Numerous figures were carved in relief on the sepulcher's sides. Not only the glory of Olympus, but Adam and Eve. The fall and burning of Troy. Paris. Helen. Esther. Haman. Judith. Holofernes. Venus. Pluto. Bacchus. Persephone. Abraham. John the Baptist's head on a platter. Peter with the key to heaven. All the oppositions of classical and biblical culture were here intertwined, "coupled glaringly," marmoreally reconciled. "The Grecian sense of joy—the godly mind / of old Judea!"

Staring at this wondrous pantheon, it occurred to him that *he* was the dead figure in the casket. At the same moment he observed, at the tomb's head, "a strangely formed, mysterious new flower" with violet-gold leaves that breathed the spell of love's power—the passionflower, which was supposed to have sprung from Calvary on the day of the crucifixion. The flower sorrowfully bowed its head, brushing the poet's hand, then transformed into a woman—into the Mouche. The two didn't speak, but his heart knew her thoughts all the same. It was an eloquent, silent dialogue. Everything "said without a metaphor or trick." The harmonic delight was complete.

He didn't know how long he lay in that state of bliss, "dreaming my dream of peace," among those beautiful, conjoined opposites, but at last the quiet dissolved. A silent grave alone could give such peace, Heine wrote. "Raw life inanely gives not happiness / But spasms of passion, pleasure without peace."

All at once, he heard a wretched tumult, a terrible jangling filled the air, wild shouts assailed his ears. His flower was frightened away. The noise arose from the sculptures on the bier. They'd come alive—but their resurrection was accomplished only so they could resume their horrific battle. Once more, "The wood god Pan's wild cry of fear is thrown / Against the wild anathemas of Moses!"

So it would always be, Heine realized. The mad strife would never cease. Truth would always clash with Beauty. The Nazarenes and Hellenes were locked eternally in futile combat. Their rage and cursing would have no sequel—there was no hope of transcending this nauseatingly monotonous conflict.

Gradually, over the din of gods and heroes, one sound became discernible, growing ever louder: the cry of Balaam's ass, whose brays soared above the gods and saints.

> With this heehaw-heehaw, this neighing blare,
> This belch of nasty noise, this grating croak,

The dumb beast almost filled me with despair;
At last I too cried out—and I awoke.

With the end of the dream, the poem itself concludes.

Despite her penchant for mystery, Krinitz was devoid of spiritual pretentions, and as Heine's demise approached she felt conscious only of how much vitality remained in him. February was dark, cold, and wet. At the end of one excruciating visit, he'd placed his hand on her head in what seemed a kind of blessing. "Come tomorrow, do not fail!" he told her.

But she disobeyed him. Afterward, she couldn't remember exactly what kept her away. She might have been a little feverish herself—she almost certainly was, she decided. But still she couldn't forgive herself. A few days later, on Sunday, February 17, she woke around eight to a strange noise, an intense fluttering sound, like moths on summer evenings trapped inside a windowpane. She opened her eyes—then shut them again immediately, for she had seen a terrifying black form "writhing like a gigantic insect in the dawn," seeking some means of escape.

At ten she showed up at Heine's door and learned that he had just died. "Write . . . paper . . . pencil!" he cried at the last instant, gesturing into space.

Krinitz insisted on stepping into the room where his body lay, and when she saw Heine's corpse, amazement choked her tears. She had anticipated everything, she wrote, except "this sudden silence," the infinite calm. His profile now called to mind one of those works of Greek sculpture he so venerated. He had turned into marble. All his importunities rushed back to her. His absolute placidity now weighed on her more heavily than the lead of his coffin. "I often wished to die to escape from him," she wrote, "and he revenged himself from the tomb by crushing me."

Still, Krinitz went on to become the lover of the eminent

historian Hippolyte Taine, remaining with him a decade until he deserted her for a rich bride, after which she became a translator, novelist, essayist, and a teacher in Rouen, where she wrote her forceful, short memoir of Heine's last days—which at moments seems possessed by Heine's own voice.

Théophile Gautier was among the crowd of roughly a hundred mourners who followed Heine's coffin through the foggy streets to Montmartre Cemetery on the morning of February 20, 1856. Heine's friends ought to have rejoiced that he had at last been delivered from such "atrocious tortures," Gautier wrote. Yet to think of that luminous brain, compacted of sunbeams and ideas, from which images streamed forth "like golden bees," now reduced to gray pulp, "gives a pang which one cannot accept without revolt."

His death was widely covered by newspapers in France, where notices overflowed with praise, as well as in Germany, where the announcements were often tinged with conservative misgivings. An unsigned obituary in the *Deutsches Museum* typified the ambivalence: Heine had helped to inaugurate a completely new epoch in German intellectual life, the paper reported, "even if we may not count this epoch among our happiest." His energetic abilities had successfully "brought the dreary, sickly conditions of his time to poetic expression," which ensured him "lasting memory, memory that would of course be incomparably more glowing if he had possessed character equal to his exceptional talent."

Before Heine's funeral Mathilde abruptly fled the house. She left no address. She vanished for a month without a trace—though her intimate Pauline turned up at the apartment occasionally to pick up letters and checks. The mystery of Mathilde's flight lingers; but eventually she returned and lived a quiet life devoted to Heine's memory. The family remained mostly appalled by her gauche habits. It was Gustav, Heine's brother, however, who wanted a giant marble tomb, which he boasted would cost ten thousand francs, while Mathilde fought to respect Heine's wishes by limiting the marker to a simple stone engraved with his name. So much for her crude taste.

Later, she and Pauline took a home in Batignolles with back windows looking over a garden. Along with Cocotte, she kept sixty canaries and three white lapdogs. When Heine's nephew Carl visited her, he was astonished by all the crying, chirping, and barking. He couldn't bear to stay long in the din. *C'est drôle!* she said as he fled. *Vous êtes comme votre oncle, qui n'aimait pas les bêtes.*

But it was really only the ass that Heine considered his nemesis. In a late letter to Alexandre Dumas he tried to explain why he'd felt this lifelong antipathy for the beast—developing an argument that resonates with the triumph of discord portrayed at the climax of his poem to the Mouche. It's the closest thing Heine ever wrote to a theory of the perennial obstacle to making this world beautiful.

The letter accompanied a fifty-franc bank note, a donation to a charity Dumas supported. Heine explained that the bill he was sending originated with a compatriot who had recently sent it to *him*, ostensibly to repay some old debt. He had felt driven to get rid of this bill as quickly as possible because it stank—of donkey, to be precise. Even as a child, he wrote, he'd been frightened whenever he heard a donkey bray and ran away as quickly as he could. The roars of tigers and lions didn't make him tremble. The mewing of cats, grunting of pigs, and barking of dogs might disturb him, but only the donkey filled him with real terror. Most unbearable of all was the noise of a donkey that had been angered by some scoundrel who put pepper in its rear end, Heine observed. Unlike certain friends of his, he couldn't laugh at the terrible *hee-haw, hee-haw* that ensued then—"as horrible as it is baroque and scurrilous, at all these unspeakable and almost sublime accents of stupidity emitted by an enraged donkey in his impotent rage."

It was true, he continued, the original fault lay with those jokers who'd placed powder in the animal's behind. Typically, we associate the donkey with a certain honesty: it is "too stupid, too insipid, too silly for us not to take him for honest." But nonetheless, the tortured donkey was also to blame, since "his desperate cries reveal all there is of arrogance, envy, impertinence, ignoble rancor, bad faith and even trickery profoundly hidden in the entrails of the absurd animal."

Heine explained that his parable referred not just to the man who'd sent him the fifty-mark note but to a whole category of people who qualified as poetry's mortal adversaries. The persistent ugliness of the world, despite its glorious promise, is ultimately the fault of two groups of men: those who rile up dumb brutes for a laugh, and the egoistic, deceitful monsters who heedlessly inflict their own misery on the rest of the universe, turning ignorance and suffering into a badge of honor that entitles them to make the world resound with the ghastly clamor of their humiliation, until nothing can be heard but a cacophony of idiotic, misdirected fury.

Epilogue

UP IN THE BRONX, at the end of a narrow, flat park, bordered east and west by nondescript apartment buildings, stands a dramatic white statue of a woman on a pedestal ringed by three voluptuous mermaids. Submarine animals spout and slither around their bare limbs. One face of the pedestal displays a bas-relief of a sphinx embracing a naked young man; another shows a nude ephebe impaling a dragon; the third features a cameo profile of a sober-looking man framed by a crescent laurel above the name Heinrich Heine. The mermaids are said by some to represent Poetry, Melancholy, and Satire, although others claim that the third mermaid symbolizes Heine's particular affliction, *Judenschmerz*—literally "Jewish pain," a term coined in his lifetime to represent the misery of being attacked as a Jew even after one's formally shed that identity by converting. The central figure, perched contrapposto on a rock, combing her long hair with one hand, and clasping the folds of her windswept drapery with the other, is the Lorelei.

It's quite a statue. Not really *good*, let alone tasteful, the memorial is yet arresting—bountiful in its imagery, with a louche sensuality accentuated by the mermaids' surprisingly low-slung, cleft fishtails.

The sculpture, by the Berlin artist Ernst Herter, was unveiled in 1899 with a parade of banner-hoisting German societies to a crowd of as many as six thousand people. Speeches were delivered by local dignitaries. The first speaker remarked that in paying homage to "this champion of religious and political freedom we honor ourselves." Ralph Guggenheimer, the presiding German-American philanthropist, spoke of why New York City was the Heine monument's rightful home. "Whatever may be the faults of our political and social life, we are at least free from that insularity which narrows the horizons both of a nation and an individual," he declared. "We are justly proud of the fact that the most characteristic feature of the American mind is cosmopolitanism." To reinforce Heine's status as "the prophet and torchbearer of modern thought," Guggenheimer cited Heine's own injunction: "Place on my coffin a sword, for I was a brave fighter in the liberation war of humanity!" It was partly through Heine's influence that they could stand together this day "in the vanguard of the world's progress, under the aegis and inspiration of a government that safeguards for us all the freedom of the press, the freedom of the intellect, and liberty of conscience." Not far away, one German emigrant had placed an inscription on the façade of his house to honor the monument's dedication: *Fanaticism sleeps in peace; Heinrich Heine's statue covers it.*

Before the year was out, representatives from a Christian women's abstinence organization mounted a court case against the statue for indecency. That same year a vandal chopped off the arms of its female figures. In the ensuing decades, fresh protests were mounted against the "pornographic spectacle." It was repaired, but moved from the south end of the park to the less conspicuous north side in 1940. It sustained further damage in subsequent years—at one point the mermaid representing Poetry was decapitated. Later, the sculpture was painted black, then red. By the mid-1970s, the Heine memorial was entirely covered in graffiti and was said to be the single most vandalized statue in all New York City—a remarkable distinction for the era. In the 1990s, following multiple fund-raising campaigns, the memorial was restored again and moved back to the park's south end, where it sits today suffering the preferred form of contemporary defilement: immaculate neglect.

I went up to see the statue for the first time in the aftermath of the 2016 elections. I was wondering what, if anything, Heine's revolutionary imagination had left behind that could be used as a weapon, or balm, in the hour of crisis. I walked around the statue again and again, orbiting the burst of carved marble as if I were performing some ritual. As if when I completed a certain number of turns, Heine's lips on the north face of the plinth would be charmed open, and he would provide that clarion answer to the meaning of life, which the sphinx had so notoriously withheld.

Sparrows hopped about the heads of the mermaids. Two women sat on a bench just outside the low iron fence encircling the statue, eating, taking turns patting an infant, and talking intently. An older man with a hat and a cane sat on a bench a little farther away, beside a transistor radio playing salsa. Two women in gray coats and burqas descended the steps leading down to 161st Street. Another woman in a heavy jacket rocked a big stroller back and forth while talking at the branches of a dead tree through her cellphone.

When I looked up again at the Lorelei, I realized that—whether originally or in consequence of some strangely fortuitous repair—the figure's right eye was open, while her left eye was shut. The juxtaposition appeared emblematic of Heine's commitment to dreaming without eclipsing reality.

How surprising it seemed that the first public monument to Heinrich Heine ended up here. The sculpture was supposed to have been erected in his hometown of Düsseldorf, where, in 1887, a committee was established to create a memorial that would be unveiled ten years later, on the one hundredth anniversary of his birth. Empress Elisabeth of Austria, the consort of Franz Josef and a rebel against the stifling protocols of royal life, worshiped Heine's work. Whenever she traveled, she carried with her twenty volumes of his writings. Petals of the flowers she pressed between the pages of each book still fall from the pages when they're opened in archives. Elisabeth's enthrallment didn't stop with immersion in Heine's work: she wrote her own poetry, and believed that she could summon his voice through her pen. Elisabeth became a major supporter of the memorial project, exciting a furor in the antisemitic, nationalistic press. "Let Jews and those who are enslaved to Jews rave about this shameless Jew," raged one pan-German paper. But Elisabeth persisted. When the liberal press championed her cause for its own political purposes, she was equally unmoved, remarking, "What I love in him is his boundless contempt for his own humanity and the sadness worldly matters inspired in him."

The memorial committee was torn between two visions for the monument: one, Herter's plan for the Lorelei, the other a more traditional depiction of Heine himself. Elisabeth wanted the human semblance. The Lorelei was preferred by the committee, and Elisabeth accepted its judgment. But as the project advanced, Düsseldorf authorities began receiving more and more letters of protest against the statue, increasingly on overtly antisemitic grounds. Then someone began picking out the sculpture's subtle jibes: the nude youth killing the dragon was piercing him with a quill, not a lance, and the dragon wore a wig of exactly the sort favored by Düsseldorf's officials.

The outcry against the project grew louder. Elisabeth pulled out, some say after a direct intervention by statesman Otto von Bismarck. Instead, she commissioned a Swiss sculptor to carve an image of Heine in his last days for her own palace, Achilleion, in Corfu. In this work, the poet holds a marble sheet of paper carved with a stanza from one of his poems beginning, *What does the lonely tear desire?* The sculpture faces the sea, and Elisabeth described the spot's refreshing tranquility as the ideal eternal resting place for Heine. Eight years later, she was assassinated with an industrial needle by an anarchist on a mission to kill any royal personage he could find. Her property was acquired by Kaiser Wilhelm, who immediately arranged for the statue's removal. It drifted—arriving in Hamburg, then getting shipped out again and warehoused at various undistinguished locations—even being used at one point as an advertising prop for a Heinrich Heine coffeehouse. Finally, in 1939, it was accepted for a park in Toulon, just as the wanderings of Europe's living Jews were reaching a finale.

By then, the official Nazi line on Heine had been determined: he represented the archetypal Jew with "the capacity to adapt himself to an alien environment, to assume its characteristics and thus to shield himself," declared the authoritative *Nationalsozialistische Monatshefte.* Heine's poetry was only cunning bricolage, "not genuine, organic, complete and sprung from deepest experience, but only manufactured sham, effect and merely external semblance." His work was to be erased from all literary anthologies, school textbooks, and histories.

After Düsseldorf rejected his Lorelei sculpture, Herter had started collecting funds independently to complete the work. He tried to present it to the city as a gift, but Düsseldorf still declined. Mainz and Frankfurt were considered possible destinations for the sculpture, but both rejected it, as did Berlin and Hamburg. In 1893, a German-American choral society dedicated to "the perpetuation of love for some characteristic elements of German civilization" stepped in and purchased the work for the Grand Army Plaza at Fifth Avenue and West Fifty-ninth Street at Central Park. It arrived in America in sixty-four crates. However the Fifth Avenue siting was suddenly withdrawn, probably because of the mermaids' nudity. People thought it might then go to an amusement park on Glen Island, north of the city. But somehow it landed way uptown.

On the one hand, then, America welcomed the memorial that Germany's nationalistic prejudices wouldn't accommodate. On the other, once it was erected in New York, the statue was almost entirely demolished in decades of attacks driven by moralistic intolerance and senseless destructiveness. Still, there the statue stands, in the city's northernmost borough, where new political voices are beginning to make themselves heard, and the question remains: yes, Heine loved freedom and championed the struggle for progress, but what can we actually take from his work when we find ourselves in a state of desperate need? Is there a single recommendation the poet made that gives us something which can impel us to action?

I don't know which revolution of the sculpture I was on when I absorbed what the Heinrich Heine monument was facing. Just across 161st Street stands the monolith of the Bronx Supreme Court of Justice. Built in 1931, it's a massive gray slab with Doric pillars and a heroic architrave. Gold rectangles gleam between the dark windows up and down its colossal façade. The juxtaposition of the sculpture and the building is stunning: Heine's mythic Lorelei stares straight out at the giant seat of justice, as if that edifice were the vessel to which she were singing.

One of the people Heine befriended in his Paris years was Karl Marx. They met in the fall of 1843, through the intervention of a mutual acquaintance from Hegelian circles, and immediately struck up a companionship, though Heine was more than two decades Marx's senior. Eleanor, Marx's daughter, recalled the two men spending time together almost daily, sometimes collaborating intently on the revision of a poem. She also recounted a family legend that Heine had shown up at their apartment one night to find both Karl and Jenny Marx paralyzed with panic as their baby daughter suffered a fit of convulsions. Heine took command of the situation, telling them the child needed to be bathed in warm water. He proceeded to take responsibility for the child himself, bathing and warming her until the seizure passed. Jenny credited Heine with saving their daughter's life. In this way, it may be that Heine literally helped transmit Marx's legacy to the future.

Heine recognized Marx's genius, calling him the most intelligent and determined of the German refugees in Paris, though he also discerned a ruthless intransigence in him that seemed ominous. "A man is very little, if he's nothing but a razor," he observed, classifying Marx among the godless men who deify themselves. Nonetheless, Heine insisted that Marx's movement was the only party worth paying attention to. On this ship of fools, the communists were the one group inspired by "daemonic necessity," who could achieve something *essential* for humanity, even if it came at the expense of the beautiful creations he himself could never renounce, any more than he could strip his poetry of music.

For a time, Marx and Heine wrote for the same journal. They spent hours in conversation, and in public invariably referred to each other in admiring tones. Among friends, though, Marx was always a little condescending toward Heine's political ideas. "Dear old Heine," as he referred to him in letters, plainly had no grasp on policy. However, Marx determined, poets were strange fish, and "not to be judged by ordinary, or even extraordinary, standards of conduct." When he was about to leave

Paris in 1845, Marx wrote Heine that of all the people he was leaving behind, those he left with most regret were the Heines, adding that he wished he could pack him along in his suitcase.

Because Heine's unsystematic political pronouncements had no obvious means of being implemented, and because among devout Marxists, there has been little appetite for accepting the notion of Marx's own susceptibility to an ideologically renegade, aesthetical voice, the traditional assumption has been that the path of influence went from Marx to Heine. Heine was invigorated by Marx's radicalism, the argument goes, and works such as Heine's poem on the plight of the Silesian weavers, whose oppression deeply concerned Marx, seem to bear out this view. More recent scholarship, however, has looked at the influence of Heine on Marx as a writer—and on Marx's style as indivisible from the substance of his pronouncements. From this perspective, the conclusion has been that actually the stronger tide of influence runs in the opposite direction.

Long before the two men met, Marx envisioned a career for himself as a poet and novelist, and all through his early years, he had devoured Heine's writing. The themes and formal techniques of his own youthful book of poems are demonstrably indebted to Heine's *Book of Songs*. Marx's uncompleted novel *Scorpion and Felix* owes much to Heine's *Pictures of Travel*. Its biting caricatures and jarring cadences—the way it segues without warning between rhetorical postures and genres—evokes Heine's style. Heine was instrumental in the process whereby Marx came to see literature as embracing not just belles lettres and philosophy but also popular forms, like feuilletons. Why should these idioms be mutually exclusive? Why be afraid of any potential cross-fertilization? Might not the freedom to be stylistically inclusive be correlative with the transcendent prospects of liberty, even as a stunted, rigid mode of expression will betray shackled cognitive processes? Just so, German censorship had "retarded the development of the German mind and spirit in a disastrous and irresponsible way," Marx wrote. And he retained his commitment to a bravura style even after he turned to more exclusively political writing.

One can feel in Marx's inventive satire, captivating imagery, irony, bold, fast shifts of tone, and epigrammatic flourishes the live current of Heine's spirit. Above all, as scholars have shown, Heine's particular vein of comedy, which makes the reader a coconspirator in exposing the emperor's nakedness, helped inspire Marx's own rhetorical ploys for placing readers preemptively on his side of the barricades. Both writers suggest that when confronted with tyrannical might, there's no weapon more effective in mobilizing solidarity than fearless, visionary irreverence. Marx explicitly acknowledged as much in various writings, invoking Heine's example for that purpose in *Das Kapital*. At least one famous Marxian adage—"philosophers have only interpreted the world . . . the point is to change it"—has a distinctly Heinesque ring to it. Heine helped give Marx his voice in the years when his theories were germinating, and Marx continued to channel Heine's electric, metamorphic tone for the whole of his career. Without the already liberated *sound* of his argument, it's fair to wonder whether Marx's call to freedom would have echoed so forcefully.

Other thinkers, activists, and writers from different backgrounds have shared that response to Heine's work. William Dean Howells, the American author, recounted in an essay that before his discovery of Heinrich Heine, he was under the impression that literary expression should be "different from the expression of life; that it must be an attitude, a pose." Heine, he avowed, "undid my hands. . . . He forever persuaded me that though it may be ingenious and surprising to dance in chains, it is neither pretty nor useful." The German historian Fritz Stern, who sailed for America in 1938, fleeing what he called the "jubilant, Hitler-enthralled Germany," came to feel that Heine had provided "the perfect epitaph" for the moment: *Die*

Freiheitsliebe ist eine Kerkerblume, "The love of freedom is a prison-flower." Isaiah Berlin visited a politically despondent Boris Pasternak in the mid-1950s; "At least I can say, like Heine, 'I may not deserve to be remembered as a poet, but surely as a soldier in the battle for human freedom,' Pasternak told Berlin before thrusting the manuscript of *Dr. Zhivago* into his hands, hoping it could be published abroad. More recently, in the spring of 2019, a new musical drama had its premiere in Paris: *Zauberland*, about the flight of a pregnant Syrian refugee from Aleppo to Cologne, which features the suite of Heine's *Lyrical Intermezzo* poems that Schumann first scored: evidence of Heine's persistent bearing on the struggle for liberty.

Under the influence of Heine's iconoclastic brio, writing becomes a revolutionary vocation even beyond what is inscribed on the page. His gift to the future is less prescriptive than aural.

Looked at through the lenses of hidebound tradition, the figure of the Lorelei singing to the Bronx Supreme Court of Justice might seem a seductive female spirit striving to drive that institution to distraction so that it founders on the rocks leading up to her perch. But Heine himself never settled for the conventional interpretation—why should we? Perhaps it's time to reimagine the nature of that elusive siren, along with her presumptive prey. What's been missing, hitherto, is a true exchange.

One critical aspect of the classic Lorelei paradigm is the monumental passivity of the boatman. He responds to the Lorelei's music with an unrequitable aching in his heart that triggers fatal inattention, which then causes him to drown. Yet what if the lethal element was not inherent to this melody but arose only through the man's senseless response to it? Suppose the female spirit's music was not intended just to repeat some age-old trope of temptation, but was instead issuing a challenge to help her break the whole fatal order of things? What if, instead of just sitting in his boat, or mechanically filling his chair in the court of justice, the figure of authority responded to the lyric actively? Let it inside? Let justice itself be scored to sublime song? What if the boatman left his vessel willfully and swam to the rock where the woman sits impatiently waiting for her absent, brave counterpart? What if justice came striding out of that building into the park with the Lorelei? What if we heard the duet between them reverberate over the Bronx, America, and the rest of creation, until everyone took up the chorus?

Paraphrasing Marx, the point of poetry is not to mirror the world but to make it start dancing. As Heine himself wrote in the midst of French revolutionary ferment: "We are dancing here on a volcano—but we dance."

THE MUSIC, allusive depth, intricate wordplay, brio, and mutability of Heine's voice have made English translations of his work notoriously challenging. Some believe that his poetry defies translation altogether. Few believe that any extensive translations of his prose do it justice. Many believe that here and there one or another translator gets a verse or prose passage just about right. Taking courage from Heine's own hybrid approach—his free-spirited constellations of disparate language registers, genres, and influences—I've drawn from the work of multiple translators, in consultation with the German originals, to try to convey a sense of the exhilaratingly imaginative sound of his voice.

With respect to Heine's poetry, I relied primarily on *The Complete Poems of Heinrich Heine*, trans. Hal Draper (Oxford: Oxford University Press, 1982). While Draper's career was devoted to writing prolifically on the history and philosophy of Karl Marx (his five-volume work *Karl Marx's Theory of Revolution* is a magisterial study), he succeeded over a thirty-year period in also creating the most complete and critically respected edition of Heine's poetry in English. I am enormously grateful to the Center for Socialist History (http://csh.gn.apc.org/TopWindow/pages/WebsiteTop.htm), for giving me permission to quote from Draper's translations. In addition to this work, I relied on *The Poems of Heinrich Heine*, trans. Louis Untermeyer (London: Cape, 1938), Aaron Kramer's translations in *The Poetry and Prose of Heinrich Heine*, ed. Frederic Ewen (New York: Citadel, 1948), and the poems translated in various critical studies of Heine, especially S. S. Prawer's *Heine's Jewish Comedy* (Oxford: Oxford University Press, 1983). I am also extremely grateful to Richard Stokes, Professor of Lieder at the Royal Academy of Music, for giving me permission to quote from his superb translation of Heine's *Lorelei*. I was fortunate as well to have Jeff Dolven contribute to this project. His rendering of Heine's four-line lyric beginning *Selten habt Ihr mich verstanden* is included here. Several thoughtful suggestions from Christian Brammer have been incorporated into this translation.

The most extensive English translation of Heine's prose is the twelve-volume collection *The Works of Heinrich Heine*, trans. C. G. Leland and others (London: Heinemann, 1891–1905). Old-fashioned and expurgated, in places it yet has verve and evocative wit. In addition to Leland, I cite from Heine's prose writings in numerous other translations, including *Heinrich Heine's Memoirs, from His Works, Letters, and Conversations*, ed. Gustav Karpeles, trans. Gilbert Canaan (London: Heinemann, 1910); *The Harz Journey and Selected Prose*, trans. Ritchie Robertson (London: Penguin, 1993); *On the History of Religion and Philosophy in Germany and Other Writings*, ed. Terry Pinkard, trans. Howard Pollack-Milgate (Cambridge: Cambridge University Press, 2007); *Ludwig Börne: A Memorial*, trans. Jeffrey L. Sammons (Rochester, NY: Camden House, 2006); *Heinrich Heine: A Bibliographical Anthology*, ed. Hugo Bieber, trans. by or selected by Moses Hadas (Philadelphia: Jewish Publication Society of America, 1956); and *The Poetry and Prose of Heinrich Heine*, ed. Frederic Ewen, with prose translations by Frederic Ewen (New York: Citadel, 1948). For the German original I used the sixteen-volume edition published by Hoffmann and Campe in conjunction with the Heinrich-Heine-Institut between 1975 and 1997 under the editorial direction of Manfred Windfuhr.

Of the numerous impressive English-language critical and biographical studies of Heine, Prawer's *Heine's Jewish Comedy* offers a uniquely ambitious approach to his life story and work. I am indebted to this book, as well as to Prawer's *Heine: The Tragic Satirist, a Study of the Later Poetry* (Cambridge: Cambridge University Press, 1961), and his *Frankenstein's Island: England and the English Writings of Heinrich Heine* (Cambridge: Cambridge University Press, 1986). Two short biographies, *Heine* by Ritchie Robertson (New York: Grove, 1988) and Ernst Pawel's *The Poet Dying: Heinrich Heine's Last Years in Paris* (New York: Farrar, Straus and Giroux, 1995), provide important insights into Heine's significance that complement Jeffrey L. Sammons's excellent full-length study, *Heinrich Heine: A Modern Biography* (Princeton: Princeton University Press, 1979). I also drew on material in Philip Kossoff, *Valiant Heart: A Biography of Heinrich Heine* (New York: Cornwall, 1983). Older biographical studies such as William Stigand's two-volume work, *The Life, Work, and Opinions of Heinrich Heine* (London: Longmans, Green, 1875); Ludwig Marcuse's *Heine: A Life, between Love and Hate*, trans. Louise M. Sievelking and Ian F. D. Morrow (New York: Farrar and Rinehart, 1933); Louis Untermeyer's *Heinrich Heine: Paradox and Poet* (New York: Harcourt, Brace, 1937); and Max Brod's *Heinrich Heine: The Artist in Revolt*, trans. Joseph Witriol, with Heine's own poetry and prose translated in this volume by various other authors, including C. G. Leland and Emma Lazarus (New York: New York University Press, 1957), were also helpful sources. *Heinrich Heine: Poetry and Politics* by Nigel Reeves (Oxford: Oxford University Press, 1974) and *A Companion to the Works of Heinrich Heine*, ed. Roger F. Cook (Rochester, NY: Camden House, 2002), were particularly helpful critical works. *Heine and Critical Theory* by Willi Goetschl (London: Bloomsbury Academic, 2019), offers a wealth of material, contextualizing Heine's reception, which benefited my study. Elise Krinitz's personal memoir of Heine's last days, published under the pseudonym Camille Selden and first translated into English by Clare Brune (London:

Remington, 1884), is a remarkable work—essential for gaining a sense of Heine's living presence at the end.

Of the many books that were important to expanding my understanding of the era and key figures in Heine's life, Heidi Thomann Tewarson's outstanding study *Rahel Levin Varnhagen: The Life and Work of a German Jewish Intellectual* (Lincoln: University of Nebraska Press, 1998) was invaluable in conjuring the atmosphere and conversations that shaped Heine's outlook as his work reached maturity. I also benefited in particular from James J. Sheehan's *German History, 1770–1866* (Oxford: Oxford University Press, 1989); *Tradition and Revolution: German Literature and Society, 1830–1890* by Eda Sagarra (New York: Basic, 1971); *The Pity of It All* by Amos Elon (New York: Picador, 1993); and Ritchie Robertson's *The "Jewish Question" in German Literature, 1749–1939* (Oxford: Oxford University Press, 1999).

In addition to material drawn from these and other texts, my portrait of Heine's world was enriched through time spent with a wide range of visual material from the era, especially the collections in the Alte Nationalgalerie and the Deutsches Historisches Museum in Berlin, the Goethe-Nationalmuseum in Weimar, and the Heinrich-Heine-Institut in Düsseldorf. The director of the latter institution, Dr. Sabine Brenner-Wiczek, gave me a helpful introduction to the collections, and two affiliated archivists, Jan von Holtum and Christian Liedtke, assisted with my textual research.

Ileene Smith edited the manuscript with great perspicacity, for which I'm deeply grateful. Heather Gold at Yale University Press provided much needed assistance with numerous aspects of the book's production. I'm also thankful to Dan Heaton, who copyedited the book with great skill and sensitivity. I wish to extend a special thank you to Michael Hofmann, who at an early stage of my work kindly shared his illuminating perspective on the pleasures and significance of Heine's writing. I hope one day he will undertake the translations of Heine's work that, with his vibrant inflection, could inspire a new audience of readers in the English-speaking world.

Select References by Chapter

Chapter One

Heine's description of the preparation for Napoleon's entry into Düsseldorf and the event itself appears in chapters 6–8 of his *Ideas: The Book of Le Grand*, quoted here in Robertson's translation from *The Harz Journey and Selected Prose*, 101–114. Sudhir Hazareesingh's *The Legend of Napoleon* (London: Granta, 2004) provides useful perspective on Heine's fascination with the emperor. For Heine's discussion of the world revolution and the giant battle between the haves and have-nots (as well as his most extensive remarks on communism), see his *Lutezia*, the compilation of articles written for the Augsburg *Allgemeine Zeitung* between 1840 and 1843 on French politics, life, and culture. Leland translates the book as the second half of *French Affairs: Letters from Paris*, vol. 8 of *Works*. The Paganini scene appears in the "First Night" of his *Florentine Nights*, quoted here in the translation based on Leland anthologized in *The Sword and the Flame*, ed. Alfred Werner (New York: Thomas Yoseloff, 1960). Heine describes the world as the dream of a drunken god in chapter 3 of *Ideas: The Book of Le Grand*.

Chapter Two

Betty Heine's remarks about her "ordinary face and figure" are cited in Kossoff, *Valiant Heart*, 19. Her instructions to her children appear in Marcuse, *Heine*, 26. I was assisted in filling out my portrait of Heine's family by numerous people at the Heinrich-Heine-Institut in Düsseldorf who kindly answered many queries for me. Heine himself writes about his parents and family in his *Memoirs* (1853–1854). I relied primarily on Robertson's translation, 295–338 in *Harz Journey*.

Chapter Three

Heine's comments on his birth can be found in his "Thoughts and Reflections," Bieber and Hadas, *Heinrich Heine*, 35, which is also the source for his reference to Judaism as an "unlucky genealogical communication," 37. "I dream with open eyes" is cited by

Sammons, *Heinrich Heine*, vi. Heine describes the Jews as mummified in chapter 13 of *The Town of Lucca*, which forms the third part of his radically innovative Italian travelogue. He muses on being just a "shadowy image in a dream" in chapter 3 of *Ideas*. I've modified Leland's translation here. Untermeyer cites Heine's quip about no Jew believing in another Jew's divinity, *Heinrich Heine*, 131.

Chapter Four

Heine reminisces about his father in his *Memoirs*. Samson Heine's advertisement is reprinted in Prawer, *Frankenstein's Island*, 3–4. Most of Heine's writings on England are collected in his *English Fragments*, an eleven-part compilation of his reportage from England, parts of which are translated in Werner's *The Sword and the Flame*. Heine's remarks on "Egoistic England," are from his first series of articles on French affairs for the *Allgemeine Zeitung*, spanning 1830–1832, titled, collectively, *Conditions in France*. Heine called Shakespeare "at once Jew and Greek" in his *Ludwig Börne*. He exalts Pegasus in section 3 of his epic poem *Atta Troll* (1842–1847).

Chapter Five

Heine summarizes parts of his early education in *Ideas*. His boast about outperforming schoolboys in ancient Rome when it comes to the trysts of Venus appears in chapter 7, quoted here in my modification of Leland, *Works*, 2, no. 1, p. 312. Caulaincourt's position on the invasion of Russia is described in Harold Nicolson's *The Congress of Vienna: A Study in Allied Unity, 1812–1822* (New York: Viking, 1946), 3–6. Napoleon's remarks to Fouché on unifying Europe are quoted, among other places, in Adam Zemoyski's *1812: Napoleon's Fatal March on Moscow* (London: Harper Perennial, 2004), 9–10. For the firsthand description of the arrival of Russia's winter I drew on Philippe-Paul comte de Ségur's *History of the Expedition to Russia* (London: H. L. Hunt and C. C. Clark, 1826), 2: 143. Heine's description of Napoleon as a potential George Washington appears in his *French Painters*, originally a series of essays and reviews written in the fall of 1831 for his publisher Cotta's *Morgenblatt*, which became the first volume of his four-part anthology, *The Salon* (vol. 4 in Leland, *Works*). His caricature of Wellington is from *English Fragments*, cited here in Prawer's translation from *Frankenstein's Island*, 108.

Chapter Six

Heine's remarks on the Rothschilds' teeth are from a February 4, 1840, article in the *Augsburg Gazette*, cited in Prawer, *Jewish Comedy*, 329. He compares the family to other great European levelers like Robespierre in his *Ludwig Börne*. Heine also reflects on the Rothschilds in his *Baths of Lucca*, among other places. His likening of the corpus juris to a "Bible of selfishness" is cited in Brod, *Heinrich Heine*, 77. Heine's letter to Embden is dated February 2, 1823.

Chapter Seven

The line from Heine's *Florentine Nights* about Mademoiselle Laurence's dance with its "eerie premonition of rebirth" is quoted in Lucia Ruprecht, *Dances of the Self in Heinrich von Kleist, E. T. A. Hoffman, and Heinrich Heine* (New York: Routledge, 2016). Heine describes his schoolroom announcement of his Jewish ancestry in his *Memoirs*, which is also where he writes about his exposure to systems of free thought.

Chapter Eight

Heine reminisces about his childhood impressions of God in book 3 of his *History of Religion and Philosophy in Germany*. I'm citing John Snodgrass's translation (Albany: State University of New York Press, 1986). Heine reflects on reading *Don Quixote* in chapters 16 and 17 of *The Town of Lucca*. His ruminations on his father appear in his *Memoirs*. Many of Heine's thoughts on Cervantes over the years are compiled in "Heine on Cervantes and the *Don Quixote*," *Temple Bar* 48 (1876): 235–249.

Chapter Nine

The portrait of Simon van Geldern is drawn primarily from Heine's *Memoirs*, Sammons's *Heinrich Heine*, and L. Rosenthal's

"Simeon van Geldern, Heinrich Heine's Famous Great-Uncle," in *Studia Rosenthaliana* 6, no. 2 (1972): 180–203.

Chapter Ten

Heine's prose writings on the North Sea form the third section of his collected writings on the region, which itself is part of his *Travel Pictures*. The first two parts contain some of Heine's only work in free verse. Sammons points out the Homeric basis for this project in *Heinrich Heine*, 116–117, in addition to noting that Heine's extensive writings on the region are credited with expanding North Sea tourism in general and the chic reputation of Helgoland in particular. Heine's remarks on the homeland of crocodiles are from chapter 13 of *The Town of Lucca*. The quoted lines are Prawer's translation in *Heine's Jewish Comedy*, 160. The poem about Heine's double is cited here in Draper's translation, no. 20 from his grouping of the *Homecoming* collection in *Complete Poems*. Heine's comments on dreaming and the Jews appear in the twelfth chapter of his partly autobiographical fiction *Memoirs of Herr von Schnabelewopski*. I am drawing from Werner's revised edition of Leland's translation, *The Sword and the Flame*, 152–198.

Chapter Eleven

Heine writes to Friederike Robert about his uncle in a letter dated October 12, 1825, and calls himself a "free and unpretentious bard" in a letter to Christian Sethe, dated October 27, 1816. He reflects on lizards in the first chapter of *The Town of Lucca*. His comparisons of Hamburgians to numbers appear in chapter 4 of his *Memoirs of Herr von Schnabelewopski;* most of his reflections on Hamburg and its residents appear in chapter 3 of that work.

Chapter Twelve

Heine's line about Hamburg's "Diplomatic cocks-of-the-walk" is from a letter to Sethe, dated October 27, 1816. His poem about false looks is no. 16 from *Lyrical Intermezzo*, trans. Draper, *Complete Poems*, 56–57. The poem beginning "My songs are filled with poison" is no. 51 from the same cycle, 69 in Draper. The verses beginning "A young man loves a maiden," are also from *Lyrical Intermezzo*, no. 39 in Draper's translation. I've also drawn from Draper's version of "Affrontenburg: The Castle of Indignity," 707–709. Susan Youens writes eloquently about Heine's poetry crossing time zones in *Heinrich Heine and the Lied* (Cambridge: Cambridge University Press, 2007), esp. 32–33. Kate Hillard's comments on Heine are quoted in H. B. Sach's *Heine in America* (Philadelphia: Publications of the University of Pennsylvania, 1916), 39. Heine describes the world as "stupid and insipid" in a letter to Varnhagen von Ense, dated October 19, 1827.

Chapter Thirteen

Heine's reminiscences about Red Sefchen can be found in his *Memoirs*, 327–338; the references here are from Robertson's *The Harz Journey and Selected Prose*.

Chapter Fourteen

I drew on numerous old travel guides in depicting Heine's tours of Germany and farther afield across the continent. Editions of John Murray's *Handbook for Travellers on the Continent* from the first half of the nineteenth century were particularly helpful. Most of Heine's writing on Schlegel and Herder can be found in his study *The Romantic School*. I'm drawing here in part on S. L. Fleishman's translation of that work (New York: Henry Holt, 1882). Alexander Dumas wrote a book about Karl Ludwig Sand that describes his execution in detail. George S. Williamson's essay "What Killed August von Kotzebue? The Temptations of Virtue and the Political Theology of German Nationalism, 1789–1819," *Journal of Modern History* 72 (2000): 890–943, complicates the portrait of Kotzebue's reactionary politics with respect to the dangers Kotzebue perceived from rising Germany nationalism. I also drew on Shlomo Avineri's essay "Where They Have Burned Books, They Will End Up Burning People," in the *Jewish Review of Books*, Fall 2017. Heine's comments on the Wartburg Festival can be found in his *Ludwig Börne*. I'm quoting here from the closing stanza's of Draper's translation of *Germany: A Winter's Tale*, section 27, *Complete Poems*, 536.

Chapter Fifteen

Sammons quotes from Heine's letter to Rousseau and Friedrich Steinmann, another budding litterateur from Bonn, in *Heinrich Heine*, 69. He also cites Heine's remarks about dueling, 74. Brod quotes Rousseau's description of Heine, *Heinrich Heine*, 86.

Chapter Sixteen

Heine describes his return to Düsseldorf in Chapter 10 of *Ideas: The Book of Le Grand*. Prawer summarizes many of the ways Sterne influenced Heine in *Frankenstein's Island*, in particular 34–36. Marcuse quotes Heine on the "dry parochial vanity" of Göttingen, *Heine*, 74. "Botching it up for modern use" is quoted in *Memoirs*, 112. The reflections on Göttingen's aristocratic inhumanity appear in Heine's *North Sea* prose studies, later anthologized as the second volume of his *Travel Pictures*. Blumenbach's work is helpfully contextualized in the essays collected in *Johann Friedrich Blumenbach: Race and Natural History, 1750–1850*, ed. Nicolaas Rupke and Gerhard Lauer (New York: Routledge, 2018). Heine's letter to Steinmann about being effectively expelled from university is dated February 4, 1821. His ruminations on the freedom bestowed by masks appear in the second of his *Letters from Berlin*, dispatches to the *Rheinisch-Westfälischer Anzeiger*, published serially from February to July of 1822.

Chapter Seventeen

Heine's ruminations on Berlin's rigidity appear in chapter 2 of his *Journey from Munich to Genoa*, the first part of his Italian travelogue. Brod cites Gubitz's reminiscences of his first meeting with Heine, *Heinrich Heine*, 91–92. Schleiermacher's possible authorship of the comments on Heine's early poems is discussed in Bieber and Hadas, *Heinrich Heine*, 106.

Chapter Eighteen

Heine writes of genius and the new word in book 3 of his *History of Religion and Philosophy in Germany*. His criticism of his own verse dramas is cited in George Eliot's important essay on Heine,

German Wit: Henry Heine. Heine's poem on "stars and flowers by the ton" is no. 20 from *Youthful Sorrows,* in Draper, *Complete Poems,* 45. Robertson provides excellent context for Heine and the great soup question in *Heine,* 63–75. Sammons cites the letter to Immerman in which Heine describes poetry as a "beautiful irrelevancy," *Heinrich Heine,* 85. My quotations from Heine's *Letters from Berlin* come primarily from Elizabeth A. Sharp's translation in *Heine in Art and Letters* (London: Walter Scott, 1895), 98–170. The poem cited at the end of the chapter was originally published in Heine's *The Salon.* I've used Prawer's translation from *Jewish Comedy,* 249.

Chapter Nineteen

Heine writes to Immanuel Wohlwill of being in the "gloomy pits" in a letter dated April 7, 1823. "I dreamed I am" is the opening of poem no. 66 from Heine's eighty-eight-poem cycle *The Homecoming,* here in Kramer's translation from Ewen, *Poetry and Prose,* 90–91. Heine's letter to Moser on his "sentimental attachment" to Judaism is dated August 23, 1823. "To Edom" was included in a letter to Moser, dated October 25, 1824. Heine writes about the distinction between Hellenes and Nazarenes in *Ludwig Börne.*

Chapter Twenty

My portrait of Hegel benefited from material gathered in *The Cambridge Companion to Hegel and Nineteenth Century Philosophy,* ed. Frederick C. Beiser (Cambridge: Cambridge University Press, 2008). Hegel's toast to July 14, 1789, is cited there, 40. I also drew on Terry Pinkard's *Hegel: A Biography* (Cambridge: Cambridge University Press, 2000). An insightful discussion of Hegel's *Doppelsatz* and Heine's relationship to the concept appears in Robert Stern's *Hegelian Metaphysics* (Oxford: Oxford University Press, 2009), 81–116. I also relied on the analysis in Robert R. Williams's *Hegel's Ethics of Recognition* (Berkeley: University of California Press, 1997), esp. 22–26. Heine describes Hegel's "serio-comic visage" in his *Confessions,* which Sammons characterizes as Heine's "spiritual autobiography," from a post-1848 perspective, *Heinrich Heine,* 318. The poem beginning "Life in this world is a fragmented business" is from *The Homecoming*, no. 57 in Untermeyer's translation in *Poems*, which I've used here with a revised first line. The letter in which Heine reports that he is not an idea is to Moser, dated May 1823, in Ewen, *Poetry and Prose*, 348–349.

Chapter Twenty-one

Prawer's *Jewish Comedy* references Friederike von Hohenhausen's description of Gans as a "spiritual Antinous," 40. Prawer analyzes their relationship through the book, esp. 10–43. I also drew on Warren Breckman's essay "Eduard Gans and the Crisis of Hegelianism," *Journal of the History of Ideas* 62 (2001): 543–564. The story of Gans's struggle with the Prussian bureaucracy is recounted in *Divided Passions: Jewish Intellectuals and the Crisis of Modernity* (Detroit: Wayne State University Press, 1963), esp. 39–41. The description I quote regarding Berlin's arsenal is from Augustus Bozzi Granville's *Saint Petersburgh, a Journal of Travel to and from that Capital* (London: Henry Colburn, 1828), 281. Michael Meyer's *The Origin of the Modern Jew* (Detroit: Wayne State University Press, 1967) was another source for my account of Gans and the Society. Gans's remarks about "complete negation" appear on 167. I also drew from speeches by Gans cited in *Eduard Gans and the Hegelian Philosophy of Law* by Michael H. Hoffheimer (Dordrecht: Kluwer Academic, 1995). On the history of the Society see for example, H. G. Reissner, "Rebellious Dilemma: The Case Histories of Eduard Gans and Some of His Partisans," for the Leo Baeck Institute, 1957, vol. 2, pp. 179–193.

Chapter Twenty-two

Heine's reflections on the Society appear in his obituary of Ludwig Marcus, parts of which are excerpted in Ewen, *Poetry and Prose*, 685–690, as well as in Prawer's *Jewish Comedy*, 466–481—the latter including significant commentary. The quotation from Zunz is taken from *Leopold Zunz: Creativity in Adversity* by Ismar Schorsch (Philadelphia: University of Pennsylvania Press, 2016), 18–19. Heine describes Zunz's pockmarks in a letter to Wohlwill, dated April 1, 1823. This is the same letter in which Heine describes not having the strength to wear a beard. In discussing Hegel's relationship to the Jews, I drew on Nathan Rotenstreich's "Hegel's Image of Judaism," *Jewish Social Studies* 15, no. 1 (1953): 33–52. Heine's description of the world as "a great stable" is cited in *Work on Myth* by Hans Blumenberg (Cambridge: MIT Press, 1985), 46. Sven-Erik Rose cites the critique of the Society by Isaac Markus Jost in an insightful discussion of Hegel's relationship to the organization, "The Verein and Hegel's State," in his book *Jewish Philosophical Politics in Germany, 1789–1848* (Waltham: Brandeis University Press, 2014), 56–64.

Chapter Twenty-three

Tewarson cites Rahel's account of her first dream, *Rahel Levin Varnhagen*, 116–118. Her illuminating discussion of Rahel's views on sociability appear in an account of Rahel's first salon, 34–45. Heine's letter on macaroni and spiritual food is cited there, 193–194. Rahel's remarks on her letters' roots appear in Kay Goodman's "Poesis and Praxis in Rahel Varnhagen's Letters," *New German Critique*, no. 27 (1982): 123–139. Another source for my account of the Berlin salons was *Jewish Women and Their Salons: The Power of Conversation* by Emily D. Bilski and Emily Braun (New Haven: Yale University Press, 2005.) Brod recounts the story of Heine's unfortunate recitation, *Heinrich Heine*, 94. He also quotes Herz's comment on the *salonnière's* predicament, 103. His citation from Karl Varnhagen's letter on Heine's defects appears on 126. Nietzsche's remarks on Goethe and Rahel are quoted in Barbara Hahn's "Demarcations and Projects: Goethe in the Berlin Salons," anthologized in *Goethe in German-Jewish Culture* from the Wisconsin Workshop, ed. Klaus L. Berghahn and Jost Hermand (Rochester, NY: Camden House, 2001), 31. The collection also contains Hermand's informative essay "A View from Below: Heinrich Heine's Relationship to Johann Wolfgang von Goethe," 44–65. Rahel's dream about "enduring wrong" is quoted in Tewarson, *Rahel Levin Varnhagen*, 120–121. Rahel likened herself to a supernatural being in a long letter to David Veit, dated March 21–25, 1795. Heine's letter about their "innermost secret" is dated February 5, 1840.

Chapter Twenty-four

Heine's story about Gans and the flowers is quoted in Prawer's *Jewish Comedy*, 32. He discusses Rahel's literary style in *Ludwig Börne*, 2–4 in Sammons's translation. Rahel's discussion of her own writing style is deftly examined by Liliane Weissberg in "Writing on the Wall: Letters of Rahel Varnhagen," *New German Critique*, no. 36 (1985): 157–173. I also drew on Weissberg's essay "Stepping Out: The Writing of Difference in Rahel Varnhagen's Letters," *New German Critique*, no. 53 (1991): 149–162. Carlyle's remarks on Heine are quoted by Sol Liptzin in "Heinrich Heine, 'Blackguard' and 'Apostate': A Study of the Earliest English Attitudes toward Him," *PMLA* 58 (1943): 170–180. Heine's remarks about "Catholic harmony" are quoted in Prawer's *The Tragic Satirist*, 17. Heine's letter describing the effect on him of Rahel's correspondence is dated July 29, 1829, cited in Prawer's *Jewish Comedy*, 212–213. Rahel's extraordinary letter on Germans and Jews is quoted in Tewarson, *Rahel Levin Varnhagen*, 160–161.

Chapter Twenty-five

Heine tallies archetypal German comforts in *The Salon*, in Leland, *Works*, 4: 7–8, and writes about "German constancy" in *The Romantic School*, 145, in Fleishman's translation. He remarks that German is to him "what water is to a fish" in a letter to Christiani, dated March 7, 1824, Bieber and Hadas, *Heinrich Heine*, 169–170. Prawer discusses the Heinestrophe in *The Tragic Satirist*, 55. A useful overview of Goethe and the daemonic in relation to "Der Fischer" can be found in *Schubert's Goethe Settings* by Lorraine Byrne Bodley (London: Routledge, 2003), 215–220. I use Edwin Zeydel's translation of "Der Fischer." Brod quotes Rahel's letter warning Heine not to be a Brentano, *Heinrich Heine*, 124. Rahel's letter to her brother is cited in Tewarson, *Rahel Levin Varnhagen*, 160–161. Heine's letter to Moser about being a "water poet" is dated January 21, 1824, Bieber and Hadas, *Heinrich Heine*, 167–168. I use Richard Stokes's admirable translation of Heine's "Lorelei," which is anthologized in his volume *The Book of Lieder* (London: Faber, 2005). My discussion of the poem benefited from Ignace

Feuerlicht's essay "Heine's 'Lorelei': Legend, Literature, Life," *German Quarterly* 53, no. 1 (1980): 82–94. Heine categorizes himself as a member of the "party of action" in *The Romantic School*. Hegel's demotion of art relative to truth appears in part 1 of his lecture "The Idea of Artistic Beauty, Or the Ideal." Robertson cites Heine's 1823 statement on art in *Heine*, 4. The three poems quoted are from Heine's *Homecoming* cycle, the first two in Draper's translation, no. 21 and no. 39, respectively; the third in Jeff Dolven's translation. Prawer quotes from Heine's letter about his book's dedication in *Heine's Jewish Comedy*, 36.

Chapter Twenty-six

Heine compares Byron to Prometheus in a letter to Christiani, dated May 24, 1824. Gans's expression of disappointment is cited in Stigand, vol. 1, p. 118. My quotation from Goethe's "A Winter Journey in the Harz" is drawn from *The Essential Goethe*, ed. Matthew Bell (Princeton: Princeton University Press, 2016). Nicholas Boyle describes Goethe's encounter with the Montgolfier brothers in *Goethe: The Poet and the Age*, vol. 1 (Oxford: Oxford University Press, 1991), 346. Goethe's reflections on true poetry appear in *The Autobiography of Goethe: Truth and Poetry from My Life* vol. 3, ed. Parke Godwin (New York: Wiley & Putnam, 1847), 125. Heine refers to the Bible as the "portable fatherland" in his *Ludwig Börne*, among other places. Prawer cites Heine's description of "the wild hunt of time" from that same work, *Heine's Jewish Comedy*, 348. I've drawn primarily on Robertson's translation of *The Harz Journey*, except for the extended passage on the migration of the "young dollar," which is my own modification of Leland's translation in vol. 2, pp. 80–81.

Chapter Twenty-seven

Heine's letter to Goethe is dated October 1, 1824, in Ewen, *Poetry and Prose*, 355. My citations from Goethe's *Theory of Colors* are from Bell's *Essential Goethe*. In discussing Goethe's sociability I draw primarily from the condensations of Goethe's dialogues with contemporaries collected in *Goethe: Conversations and Encounters*, ed. and trans. David Luke and Robert Pick (Washington, DC:

Regnery, 1966). His "negating propensity and skeptical neutrality" are noted by Friedrich von Müller, a statesman friend of Goethe's, in his diary notes for March 27, 1824, 129 in this volume. Goethe's remarks on conversation are cited in the above volume on 7. Heine tells the story of his encounter with Goethe at the end of book 1 of *The Romantic School*.

Chapter Twenty-eight

Many of Heine's reflections on Luther appear in the first book of his *On the History of Religion and Philosophy in Germany*. His statement about not belonging to the materialists is drawn from the collection of articles he wrote on German literature for the French, which appeared in a French journal between March and May of 1833; Prawer's *Jewish Comedy*, 257. Stigand recounts Heine's dream about hexameters in *Life, Work, and Opinions*, 1: 162, where the 1824 letter in which Heine's fantasizes about becoming Japanese also appears, 182–183. Bieber and Hadas quote Heine's aphorism about the baptismal certificate as a ticket of admission, *Heinrich Heine*, 196. Heine's July 31, 1825, letter to Charlotte Emden hinting at his conversion appears on the same page. His letter of December 14, 1825, to Moser in which he describes "glowing kugel" is on 203. The lines I cite from Heine's *To an Apostate* appear in Brod, *Heinrich Heine*, 129.

Chapter Twenty-nine

I've used Draper's translation of Heine's "Sea-sickness," a supplemental work to his "North Sea" series, *Complete Poems*, 177–178. Heine writes about church hypocrisy and Goethe near the opening of his North Sea travel piece from 1826. His gloomy letter to Rudolph Christiani, dated December 1825, can be found in Bieber and Hadas, *Heinrich Heine*, 204–205, as can his December 18, 1825, letter to Moser in which he describes "toadying up to rich Jews," 204. The remarks about Salomon's house appear in a letter to Heine's brother Max cited in Stigand, *Life, Work, and Opinions*, 1: 237. Heine's comments about Hamburgian thick-headedness were made to Adolph Stahr and are quoted in the same volume, 236. Campe's lines about the future belonging to the young are cited there as well, 240. Sammons quotes Campe's letter from July 12, 1833, to Heine about his limited appeal, *Heinrich Heine*, 122. For Sammons's broader discussion of Heine's relationship with Campe and the state of book publishing during Heine's lifetime, both 118–123 of the biography and his essay "Thinking Clearly about the Marriage of Heinrich Heine and his Publisher Julius Campe," anthologized in *Publishing Culture and the "Reading Nation": German Book Publishing in the Long Nineteenth Century*, ed. Lynne Tatlock (Rochester, NY: Camden House, 2010), were valuable sources, as was Tatlock's introductory essay to the same volume, which contains useful data on rates of German book production. I quote from Draper's translation of *Germany: A Winter's Tale*, *Complete Poems*, 481–536.

Chapter Thirty

Heine's comments on "the hubbub of a common European brotherhood," which derive from the introductory remarks to the reprinting of his "New Spring" cycle, are quoted by Prawer in *The Tragic Satirist*, 18. Heine discusses the end of the Goethean era in art in an 1828 review of Wolfgang Menzel's *Die Deutsche Literatur*. Ben Hutchinson provides important perspective on these themes in his *Lateness and Modern European Literature* (Oxford: Oxford University Press, 2016), esp. 119–126. Heine's paean to emancipation appears in chapter 29 of his *Journey from Munich to Genoa*. He writes on the difference between poets and historians in chapter 7 of this work. Brod quotes Heine's letter to Robert, *Heinrich Heine*, 253–254. Heine expresses his reservations about political poetry in the preface to *Atta Troll*. Stigand recounts the story of the appearance of Heine's residence, *Life, Work, and Opinions*, 1: 336. Heine's remarks about china and domesticity are quoted in Robertson's *Heine*, 21. Heine's letter to Moser from July 28, 1826, reflects on the mystery of the Wandering Jew.

Chapter Thirty-one

Heine's dream of bliss pops up in many places, including a footnote to chapter 5 of Freud's *Civilization and Its Discontents*, 57, in the James Strachey translation (New York: Norton, 1961). Heine's astonishing comparison of murdered Judaea to the dying Nessus appears in Prawer, *Heine's Jewish Comedy*, 146–147. Heine's letter to Campe on his reception during his travels is dated December 1, 1827; Bieber and Hadas, *Heinrich Heine*, 245–246. His ruminations on *The Merchant of Venice* appear in his essay on Jessica in *Shakespeare's Maidens and Women*, which had been commissioned by a French publisher in 1838 to accompany a collection of engravings. He describes himself as "all sword and flame" in *Ludwig Börne* and in an unpublished hymn. Brod quotes Heine's letter to Christiani mourning the loss of his father, *Heinrich Heine*, 254. Brod also provides background on the Platen quarrel, esp. 241–253, as does Sammons's *Heinrich Heine*, 141–147. Jefferson S. Chase's *Inciting Laughter: The Development of "Jewish Humor" in 19th Century German Culture* (Berlin: Walter de Gruyter, 2000) includes examples of Platen's antisemitic jabs against Heine outside of *The Romantic Oedipus*, 139–180. Heine writes Immerman about Platen at the end of December 1829; Bieber and Hadas, *Heinrich Heine*, 258. His two letters to Varnhagen on the subject, the first dated January 3, 1830, the second February 4, can be found in the same volume, 258–260. His ruminations on the oddity of his destiny appear in Sammons's translation of *Ludwig Börne*, 27. He calls America that "enormous freedom prison" on 29 of the same work. Scholars have generally concluded that Eckermann mistook the date of his conversation with Goethe, and that this error contributed to the misidentification of Heine as the subject of Goethe's critique; however, the issue has not been definitively resolved. Eckermann added Platen's name to the text only in 1836, after Platen's death. Was it easier to impugn the dead Platen than Heine, whose fame was then sharply in the ascendancy? Or had Eckermann shielded Platen until his death? Whichever is true, the public consensus that Goethe must have meant Heine is itself instructive. I am grateful to Peter Filkins for alerting me to the discussion of this issue in *Italy in the German Imagination: Goethe's "Italian Journey" and Its Reception by Eichendorff, Platen, and Heine* by Gretchen L. Hachmeister (Rochester, NY: Camden House, 2002), esp. 204.

Chapter Thirty-two

Heine described himself as a supernaturalist in a review of Delacroix for his discussion of the 1831 Salon. His letter from Helgoland forms part of *Ludwig Börne*. Prawer quotes Heine's journal observation about anti-Jewish actions and business people, *Heine's Jewish Comedy*, 222–223. His ruminations about Jewish weakness are cited in Brod, *Heinrich Heine*, 143. Rahel's remarks on revolution and the future appear in Tewarson, *Rahel Levin Varnhagen*, 185, as does Rahel's letter to Heine about the need for the pocks to be extirpated, 199. Rahel's ruminations on the "old great wound" appear 223–224. Ewen quotes Heine about the sun as a Prussian cockade, *Poetry and Prose*, 401. Isaiah Berlin's *Karl Marx: His Life and Environment* (Oxford: Oxford University Press, 1978) contains useful background material on Saint-Simon, esp. 66–69. Georg G. Iggers's essay "Heine and the Saint-Simonians: A Re-Examination" in *Comparative Literature* 10, no. 4 (1958): 289–308, offered important perspective on the subject. Robertson's *Heine* also offers an excellent survey of Heine's relationship to Saint-Simon and the movement, esp. 36–49. Contemporary perceptions of Rahel as well as insight into the early appeal of Saint-Simon can be found in Albert Brisbane's *Albert Brisbane: A Mental Biography* (Boston: Arena, 1893), 84–85. Sammons quotes Heine's Saint-Simonian flourish in the course of his own important discussion of Heine's relationship to the movement, *Heinrich Heine*, 159–168. Sammons also quotes Heine's letter to Varnhagen about his new religion, 155. Heine writes of the divine rights of humanity in his *History of Religion and Philosophy in Germany*.

Chapter Thirty-three

Heine's joy on first arriving in Paris is communicated in the second of his *Florentine Nights*, among other places. His comparison of himself to a fish in water appears in a letter to Ferdinand Hiller dated October 24, 1832, in *Heinrich Heine: Selected Prose*, ed. Hermann Kesten, trans. E. B. Ashton (New York: L. B. Fischer, 1943), 310–311. Heine's remarks on the Napoleon cult are quoted by Hazareesingh, *The Legend of Napoleon*, 199. Warren Breckman's

Marx, the Young Hegelians, and the Origins of Radical Theory (Cambridge: Cambridge University Press, 1999) includes an important discussion of Saint-Simon's influence on Heine's peers. Enfantin's remarks on pantheism in a political language are quoted there on 164. Heine writes about Louis Phillipe in a number of letters compiled in *Lutezia*. His letter to Varnhagen about dragging the Fatherland around on his soles is dated June 27, 1831. Börne welcomes Heine to Paris in Sammons's translation of *Ludwig Börne*, 51. Heine's citations from Börne's letters span 114–119. Heine writes of a future smelling of Russian blood in the July 12, 1842, dispatch in *Lutezia*. Heine's poem "The Roving Rats" appears in Draper, *Complete Poems*, 783–784.

Chapter Thirty-four

I quote from Ellen Marriage's translation of Balzac's *Lost Illusions*. My portrait of Heine's Paris benefited enormously from material gathered in Eric Hazan's marvelous *The Invention of Paris: A History in Footsteps*, trans. David Fernbach (London: Verso, 2010). Heine's observations about Paris filled with rosy light appear in the second of his *Florentine Nights*. His reference to Madame de Staël occurs in his February 10, 1832, dispatch from France, quoted in Stigand, *Life, Work, and Opinions*, 2: 88. Heine's reflections on life being neither a means nor an end occur in his fascinating essay "Differing Conceptions of History." I cite from Robertson's translation in *Harz Journey*, 195–196, which also includes Heine's sharpest formulation of Saint-Just's pronouncement on the people's right to bread. Stigand cites Heine's May 1832 letter to Varnhagen on Saint-Simonianism, *Life, Work, and Opinions*, 2: 137. Heine's prophecy of the coming of "happier and more beautiful generations" occurs in his *History of Religion and Philosophy in Germany*; I use Robertson's translation from *Heine*, 47. Heine's moving description of the cholera epidemic in Paris appears in the April 19, 1832, entry of his *Letters from Paris*, in Leland, *Works*, 7: 155–185. Heine's famous prophecy about the resurrection of Germany's old stone gods appears at the close of book 3 in his *History*. His condolence letter to Varnhagen is dated March 28, 1833; Ewen, *Poetry and Prose*, 406–407. Brod quotes the line about Germans in France from Heine's memorial to Ludwig Marcus, *Heinrich Heine*, 278. Heine's wistful remarks about the kind of beautiful lyrics and light prose he'd hoped to write appear in the preface to *The Salon*, vol. 1 (1833), which is also the source for his citation from Rahel's letter; Ewen, *Poetry and Prose*, 408–415.

Chapter Thirty-five

Stigand quotes Heine's April 1835 letter to Lewald about Mathilde, *Life, Work, and Opinions*, 2: 229–230. This volume is also my source for Heine's letter to Campe of July 2, 1855, in which he describes his relief at being apart from Mathilde, 230. Brod cites Weill's reminiscence about Mathilde, *Heinrich Heine*, 203–204. Marcuse excerpts from Heine's love letters to Mathilde, *Heine*, 264–265, including the letter about missing her "fat little behind." Heine's letter to his mother about Mathilde's honorable qualities is dated March 8, 1842. He tells August Lewald that he has always been against renunciation in a letter dated January 25, 1837; Bieber and Hadas, *Heinrich Heine*, 339–340. Lewald is also Heine's correspondent for a letter dated May 3, 1836, in which he praises the "consistent inconsistency" of Mathilde's whims. Heine complains to Heinrich Laube about being condemned to love only the most foolish in a letter dated September 27, 1835; 337–338 in the same volume. This anthology also contains Heine's letter to Varnhagen, dated January 3, 1846, in which he describes his plan to savage his family in the press, 405–406. Heine describes his dedication to honoring Mathilde's inherited Catholicism in his *Confessions*. Untermeyer records details of Heine's "Wanted" poster, *Heinrich Heine*, 301. Prawer's *The Tragic Satirist* references Heine's desired tombstone inscription, 55. Heine's paean to the "god that dwells within people" is from the preface to his *Germany: A Winter's Tale*; Draper, *Complete Poems*, 482–483. I am indebted to Christian Brammer for research into relative currency rates in connection with Salomon's legacy. Heine's ruminations on pantheism occur near the opening of *The Romantic School*, cited in Stigand, *Life, Work, and Opinions*, 2: 139. The 1851 postscript to *Romanzero* expands on these ideas, parts of which are quoted in 2: 364–366 in Stigand. The first volume of Stigand's biography is also one source for Heine's account of his last visit to the Venus de Milo. Sammons describes the incident as well. Heine discusses his feelings of kinship with Uncle Tom in his *Confessions*. I am grateful to Dr. Sabine Brenner-Wiczek of Düsseldorf's Heine Institute for an enlightening discussion about the discoveries concerning Heine's retracted process of self-censorship, made in the course of analyzing the latter manuscript. My quotations from *Atta Troll, Germany: A Winter's Tale*, and four shorter works are from Draper's translations in *Complete Poems*: "The Slave Ship," 704–707; "Supplement to 'Lazarus,'" 709–715; "Miserere," 813–814; "Parting Word," 814. Heine writes Gustav Kolb about the destruction of his generation's "beautiful ideals" in a letter dated January 13, 1852.

Chapter Thirty-six

In addition to Krinitz/Selden's memoir of Heine's last days, Pawl's *The Poet Dying* and Sammons's *Heinrich Heine*, 341–343, were important sources for my account of his final period. Draper's translation of Heine's poem "Lotus Flower" appears in *Complete Poems*, 819–820. Heine's final masterpiece, "For the Mouche," is on 821–825 of that same volume. Untermeyer quotes from some of Heine's letters to and about Krinitz, *Heinrich Heine*, esp. 346–347. Gautier's ruminations on Heine's death are cited in Stigand, *Life, Work, and Opinions*, 2: 423. The anonymous obituary from *Deutsches Museum* is quoted in *The Poet as Provocateur: Heinrich Heine and His Critics*, by George F. Peters (Rochester, NY: Camden House, 2000), 69–70. *The Family Life of Heinrich Heine* by Heine's nephew Baron Ludwig von Emden, trans. Charles de Kay (New York: Cassell, 1892), contains a lively summary of Mathilde's life after Heine's death, esp. 319–322. Heine's letter to Dumas is dated February 8, 1855, and was published in *Le Mousquetaire* of February 14, 1855. I quote from Mitchell Abidor's translation.

Epilogue

An account of the unveiling of the Lorelei statue with partial transcripts of the speeches delivered on this occasion appeared in the *New York Times* on July 9, 1899. The statue stands today in Joyce Kilmer Park, which borders the Grand Concourse between 161st and 164th Street. Additional material appears in "Sturm und Drang over a Memorial to Heinrich Heine," a *Times* article by Christopher Gray, dated May 27, 2007. I'm very grateful to Samuel Goodman, urban planner and lifelong resident of the Grand Concourse in the Bronx, for providing me with a wealth of information regarding the statue's peregrinations and fortunes over the twentieth century. An excellent summary of the Empress Elisabeth's relationship to Heine and the Heine memorial can be found in Michael Stanislawski's *Zionism and the Fin de Siècle: Cosmopolitans and Nationalism from Nordau to Jabotinsky* (Berkeley: University of California Press, 2001), 77–80. Brigitte Hamann's *The Reluctant Empress: A Biography of Empress Elisabeth of Austria*, trans. Ruth Hein (New York: Alfred A. Knopf, 1986) was also a helpful resource for understanding Elisabeth's obsession with Heine. Hamann quotes Elisabeth's reasons for admiring the poet. The article in the *Nationalsozialistische Monatshefte* on Heine is by Wolfgang Lutz. Harry Slochower quotes from the essay in "Attitudes towards Heine in German Literary Criticism," in *Jewish Social Studies* 3 (1941): 355–374. Zvi Tauber's essay "Remarks on the Relationship between Heine and Marx in 1844," anthologized in *Ethnizität, Moderne und Enttraditionalisierung*, ed. Mosheh Tsukerman (Tel Aviver Jahrbuch für deutsche Geschichte, 30, 2002: Wallstein Verlag), provides valuable context on their friendship, as does Prawer's *Karl Marx and World Literature* (Oxford: Oxford University Press, 1976), which quotes Heine on the limitations of a man who is only a razor, 150. The book is also my source for the citation from Marx about German censorship, 44. I further relied on David Leopold's *The Young Karl Marx: German Philosophy, Modern Politics, and Human Flourishing* (Cambridge: Cambridge University Press, 2007), which recounts Marx's line about poets as "strange fish" from Jenny's reminiscences on 31. Nigel Reeves's essay "Heine and the Young Marx," from *Oxford German Studies* 7 (1972): 44–97, includes a revealing assessment of Marx's knowledge of Heine's writing. Howells's account of Heine's influence on him can be found in his *My Literary Passions*, published 1895. Fritz Stern remarked on Heine's "perfect epitaph" in his memoir *Five Germanys I Have Known* (New York: Farrar, Straus and Giroux, 2007). Isaiah Berlin's account of visiting Pasternak appears in "Conversations with Akhmatova and Pasternak," anthologized in Isaiah Berlin, *The Proper Study of Mankind* (New York: Farrar, Straus and Giroux, 1998), 537–538. *Zauberland* premiered at the Théâtre des Bouffes du Nord in April 2019, with music by Robert Schumann and Bernard Foccroulle, text by Heinrich Heine and Martin Crimp, and stage direction by Katie Michell.

Heine's line about dancing on a volcano is from the 42nd dispatch in *Lutezia*, dated February 7, 1842. The first part of the exclamation originated with a French diplomat on the eve of the 1830 Revolution.

INDEX

INDEX

JEWISH LIVES is a prizewinning series of interpretative biography designed to explore the many facets of Jewish identity. Individual volumes illuminate the imprint of Jewish figures upon literature, religion, philosophy, politics, cultural and economic life, and the arts and sciences. Subjects are paired with authors to elicit lively, deeply informed books that explore the range and depth of the Jewish experience from antiquity to the present.

Jewish Lives is a partnership of Yale University Press and the Leon D. Black Foundation. Ileene Smith is editorial director. Anita Shapira and Steven J. Zipperstein are series editors.